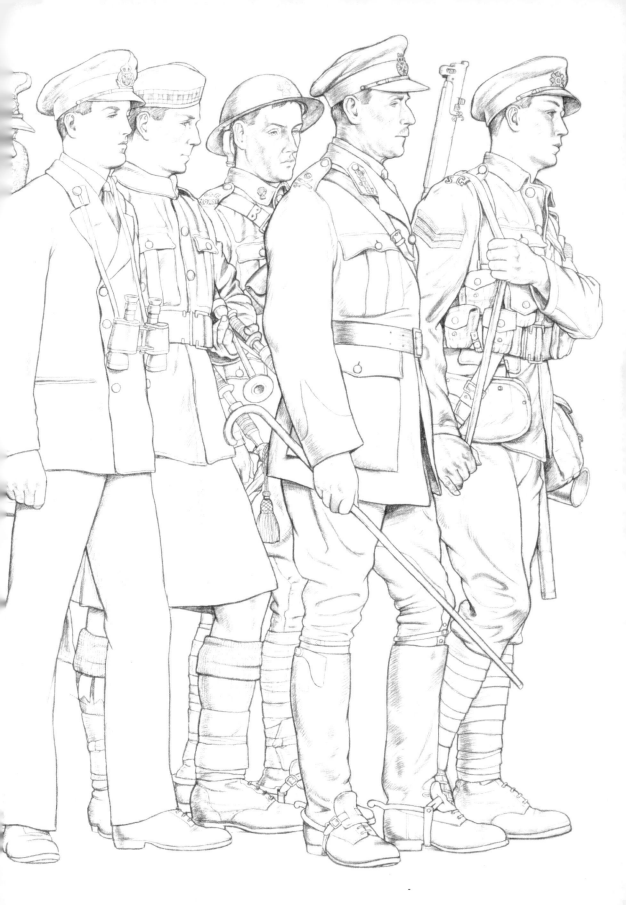

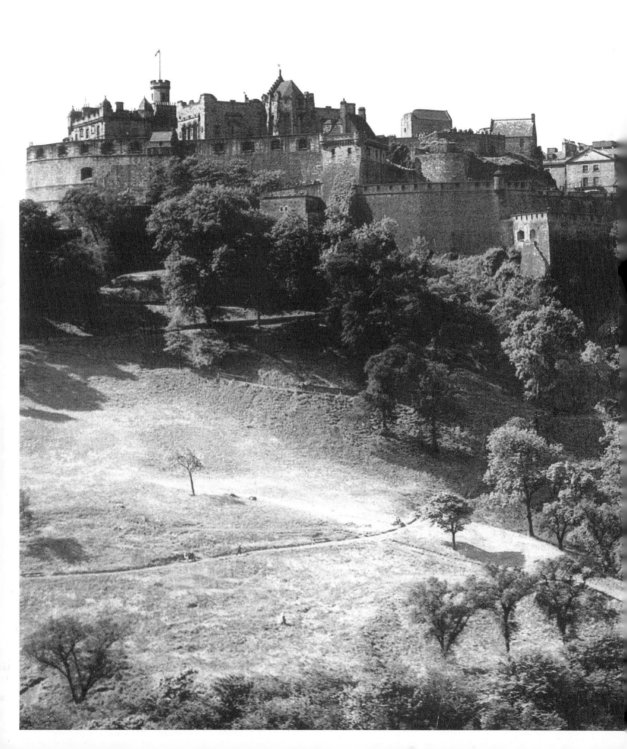

The Thin Red Line

WAR, EMPIRE AND VISIONS OF SCOTLAND

Stuart Allan and Allan Carswell

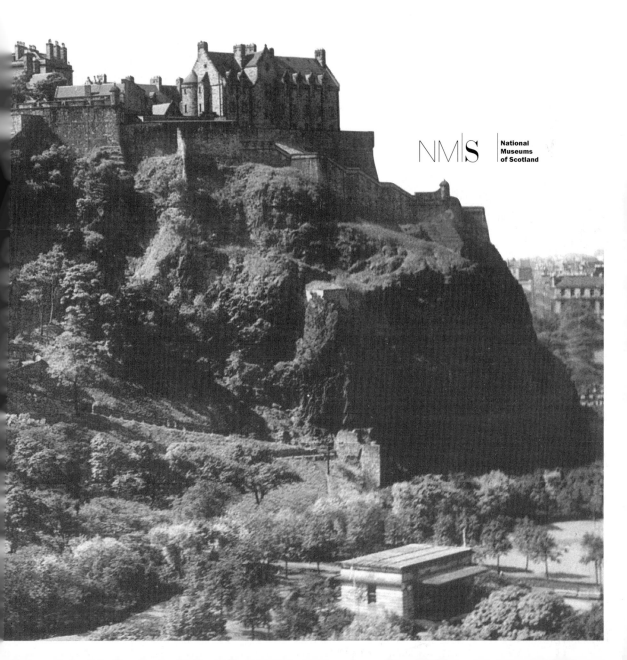

NM|S **National Museums of Scotland**

ACKNOWLEDGEMENTS

Dedicated to the collectors, former curators
of the National War Museum of Scotland:

Major I H Mackay Scobie, Major H P E Pereira,
W A Thorburn, A V B Norman,
R G Ball, W G F Boag,
Stephen Wood and Charles J Burnett

THE AUTHORS ARE INDEBTED TO ALL THOSE WHO HAVE ASSISTED THE production of this book with information, illustrations and advice. We particularly acknowledge the kind help of Lieutenant-Colonel (Retd) I Shepherd, Secretary of the Scottish National War Memorial; Mr W M Mackay, Free Church of Scotland; Mr R Mackenzie, assistant curator, Regimental Museum of the Argyll and Sutherland Highlanders; Colonel R P Mason, Regimental Secretary of the Royal Scots (The Royal Regiment); Lieutenant-Colonel (Retd) R J Binks, Regimental Secretary of the Royal Scots Dragoon Guards (Carabiniers and Greys); Lieutenant-Colonel (Retd) S J Lindsay, Regimental Secretary, and Mr T Smyth, Archivist of the Black Watch (Royal Highland Regiment); and the family of the late Lance-Corporal Barry Stephen, 1st Black Watch. We thank Professor Tom Devine for his foreword and for his interest in the National War Museum of Scotland.

This book benefits greatly from the photography of Joyce Smith and Neil McLean of the National Museums of Scotland for which we gratefully record our appreciation. Its production is the creative and patient work of Cara Shanley, Lesley Taylor and their colleagues at NMS Enterprises Limited – Publishing.

Finally, this book could not have been written without the help of Edith Philip, assistant curator and librarian at the National War Museum of Scotland. Like many others working in the field of Scottish military history, we owe a debt to her industry and expertise.

In acknowledging their help, we absolve our colleagues and friends of implication in any opinions expressed or errors made herein; these are entirely our own.

Published by NMSE Publishing
a division of NMS Enterprises Limited
National Museums of Scotland
Chambers Street
Edinburgh EH1 1JF

ISBN 1-901663-87-6

British Library Cataloguing in Publication Data
A catalogue record of this book
is available from the British Library.

Cover design by Mark Blackadder.
Typesetting and internal layout by NMS Enterprises Limited – Publishing.
Printed and bound in the UK by The Cromwell Press.

CONTENTS

T M Devine FRSE, FBA

Glucksman Research Professor
in Scottish and Irish Studies,
University of Aberdeen

SCOTTISH HISTORY IS INCOMPREHENSIBLE WITHOUT AN UNDERSTANDING of war, the military tradition and the impact of international strategy on Scotland's place in the world. For better or for worse the modern nation has been moulded by these forces, many of which stretch back over several centuries. But for a sustained struggle for independence in medieval times, culminating in the historic victory at Bannockburn in 1314, the Scottish nation would have been conquered and rendered impotent and dependent. It is no coincidence that two of Scotland's hero figures, William Wallace and King Robert the Bruce, are forever associated with that extraordinary period but still have resonance to this day. It was not simply a question, however, of removing the threat of subjugation. Essentially, the Wars of Independence helped to fuse the confused mix of kindred, localities and clans into a much broader entity, a nation. There is much truth in the old saying that Scotland was born fighting.

From that day to this the military factor has remained central. The old Scottish connection in the sixteenth and seventeenth centuries with Europe was forged by trade, scholarship and religion. But, above all, it was based on the age-old migration of young Scotsmen to serve in the armies of the continent. After the Union of 1707 some argue that the remarkable expansion of the British empire would have been impossible without the Scottish martial contribution and, in particular, the legendary exploits of the Highland regiments. It was much more than coincidence that when the sun finally set on the greatest territorial empire the world had ever seen, with the handover of Hong Kong to China in June 1997, the Black Watch pipes and drums ended the ceremony with 'Auld Lang Syne'.

Perhaps much more than all of this, however, is the key influence of the military tradition on how Scotland sees itself as a nation. The survival of Scottishness within the union state is often seen as the result of the 1707 treaty which preserved the pre-Union institutions of church, law and education which then became the transmitters of national identity to future generations. At least as important, nonetheless, was the Scottish soldier, distinctive in dress, playing an imperial role, but recognisably and still unambiguously Scottish. In the post-imperial era that tradition might not simply seem irrelevant but also offensive to some. But the influence lives on, whether it be in the extraordinary success of the Edinburgh Military Tattoo, the saturation coverage in the Scottish media when Scottish soldiers, airmen and sailors are on active service in the Gulf or Iraq, or the continuing controversy over the amalgamation or even the disbanding of ancient regiments, some of which can date their battle honours back as far as Blenheim, Fontenoy or Waterloo.

To explain the complexity of the military factor in Scottish history is not easy. But Stuart Allan and Allan Carswell have responded remarkably well to this challenge. They have written a book which will stimulate and inform the general reader, not least because it is written in accessible prose. The professional will also find much of interest in these pages. This is no old-fashioned blow-by-blow account of past Scottish glories. Instead, the authors relate the military past to the mainstream of Scottish history by setting the martial experience within the broader context of political, economic, social and international developments. Above all, they approach their subject with a keen, critical eye and dispassionate scholarship. I recommend the book to anyone who seeks to understand how Scotland came to be the way it is today and especially how the military factor has shaped the national story.

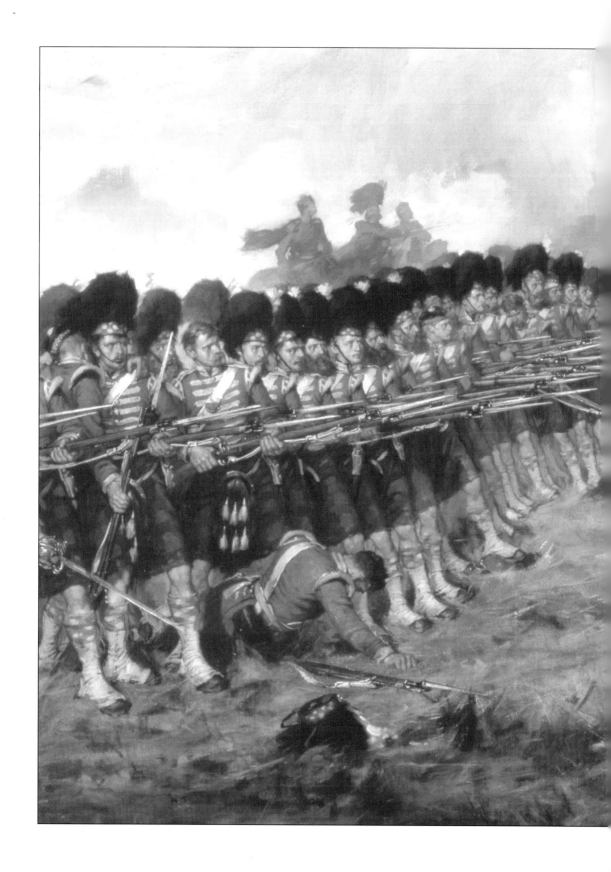

INTRODUCTION

Nemo me impune lacessit

'NEMO ME IMPUNE LACESSIT' ('NO ONE PROVOKES ME WITH IMPUNITY'). This ancient royal motto of Scotland is inscribed above the gateway of Edinburgh Castle. It is a warning about war. War and military service have been bound up with the reputation of Scotland and its people for centuries. Their influence remains something that the wider world recognises of Scotland in the present day. This book examines Scotland's military image and considers what it has meant for Scots in the years since the independent Scottish kingdom ceased to be. For most of the period with which this story is concerned, the questions of strategy, the means of waging war and the organisations that resulted were concerns not of Scotland alone, but of the British state. There is much that is common between Scotland and other parts of the United Kingdom in what, to some extent, is a historical experience that follows the fate of the British empire. Yet the story is not the same. The perspective of this book is not that of the Scottish end of British military history. Instead, it considers how these questions of strategy and military power impacted on Scottish society and culture, how these military institutions were encountered by Scots and, ultimately, what all this has meant for Scotland.[1]

The scope of this book proceeds from its origins in the creation of exhibitions at the National War Museum of Scotland in Edinburgh Castle. What follows is not, then, a work based on new research amongst primary written sources, nor exactly a new synthesis of secondary sources, but rather a response to the existence of a collection of artefacts that can be, and have been, arranged and interpreted in different ways to represent Scotland's long acquaintance with warfare. The very existence of this collection gives us our starting point, for, as will be described, the museum's creation in 1930 was part of the expression of a desire to commemorate Scotland's part and sacrifice in the First World War as a national contribution, the same impulse that three years earlier had seen the completion of the Scottish National War Memorial, also in Edinburgh Castle. That the museum's collection has grown since is in large part due to a similar impulse that has led Scots to give treasured objects, precious personal or family possessions to the museum in

Detail from 'The Thin Red Line' by Robert Gibb, 1881.

Edinburgh Castle, and not perhaps to other museums, specifically because they wanted them to be preserved in Scotland and in such a symbolically potent place.

There are different ways of approaching such a collection. In its earliest manifestation, in the days before individual regiments had their own public museums, the museum in Edinburgh Castle was principally given over to celebrating and commemorating the famous Scottish regiments – the units of the British army that epitomised the Scottish military tradition, and to acknowledging notable individual Scottish contributions in other parts of the armed services. Years of typological collecting in uniform, weapons and other military artefacts added to the collection and, in recent decades, a broader perspective of historical interpretation was applied as military museums in the United Kingdom aspired to recognition as museums of social history. A national museum of war and military history is indeed a medium of social history that can convey something of human experience in this most extreme and unusual of occupations, of the lot of the Scottish soldier, sailor or airman in war and peace. That such individual experiences have something in common with those of the Welsh soldier, the Irish sailor, or the English airman, or indeed of soldiers, sailors and airmen around the world, need not diminish interest from the Scottish perspective. But in writing this book from the standpoint of a National War Museum of Scotland, we have our own questions to ask in seeking to understand such experiences. What were the forces operating on Scotland and Scots that shaped the histories, traditions and individual experiences that have come down to us? How have war and military service influenced Scottish society and been influenced by it in turn?

The National War Museum of Scotland today forms part of the National Museums of Scotland, a body whose collections span the range of human activity in Scotland and reflect Scotland's interaction with the rest of the world. Yet the National War Museum sits a little apart, at home in Edinburgh Castle, an ancient military stronghold perched high on the rock above Scotland's capital city, a place that has often been seen as the core of the nation. The Museum's presence there is testament to the fact that the notion of a Scottish military tradition was once felt to be something absolutely central to our national history, to our national character even. Today, many of those who come to the National War Museum of Scotland are visitors to Scotland, tourists drawn to the Castle by what it represents about the country they seek to experience. That they should find there a museum that explores Scotland's military reputation comes as no surprise, for it is a reputation with which many of them are familiar, one whose symbols they can recognise in the artefacts they see. To many Scots today, this might not be the first conception of Scotland that springs to mind, to some it might even be a

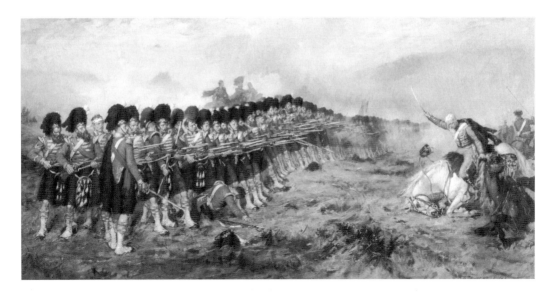

source of unease. The contention that military museums glorify or elevate war is not always easy to counter. Many of the objects used in warfare and produced to commemorate it were designed for that very purpose, and to some degree that is how they still communicate as museum exhibits, no matter how they are interpreted and placed in historical context. Yet the existence of the National War Museum of Scotland reflects the desire of Scots, many from generations that had been through hugely destructive wars, that Scotland's relationship with war should be recorded and commemorated, not because war was good or glorious, but because it was important.

The Thin Red Line by Robert Gibb, 1881, the quintessential image of the Victorian Scottish soldier, depicts the 93rd Highlanders defending the port of Balaclava during the Crimean War, 25th October 1854.

---

1   Two terms, used here and throughout, require clarification. The word 'military' has been employed in its widest definition, *ie* that pertaining to the prosecution of war, and not in the literal sense of that pertaining to soldiers (and therefore not to sailors or airmen) alone. For the sake of concision, the various, and particular, appellations 'United Kingdom', 'Great Britain and Ireland', and 'Great Britain' have largely been substituted with the terms 'Britain' or 'British'.

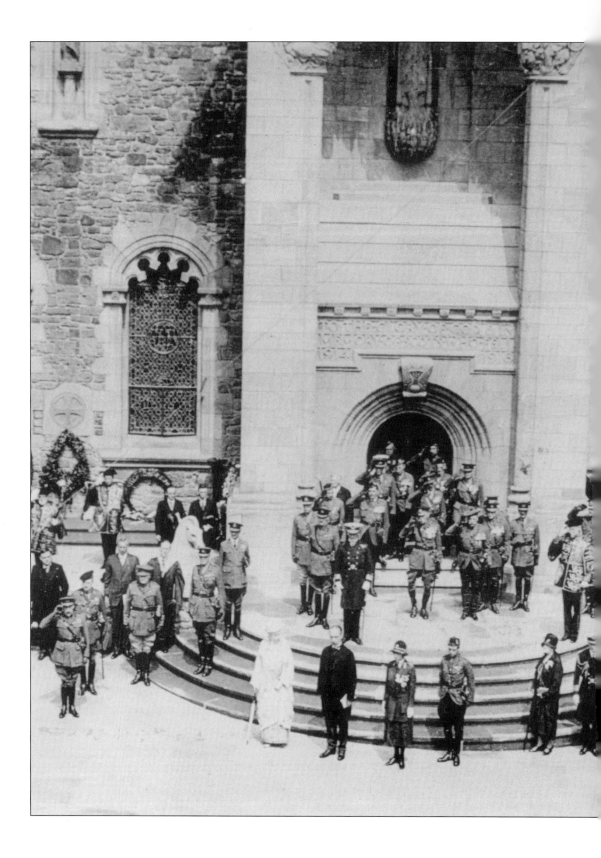

Old Scotland
for ever

THE SCOTTISH NATIONAL WAR MEMORIAL STANDS ON THE SUMMIT rock of Edinburgh Castle. At the core of architect Sir Robert Lorimer's design, within the Shrine with its stone of Remembrance and Casket containing the Rolls of Honour, the Castle Rock itself breaks up through the floor. The symbolism of the setting is elementary. We are on the 'Capitol' of Scotland, the commanding height of the nation, and it is here that the Scots have placed their reckoning with war. Opened in 1927, the Memorial commemorated over 100,000 Scots then estimated to have lost their lives in the First World War.[1] Scotland, it seemed, knew well what it had given to Britain and the empire during the conflict and would have its own, very Scottish reminder. The Scottish National War Memorial is probably the most elaborate, most artfully symbolic, most deliberately monumental, of all the memorial schemes realised in the United Kingdom in the aftermath of the conflict. In its symbolism and in its internal arrangement, the Memorial reveals something of how Scots viewed the war and Scotland's part in it.

By adapting buildings in Edinburgh Castle to this purpose, Scotland was placing its response to the war, the Great War that surely then seemed a defining national experience, firmly in the embrace of its historic past. Not for Edinburgh the knowing understatement of the Cenotaph in Whitehall or the park settings of the national memorials placed in Cardiff and Dublin. From the earliest public moves to create a national memorial, on the urging of the Duke of Atholl in 1917, the proposed schemes proceeded in agreement that, 'no nation in the wide world has in its capital a finer and more natural Monument of War than Edinburgh Castle'.[2] It is indeed striking, and perhaps telling, that the great landmark of Scotland's capital city is not a palace or a church (although it contains both), but is an ancient fortress, built high on a place of natural military strength. In the modern period, Scotland has been fortunate to avoid the continued ravages of war suffered by many countries of continental Europe, but like Prague's Hrad or Belgrade's Kalemegdan fortress, Edinburgh Castle looms large as the daily business of the town proceeds, a reminder that peace here in Scotland was not always to be taken for granted.

Dedication of the Scottish National War Memorial, 14th July 1927.

As a place of strategic importance, the Castle ceased to serve any real purpose some two hundred years ago and more. In the interim, while still used for military purposes by the British army as barracks, headquarters and prison, and much altered in the fabric for such requirements, its importance to Scotland has been more symbolic in nature. Today, in our age of mass tourism, where the Castle seems if anything an icon of our tourist industry, and in a time where patriotism is less confidently and publicly expressed, it is perhaps difficult to remember the degree to which, for much of the nineteenth and twentieth centuries, Edinburgh Castle was looked to by Scots as the kernel of their own country, as a citadel of national sacred space.

Gradually, while the British army remained in day to day occupation, the Castle was equipped better to fulfil this cultural role. When Sir Walter Scott rediscovered the Honours of Scotland (the Scottish royal crown and regalia packed away at the 1707 Union with England) in their oak chest in 1818, they were placed on view again in the Castle so that the Scots might look at them in what seemed their rightful place, or, failing seeing them, so that they might simply know they were there – in Edinburgh Castle – where they ought to be. As for the Honours, so too for 'Mons Meg', a 15th-century bombard artillery piece, the return of which from the Tower of London in 1829 ministered to the popular mood.

Where the Castle's structure was found not quite to measure up to its perceived position as repository of Scotland's national heritage, it was altered to suit, and might have been altered greatly if more grandiose schemes had been realised. When, in 1917, the need for a Scottish National War Memorial began to be expressed, there was little doubt over where it would have to go, particularly as the planned departure of the army garrison to new accommodation to the south of the city would leave many of the Castle's buildings empty. Following Cabinet approval for the general principle of creating such a monument, the Secretary of State for Scotland wrote, 'if any spot is marked out by nature and history for the dedication of a shrine in memory of men and women of Scottish birth or connection who died for King and Country, it is surely the beautiful capital of Scotland, and in that capital the Castle, whose Rock, beyond any other of Scotland's sacred places, may claim to symbolise the national soul'.[3]

In the ten years from inception to completion, the memorial scheme went through many changes and encountered some opposition (principally over fears that Lorimer's first design would radically alter the Castle skyline). The original proposal put forward in 1917 was to create in the Castle a National Historical War Museum with collections that represented Scotland's military heritage stretching back beyond the then-current conflict. Later schemes included a more comprehensive National Museum of Scotland, envisaging the transfer of collections from the existing Museum of Antiquities to join new military collections in the Castle. In the event, the creation of a memorial building took precedence, and the military museum aspect of the scheme was not realised until the 1930s.

Together, the Memorial as finally executed and the opening of its companion Scottish Naval and Military Museum in 1933, speak volumes about the place of war in ideas of Scottish national identity in the early twentieth century. One striking aspect of the Memorial is that, outside the central Shrine, the space is arranged by way of separate dedications to individual military units. This 'Hall of Honour', originally 'Hall of the Regiments', with its Rolls of Honour for each service, regiment or corps, is an arresting and affecting tribute to the sacrifice of many lives. It also seems to suggest the distinctiveness of the Scottish contribution to the First World War in a way that might not have been conveyed if the emphasis had instead been placed on the common sacrifice of the individual, a symbolic theme more readily found in other national and local places of remembrance. Scots gave of their lives, it seems to say, and Scotland gave of its historic regiments, an echo perhaps of the 'clannish-ness' which had long been regarded as a peculiar aspect of Scottish society. The same influence guided ideas about a war museum for Scotland. In London the Imperial (originally 'National') War Museum was founded to document and commemorate the First World War alone. Further afield, the same stipulation originally guided the creation, in museum form, of the Australian War Memorial in Canberra. But the war museum suggested and created in Scotland always looked further back to the accumulated glories of Scottish regiments and military heroes. In Scotland, powerful latent forces were at work – the weight of the Scottish military tradition.

If, to a large degree, Scotland's national memorial to the war was to be a monument and a museum of the Scottish regiments, shaped in the image of the Scottish military tradition, then this corresponded to the outlook of those individuals who initiated and shaped the scheme. In its efforts to raise funds the Scottish National War Memorial Committee was not overwhelmed with gifts from the broader Scottish public. Representatives sent out into 851 parishes found approval for the idea, but met a muted response in funds collected and promised. The prior call of local memorials and a 'sick-tired' weariness for collections of all kinds were amongst the factors identified in acknowledging that results had not come up to expectations.[4] This was as likely down to a lack of means as to any lack of interest, for the call went out as Scotland stood in the depth of economic slump. Ultimately, the £120,000 sum raised owed much to significant donations by a small number of private individuals (including one gift of £50,000). To a large degree, the Scottish National War Memorial was the conception and creation of the Scottish establishment. Unsurprisingly, its principal progenitors were both military men. The Duke of Atholl, Chairman of the Committee, had served with the Nile Expedition of 1898, had been awarded the Distinguished Service Order for his service in the South African War, and held brigade commands and regimental colonelcies during and after the First World War. Lieutenant-General Sir Spencer Ewart, who had been advocating a Scottish military historical museum since before the war, was General Officer Commanding Scotland, a distinguished soldier at the end of a long career. Those they cultivated for support and funds of course included the Scottish regiments themselves, to whom the idea of a national amalgam of regimental memorials, adorned with battle honours and regimental Colours, as can be seen today, appealed strongly. It would be inaccurate to call the Scottish National War Memorial triumphal or militaristic – no monument housing the names of so many dead could be that – but with a quality that is perhaps less pacific, more assertive than that of many local war memorials, it is absolutely a military memorial.

Although funds for the Memorial were hard to come by, this did not mean that the Scottish public was unmoved by what was achieved. Crowds flocked to Edinburgh Castle to pay their respects and appreciate the symbol of remembrance and nationhood that had been created. Later generations of historians and commentators have applied close scrutiny and contemporary attitudes to the causes and conduct of the First World War and have found much to condemn, so much so that in what has come down to the present day as the popular view of the war it is often only the very worst that is remembered. However, the generation that actually went through the experience, under no illusions as to the

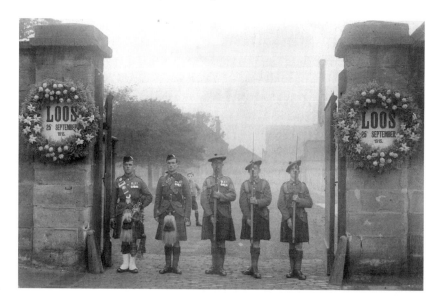

Depot of the Black Watch commemorates the battle of Loos, c.1925. With over 12,000 Scots casualties, this 1915 battle was particularly remembered in Scotland.

cost, believed overwhelmingly in the justice of the cause and the worthiness of victory. The Scottish National War Memorial and the museum it spawned corresponded to the popular mood of sober pride in Scotland's share in victory – a victory for the British empire in which Scotland was eminent and (in relation to the ultimate reversal of Germany's 1914 invasion of Belgium) a victory that was seen as a blow struck for the freedom of small nations.

The outbreak of the First World War in 1914 provided the high watermark of popular identification with an ideal of Scotland's warlike past. The celebration of Scotland as a nation of warriors and soldiers was an idea with a long heritage, but by the early twentieth century it had come to be identified in particular with the Scottish infantry regiments of the British army. Each of these had its own identity and traditions, carefully nurtured and promoted, but together they formed a pantheon of heroic reputation, of picturesque and distinctively Scottish appearance that appealed strongly to the tastes of the public in Scotland and beyond. The Royal Scots, the Royal Scots Fusiliers, the King's Own Scottish Borderers, the Cameronians, the Black Watch, the Highland Light Infantry, the Seaforth Highlanders, the Gordon Highlanders, the Queen's Own Cameron Highlanders, the Argyll and Sutherland Highlanders: all were names that meant something to any Scot who ever picked up a newspaper or had an ear for tales of national prowess. To the list was added the Royal Scots Greys and the Scots Guards, representing the Scottish elements of the cavalry and guards respectively, whose rather different social and organisational milieux did not keep them from associate membership of the magic circle of the Scottish regiments. Well before the building of monuments to the First World War the list

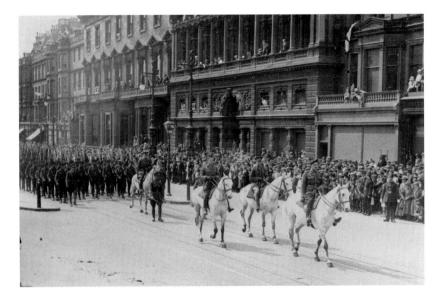

Canadian troops parade through Edinburgh in May 1919 as Scotland's capital city acknowledges a special link of kinship.

19

seemed monumental, suggestive of something eternal, as if the Scottish regiments had always been there, carrying their country's good name into battle.

During the war itself, it was through these 'historic' Scottish regiments that Scotland's part in the conflict was seen to be played out, although, as subsequent chapters will consider, Scotland's practical importance in the war effort was as much a matter of naval strategy and industrial production as of military manpower. As was the practice throughout the United Kingdom, the many thousands of Scots who volunteered for war service joined existing and new battalions of the traditional regiments and so took on, on the surface at least, their trappings and reputations. Scots of course served in number in all branches of the armed services, but in the kilted or bonneted battalions of the lowland and highland regiments they were, in short, visibly Scottish. In the case of the highland regiments in particular, appeals for recruits were couched in terms of tradition, clan and cultural loyalty referring back to the mass recruitment of highlanders into the British army in the late eighteenth century.

This appeal extended to Scottish emigrants and their descendants who in Canada, Australia, New Zealand and South Africa took on the compound of Scottish regimental identity, almost as second nature, as they went about forming their own war service units. In this they had their own precursors, as local part-time volunteer defence forces in these countries had included 'Scottish regiments' parading their ethnic identity as early as the 1860s and, in the Canadian context, recalling Scottish emigrant regiments of the previous century. These units had increasingly identified themselves not only with the cultural emblems of the Scottish regiments as a whole, but, to varying degrees, had connected themselves with individuals regiments in Scotland, wearing uniforms close to those of the illustrious Scottish originals. In at least one instance, that of the Queensland Scottish in the 1880s, the Australian unit was wearing uniform recycled from that cast off by its chosen Scottish parent, the Gordon Highlanders.[5]

The obvious explanation for the prominence of the Scottish regiments in these visions of Scottish national identity is of course that the military achievements and reputations of the regiments put them there. In a straightforward sense this is true. For generations the Scottish soldier had been a positive element in Scottish self-image. Highland soldiers specifically, formerly distrusted and tainted with memories of Jacobitism, had made themselves conspicuously useful to the army in British victories such as the storming of Quebec in 1759. But it was with defeat of Napoleon's French army in Egypt in 1801 that the presence of highland regiments came to be celebrated broadly as a talisman of British military success. Success is the operative word here, as prior to victories in India in the 1790s and the defeat of French armies in Egypt conspicuous

British military success in land warfare had been lacking for some time. But after the Egypt campaign the pictorial and literary celebration of British martial achievement, in the Penisular War, at Quatre Bras and at Waterloo, seemed almost to require the presence of the valorous highlander.

The distinctive appearance of the highland soldier of course gave an element of the picturesque, of the romantic, in the prints and paintings commemorating British military achievement that were produced for a growing market in London and beyond, but for Scots it was the positive equation between Scots and British success that was important. It was a means by which the Scottish establishment and growing middle classes could first demonstrate Scotland's loyalty to the British state and, when that ceased to be a matter of any doubt, could posit as evidence, both for their own satisfaction and for the instruction of their English brethren, that Scotland was contributing to the security and prosperity of the British empire as a full and equal partner.

Inherent in this manner of self-promotion was a piece of cultural 're-branding', for the most colourful and saleable representation of Scottish military success was the image of the highland soldier, recruited into the British army in huge numbers. It required the Scots themselves to accept and embrace the idea of the highland soldier as a desirable national symbol, representing quite a turnaround for a country in which dominant interests of government, property, religion and business had long been in the habit of looking on the highlands and its people as things alien, backward and to be feared. In the seventeenth century in particular, the highlander had been the bogeyman of Scottish lowland society. The 'highland host' was a fearsome folk memory, an army of rapacious strangers that could be brought down on the south by unscrupulous and ungodly kings. The Jacobite campaigns from 1688 to 1746 had added specific negative associations between highland military society and armed Jacobitism, complete with its perceived overtones of political and religious tyranny. The highland armies that had made the Jacobite campaigns such a potent threat were, in the late eighteenth century, a source of embarrassment, if not national shame, to Scottish vested interests. These were, however, memories of armies that had been defeated. Regimented in the British service thereafter, highland soldiers were perceived to have become politically safe. Their appearance and curiosity value became appealing in a popular culture increasingly influenced by artistic and literary appreciation of the picturesque and romantic. Better yet, they came to be associated with victory.

The landed, propertied classes in Scotland, and all those doing well out of the Union, the empire and the wars against France, wanted the Scottish military contribution to British security and conquest recognised and

A medal struck by the Highland Society of London after the British victory in Egypt in 1801, commemorating the 42nd (Highland) Regiment and the Scottish commander General Sir Ralph Abercromby.

acknowledged. Admiral Lord Duncan, for his victory over the Dutch fleet at Camperdown in 1797, General Sir David Baird for his overthrow of the dreaded Tipu Sultan of Mysore, and General Sir Ralph Abercromby for his defeat of the French at Alexandria, were lionised (and, in Abercromby's case, mourned) as Scottish national heroes, successors to the reputation of Scottish, and solely Scottish, war leaders Sir William Wallace and King Robert the Bruce. On Calton Hill, another of Edinburgh's prominent hilltops, stands the National Monument to the Scottish dead of the Napoleonic Wars, a project designed to commemorate and celebrate a distinctly Scottish and, crucially, Scottish *national* sacrifice in Great Britain's long and finally successful wars against France. However, the National Monument project came to reflect another story, for it is as an unfinished monument that the structure attracts attention as a landmark today. Among other monikers it was quickly dubbed 'Scotland's Pride and Poverty', for the work was famously abandoned in 1830 when funds raised by public subscription ran out. It might be inferred that not all people with disposable income to contribute were quite ready to associate their security and prosperity with the sacrifices and successes of armed forces recruited from other sections – the top and the bottom – of Scottish society; or, mindful of how much they had invested in what was still a fragile union, were as yet wary of going too far in acclaiming Scottish nationhood in arms. Calton Hill's incomplete acclamation in stone, like the Scottish National War Memorial of the next century, was the work of relatively few influential Scots seeking to encourage, as well as reflect, popular support for their vision of Scotland.

This view of Scottish military achievement nevertheless had a ready constituency. In addition to the high visibility of Scots and Scottish units in the regular army, substantial numbers of Scots who remained at home during the wars against France had also donned military uniform and felt a share in the victory. Responding to the threat of a French invasion, part-time volunteer units for home defence sprung up throughout Great Britain in the 1790s. Scotland's long coastline was certainly vulnerable to enemy naval activity. The volunteer infantry and mounted yeomanry units were a means by which civilians could provide for their own defence, earn extra money, contribute to the war effort on their own terms, and demonstrate their patriotism and respectability by overtly displaying that commitment. As in regular military service, Scots were disproportionately represented in the British volunteer movement.[6] In the eyes of some, this was itself evidence of continuity in Scottish national military prowess. Although the uniform of the volunteer units was similar throughout Great Britain, the most common element in the badges of local volunteer units in Scotland was a Scottish national symbol, the thistle. Sometimes it appeared with the royal cipher, or in conjunction with a specifically local symbol of identity, but the thistle alone was the most popular design choice. In penning a war song for his own volunteer regiment, the quartermaster of the Royal Edinburgh Light Dragoons, one Sir Walter Scott, exercised his highly developed sense of Scotland's historic nationhood in interrupting his flow of British patriotic bombast against the French to note,

> From high Dunedin's towers we come,
> A band of brothers true;
> Our casques the leopard's spoils surround,
> With Scotland's hardy thistle crowned ....[7]

At the end of the war with France, Scotland was brimful of men with personal experience of military life, whether as regular soldiers or sailors, volunteers or yeomen, war service fencible troops or even conscripted militia men. Few Scottish families of any class can have been without some connection to military service. As the post-war army shrunk and people returned to peacetime life, they continued to constitute a society receptive to the equation between military success and Scotland's status as a fully paid-up national partner in the Union and the British empire.

The idea stuck and, as the nineteenth century progressed, it came to be focussed on the performance of highland regiments that had remained as part of a relatively small, but highly active, imperial British army. During the Victorian period the reputation of the highland regiments really became an article of faith for Scottish patriots, since the actual preponderance of Scots in the British army was actually on the wane. The high point of Scottish recruitment into the army had come during the wars against Revolutionary and Napoleonic France. By one estimate, Scots made up 15.3 per cent of the British army in 1813 (compared to approximately 10 per cent of the total British popula- tion).[8] By 1830 the decline is evident, with another calculation giving Scots as 13.5 per cent of the army (and still as 10 per cent of the British population). By 1870 the figures suggest Scots constituting just 8 per cent of the army, despite the Scottish population rising to around 10.5 per cent of the British total.[9]

Yet from the way that highland regiments monopolised the limelight as imperial victories were reported and celebrated at home, one might never have guessed that this was the case. Re-enforced notions of highland heroism stood among the few positive features to emerge from such conflicts as the Crimean War and the Indian Mutiny, campaigns that otherwise seemed to reflect equivocally on British military and administrative organisation. News from foreign fields of battle was by then travelling fast. In 1854 reports of incompetence and maladminis- tration filed from the Crimea by *The Times* war correspondent William Russell made for dispiriting reading, but the public could at least marvel

at such feats as the 93rd Highlanders' stand against Russian cavalry at
the battle of Balaclava – in Russell's original words 'a thin red streak
tipped with a line of steel', a description that he later metamorphosed
into 'The Thin Red Line', the phrase later immortalised in the title
of Robert Gibb's famous painting. Soon afterwards, the home public
could sooth their shock over the outbreak of the Indian Mutiny by
reading of such exploits as the defence and relief of the besieged garrison
at Lucknow by highland troops. The Crimea and Indian successes of
the Highland Brigade, led by the Scottish General Sir Colin Campbell,
offered reassurance as well as relief, for, in celebrating the highlanders
in particular, contrasts were drawn between perceptions of the simple
heroism and loyalty of the highland soldier, the shameful weakness and
vulnerability of the British administration in India that had brought
things to such a pass, and, of course, the perfidy of the Indian soldiers
who had rebelled against their Queen. By this stage, the Scottish aspect
of British military endeavour was beginning to be acclaimed in print
and imagery quite out of proportion to its practical impact, sometimes
to the irritation of non-Scottish regiments who could find their own
comparable battlefield successes, even those achieved side-by-side in
highland company, overshadowed by the cult of the highland soldier.

In the small campaigns fought on the fringes of the British empire in
India and Africa thereafter, the deeds of highland regiments continued
to emerge as the leading story absorbed with enthusiasm by the British
newspaper reading public at large, and not just in Scotland. Too much
ought not to be made of differences in Victorian public attitudes towards
the military in Scotland as distinct from the United Kingdom as a whole.
The English too were fond of their admirals and generals when they
did well. It is true also that in the last decades of the nineteenth century,
with reforms in army administration and the growth of a popular
ideological element to British imperialism, the outlook of the property-
owning classes generally was much more susceptible to the idea that the
common soldier, once viewed as brutish and dissolute, could be not only
heroic, but even respectable.

Nevertheless, subtly different traditions still held sway. English notions
of English, or greater British, power and martial glory had long focussed
on the Royal Navy as the guarantor of national security and honour.
England's part in the defence and expansion of the British empire was
not a matter of doubt; the English would feel no need to be reassured
about it. There was also, as a strain in English political culture, a long
heritage of distrust in standing armies, a fear of militarism as a threat
to hard-won political and civil liberties. Indeed, expressions of English
cultural hostility to their partners in union had in the past been couched
in terms of identifying Scottish/highland soldiers as the unquestioning
arm of military tyranny, another consequence of the Jacobite wars.

Most virulent of the anti-Scottish voices was the popular radical politician and polemicist John Wilkes. Wilkes' attacks on the government in the 1760s focussed on the Scottish aristocratic background of the King's Prime Minister, the Earl of Bute, and his published libels of Bute earned Wilkes spells in prison. On the occasion of his release in 1768, public demonstrations in Wilkes' favour turned to riot. As chance had it, it was soldiers of the 3rd (or Scots) Guards who were called out to deal with the disturbance. The tumult ended with six Wilkes supporters killed, others injured, and one apparently innocent bystander pursued into a barn and shot dead. Reports of Scottish troops firing on the London crowd naturally fuelled perceptions of Scots as the enemies of liberty, a notion that reinforced the link between Scots bearing arms and a traditional English distrust of the military power of government. The regimental system of organisation that came to characterise the British army was in tune with this very concern, helping to fragment the potential for military interference in politics. As in Scotland, individual English, Welsh and, for that matter, Irish regiments had their own reputations and traditions, well-won and fiercely defended, but, unlike in Scotland, these were not melded together in the popular perception into a symbol of distinct historic nationhood within the context of Great Britain and the empire.

In the Scottish context there were no such reservations, and no longer any worries about the fragility of the Union. Although in the structure of British army organisation Scotland had no institutional status as a nation (for administrative purposes at best it was 'North Britain'), in the popular view the Scottish regiments together came to constitute something akin to an unofficial Scottish army operating within and at the forefront of the forces of the British empire. This cultural phenomenon was rooted in something more than the continuing success of those regiments on the field of battle, though it certainly fed off this. Essentially, the reputation of the Scottish regiments fitted perfectly with, and indeed was adapted to suit, the deliberate cultural redefinition of Scotland, the rediscovering and refining of Scottish history that was underway during much of the eighteenth and early nineteenth century. It was in a Scotland that had begun to be defined in literary terms by the sensational publishing success of James McPherson's mythical 'translations' of *Ossian*'s epic Gaelic poetry, by the creative codification of clans and tartans drawn up with rather dubious claims of historical authenticity, and by the vision of Scotland's heroic past drawn from the pen of Sir Walter Scott, that the image of the Scottish regiments could shine. In turn, the reputation of the regiments gave modern substance to the highland ancestral idyll.

Much has been written about the romantic makeover of Scottish historical culture during the eighteenth and nineteenth centuries, a great deal of it disparaging. The influence of wider movements in art, music and literature – the fashion for the picturesque, for historical romanticism – is seen to have created a bogus past for Scotland based on a mythical and sentimental view of Gaelic highland society. Combined with the absence in Scotland of a meaningful demand for political independence such as was to be found developing among small nations on the continent, this romantic self-image has been taken as a substitute for a 'real' national consciousness in a Scotland culturally and politically subservient to England. On the other hand, and quite conversely, for a Scotland where there was consistent and near-universal agreement among the middle and upper classes that the national destiny lay within the United Kingdom and the British empire, and for a Scotland where considerable national autonomy was enjoyed in domestic political matters by the professional and propertied classes, it is possible to read the popularising of Scottish history in this form as the expression of a type of patriotism equally as valid as one based on a demand for national sovereignty.

As in most contemporary versions of the past, the tartan-clad version of Scottish history suited the needs and interests of the present. It overlooked or neutralised much in the way of historical fact that was unhelpful, divisive or unpalatable. Such was the attractive power of its highland cultural overtones, even the memory of Jacobitism, not long since feared and derided, could be assimilated and become an acceptable subject for nostalgia. In this view the Jacobite highlanders, simple and loyal to their chiefs and kings, had fought in a tragic cause, but had fought with Scottish heroism. Tartan Scotland was a form of patriotism that could bolster Scotland's distinctiveness within the Union, could revive and reinforce the survival of the ancient kingdom of Scotland as an idea, but was one that did not undermine the British political structure on which Scottish prosperity and society was taken to rely. It was a conservative impulse, a reaction to economic forces that were

Sergeant Donald McKenzie, 42nd Highlanders, is prominent in the foreground of David Octavius Hill's painting of the *First General Assembly of the Free Church of Scotland*, indicating the respectability enjoyed by the army in Victorian Scotland.

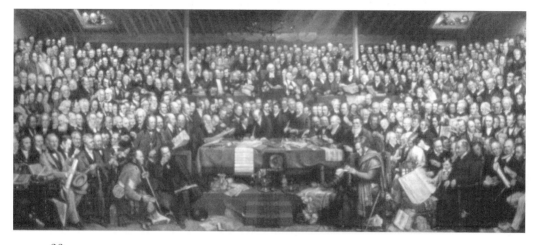

radically changing the country, but simultaneously was one that distilled an idea of Scottish identity that the rising professional and commercial classes could embrace, that actually transcended the surviving established institutions of Scottish nationhood – the aristocracy, the law and the kirk, associated in the liberal, progressive mind with a questionable past of vested interests and exclusivity. The search for a heroic past made sense to Scots who were growing prosperous, secure and confident of their future.

What is not in doubt is that the highland regiments were at the centre of the craze for Scottish antiquity. Since the publication of Major-General David Stewart of Garth's seminal work *Sketches of the Character, Manners and Present State of the Highlanders of Scotland* in 1822, the highland regiments had been classified as the direct inheritors of the ancient martial society of the highland clans.[10] Stewart's research and writings on highland tradition, characterised by a sympathetic view of the economic and social pressures which contemporary highland society faced, came after a distinguished military career as a highland officer. His interest in cataloguing and defining the history of the highland garb, among other things, was coloured by his experience of the tartan uniformity developed for the highland regiments. Essentially, Stewart's work gave the regiments an aura of antiquity and preciousness that transcended the hard facts of their existence in the British army establishment which dated only from the raising of the first highland regiment in 1739.

Like all of the regiments of the British army, their survival into the nineteenth century had always depended on military expediency: the size of army deemed necessary by government, and seniority, the age of the regiment, which determined the likelihood of disbandment when the army was reduced in size. Thus the disappearance in the late eighteenth century of a number of highland regiments, soon largely forgotten, that but for bad luck might have achieved the enduring fame associated with those that survived into the twentieth century. Similarly, when depopulation of the highlands had made recruiting there difficult, and highland dress was proving a disincentive to recruitment in other parts of the country, six regiments abruptly lost their highland status in 1809 to be dressed as normal regiments of the line.

Yet if the army authorities showed little sentimental attachment to the kilt in such circumstances in 1809, the influence of the tartan revolution began to be felt as the century progressed. Royal patronage of the highland ideal, first by George IV and, more devotedly, by Queen

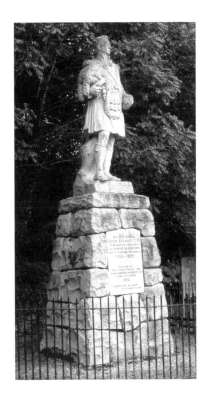

A statue of soldier and historian David Stewart of Garth was erected at Keltneyburn on the old Garth estate, Perthshire in 1925.

Victoria and Prince Albert, placed the highland regiments, their uniforms and their pipers, at the height of fashion. By the 1840s the trend was the opposite of that in 1809. Regiments who had lost the kilt lobbied their way back into tartan, albeit in the form of trews, as highland dress became a positive incentive to recruitment for fashionable officers. Perhaps less enthusiastic were the rank and file soldiers who found themselves out of pocket as a consequence of the cost of maintaining their non-standard highland uniform. Extra items, such as feathers for bonnets, were not official issue and were docked from the men's pay as regimental 'necessaries'. Such was the negative effect on recruitment, an extra kit allowance had to be introduced for soldiers in highland regiments. The army, and by extension the government, was willing to pay to have its highland soldiers conform to the dictates of fashion. To the administrators who had developed a system designed to clothe and equip modern soldiers with efficiency and economy, it must all have been vexing indeed.

Royal patronage was certainly an element in popularising and perpetuating the fashion for all things highland. The highland enthusiasms of kings and queens are often taken to have begun with George IV's visit to Scotland in 1822, when the full panoply of creative highland pageantry was in attendance, orchestrated by Sir Walter Scott. At this event, which has been lampooned for the extremes to which Scott's fantasies extended, and for the unlikely sight of the portly King in a kilt, the good name of the highland regiments was certainly invoked, not least in the influence of the aforementioned Major-General David Stewart of Garth who advised on matters of (non-military) highland costume and ceremony for the great event.

But the connection between the British army, the highland regiments and royalty went back a good deal further. In fact, it was the appeal and growing reputation of the highland regiments that did much to fill crowned heads with sentimental notions about their highland domains. It took time for curiosity to turn to affection. Stewart of Garth records the interest of George IV's grandfather George II in the appearance of the exotic new highland troops in his pay as early as 1743. Three privates of the Black Watch were called to London, presented to the King by their Colonel, and performed martial exercises with their highland weapons. Clearly this early encounter was not enough to instil in the King the sort of enthusiasm for the Gaelic world that was to be shown by some of his successors, nor to stay the hand of one of those present, the Duke of Cumberland, when the highlands suffered the consequences of Jacobite resistance to his family's government three years later. However, when the Jacobite threat passed, senior army officers with direct access to the Court were in a position to promote a more sympathetic, sentimental view. George IV had first worn highland costume in 1789 when he, as

Prince of Wales, and his three brothers had been presented with kilt, plaid and accoutrements with guidance in the proper wearing of them by Colonel John Small, a well-connected army officer. Small, from highland Perthshire, had served in two Scottish regiments and was a veteran of the American War of Independence where he had raised a battalion of highlanders from among Scottish emigrants to North America. He was later promoted to Major General, and became Lieutenant Governor of Guernsey.

John Small's desire to further the interests of his homeland also saw him become one of the founder members of the Highland Society of London. The trend for tartan owed much to the promotional efforts of this private association of highland aristocrats and gentlemen resident in London whose membership always included a strong showing of officers from highland regiments. In 1782 the Society successfully championed the repeal of the Disarming Act, the 1746 law which had outlawed the highland dress following the Jacobite defeat at Culloden (an act from which the highland regiments of the British army had been exempted). With a growing membership that included many highland officers, the Highland Society specifically identified among its objectives 'Keeping up the Martial Spirit; and rewarding the gallant achievement of the Highland Corps'.[11] It played a part in the volunteer movement in London, twice raising highland volunteer regiments during the wars against Napoleonic France. The second of these regiments, the Loyal North Britons raised in 1802, had as its commanding officer the Society's President His Royal Highness the Duke of Sussex – uncle of the future Queen Victoria. Sussex had a marked fondness for highland military dress. Both he and Victoria's father, the Duke of Kent, himself a career soldier and colonel of a (lowland) Scottish regiment, maintained highland pipers on their domestic establishments.

Highland tourism was already widely in vogue by the time of Queen Victoria's first visit to Scotland, but her enthusiastic feeling for the highlands cannot but have been encouraged by the highland military connections of her relatives and forebears. Her regular presence in Scotland thereafter brought the practical need to provide for her security, a requirement that entrenched the position of regard that the highland regiments were to enjoy in her favour. In the 1842 prelude to her purchase of a highland estate at Balmoral, Victoria's first night in the highlands was spent amidst lovingly prepared highland pageantry at Taymouth Castle, seat of the Marquis of Breadalbane. An armed highland guard was provided by Breadalbane's own tenants and retainers, but the real security presence was provided by a detachment from the depot of the 92nd Gordon Highlanders, then at Dundee. Outside the castle double sentries were posted, since the request of the civilian highlanders that they alone should guard their queen could not be countenanced. Soldier and clansman stood side by side, much as they were to continue to do figuratively in the Victorian conception of Scotland. The 92nd's regimental history mischievously recounts that when an officer of the guard 'went the rounds at night he found only his own men; the others had left that uninteresting part of the programme entirely to the redcoats'.[12]

Later, in her widowhood, Victoria was drawn to her military high-landers even when away from Balmoral. In 1872 on the Isle of Wight, she bestowed her attention on the 79th Cameron Highlanders, then stationed close to her Osborne residence. The duties of guard and ceremonial bore fruit in a royal command of 1872 that the regiment should thenceforth be designated the Queen's Own Cameron High-landers. Far to the north at Balmoral, an annual round of Royal Guard duties was established for detachments from Scottish regiments, accom-modated in the small barracks built for the purpose at nearby Ballater in 1869. Royal Guard duty at Balmoral continues today as part of the diet of the Scottish infantry regiments, a requirement which has often complicated the overall plotting of manpower resources by planners at the Ministry of Defence.

The highland takeover of Scottish military identity reached its height in the change of uniform that accompanied a major reorganisa-tion of the British army in 1881. This saw the Scottish lowland regiments fitted up with highland doublets and tartan trews for the first time (though some had been maintaining pipers in highland dress for decades). While this might have gone against the grain of regimental traditions older than the highland regiments themselves, it should not be inferred that with these dress changes the older Scottish lowland regiments were merely surrendering to a highland cultural trend that really had nothing to do with them. Historical romanticism had first embraced the highlands, but, with a similar impulse, the heroic traditions of Scotland as a whole had been looked out and brushed up no less enthusiastically. Sir Walter Scott himself had espoused the virtues of mediaeval chivalry and border tradition as much as he had those of the Gaelic world. By mid-century, interest in Scottish historical culture as a whole produced cults of appreciation for such non-highland hero figures as William Wallace, Robert Bruce and Robert Burns, stretching to such conspicuous tribute as the monument to Wallace near Stirling begun in 1861. This reassertion of Scotland's non-highland heritage carried a political message. As lowlanders and, with reference to Wallace and Burns, non-aristocratic figures, these rediscovered heroes corresponded to some of the tenets of Victorian Scottish Liberalism. But the hard-headed promotion of self-made men and doctrines of individual integrity and freedom was given a sentimental flourish with a romantic literary attachment to stories of cavaliers, border reivers

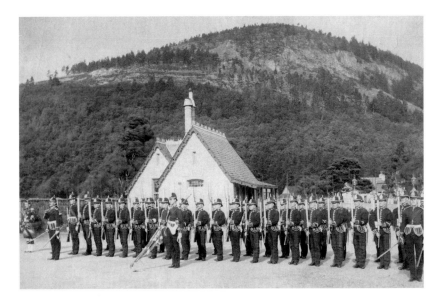

The 2nd Battalion Royal Scots provided the Royal Guard at Balmoral, 1885. On parade at Ballater, they wear their new 'Scottish' uniform.

and Covenanters – figures from Scottish history having little to do with the highlands.

Scott might have been dead many years, but his mantle was taken on by others, not least James Grant. A successful author of historical romances, and a military historian to boot, Grant was also founder of the National Association for the Vindication of Scottish Rights, an organisation asserting Scotland's nation status within the government of the Union. In his creative endeavours, Grant was first inspired by his own father's service with the 92nd Highlanders in the Peninsular War, but among the subjects of his novels were also gallant Scottish soldiers in exile serving the powers of continental Europe, and heroic tales of the religious and dynastic wars of seventeenth-century Scotland.

The Scottish lowland regiments, older than their highland counterparts, could take their place in the popular reawakening of interest in Scottish history and nationhood. They occupied in historical reality the territory covered in fiction by Grant and others: thus Archibald Murray's *History of the Scottish Regiments*, an 1862 work of non-fiction and a precedent for the many such compilations that have followed. In his book, Murray dwelt heavily on the pre-Union origins and forerunners of the lowland regiments, delving back into the religious conflicts of the seventeenth century in Scotland and beyond (on which he expressed a singular Liberal opinion) and, in the case of the Royal Scots, peering as far back as AD 882 to the Scottish bodyguard of Charles III, King of France.

This was not new information; Murray's innovation was to place the histories of the extant Scottish regiments of the British army together and present them as a discreet whole, inheritors of 'the martial achievements of the Scottish nation', part of 'the heroic tale of our ancient

glory'.[13] In the first of these phrases Murray picked up the thread from
Patrick Abercromby, a Jacobite and anti-Union propagandist whose
two-volume work *The Martial Achievements of the Scots Nation* appeared in
1715. Abercromby chronicled centuries of Scotland's independent
military endeavour, 'the military transactions wherein the Scots Nation
has ever been remarkably concerned from the foundation of monarchy
in Scotland', in the vain hope that it could yet be preserved.[14] At a
distance of 150 years, without any sense of contradiction, Murray's
book could ascribe the same tradition to the Scottish regiments by then
happily serving the requirements of the British state and its empire.
For the authors and editors of the many similar books that have followed
Murray's example (one of them the first curator of the museum in Edinburgh Castle), there was little need to make such explicit connections;
all was understood. The combining of Scottish regimental histories
into one national volume, or into a Lowland volume or a Highland
volume, was enough. The books sold, and they still do.

Looking at the tartan-clad Scottish regiments in 1881, it is easy to
see how they could have been taken to represent a glibly satisfactory
resolution of some of the problems of Scottish history. In the highland
regiments the essence of highland society seemed to have been distilled
and preserved in spite of the ravages of change and conflict that had
dogged recent highland history. If the clearing of the tenant populations
from the highland estates had worked to denude the British army of a
prime source of recruits, and to provoke angry responses to recruiting
efforts promoted by highland landowners during the 1850s, the reputation and traditions of the highland regiments had already been securely
established in an identity that could flourish independently of the society
that produced them.

By the 1880s, the Scottish newspaper-reading public was well aware
of the bitterness inherent in the long process of highland depopulation
and was broadly sympathetic towards the highland crofters in their
ongoing agitation for land reform, but as the highlands changed, the
regiments endured, giving superficial comfort and reassurance that not
all had been lost. For their part, lowland regiments clad in tartan could
appear to represent accommodation of the once bitter and violent
enmity between highland and lowland society. Among the Scottish
regiments of 1881 a regiment raised in 1689 to defend Edinburgh from a
Jacobite highland army stood alongside regiments drawing on the same
highland martial culture that had given the Jacobites their military
strength. Regiments raised in the 1670s to suppress armed presbyterian
Covenanters lined up with a regiment raised from among Covenanters
in 1689 when the fortunes of that conflict changed. They all stood for
Scotland. Their very names reflected their coherent national identity.

The 1881 reorganisation of the British army, amongst other things,

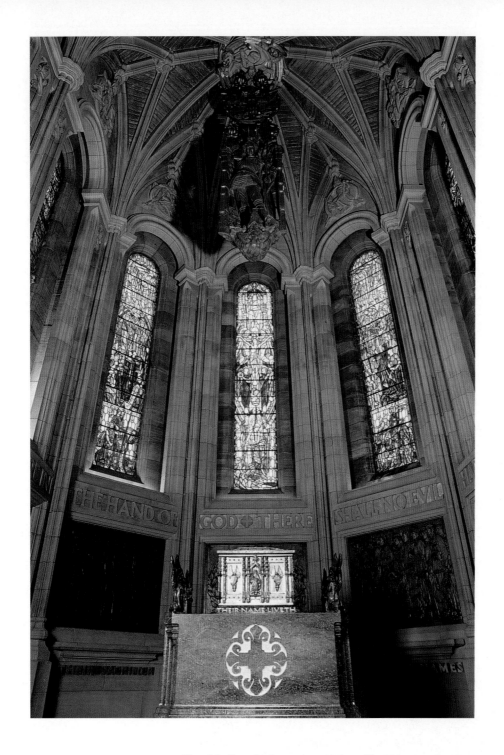

Plate 1.1 Conceived as a concentration of Scottish arts and crafts, the Scottish National War Memorial stands on Edinburgh Castle's summit rock. At its core is the Shrine, housing the Casket that contains the names of the Scottish dead.

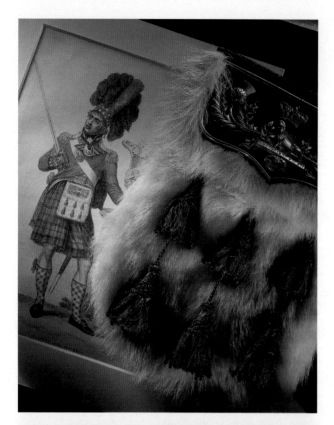

Plate 1.2 The sphinx badge on this officer's sporran commemorates the 42nd (Royal Highland) Regiment's part in the British victory in Egypt in 1801. The print was one of many produced to celebrate the success of the highland regiments and to mourn the heroic death at Alexandria of the army's Scottish commander, General Sir Ralph Abercromby.

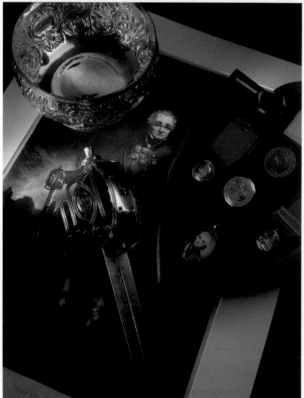

Plate 1.3 The honours of a career as a highland officer were the treasured possessions of the historian Major-General David Stewart of Garth. The medals won in Egypt, Italy and the West Indies are proudly worn in his portrait. He received the silver-hilted highland sword and silver bowl as tribute to his part in the battle of Maida, 1806.

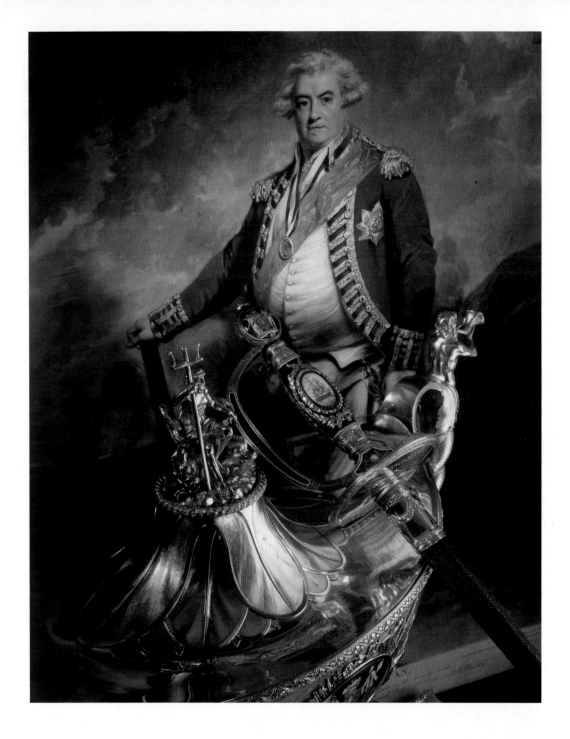

Plate 1.4 An elaborate silver-gilt soup tureen commissioned by the County of Forfar, and a gold-hilted presentation sword from the City of London, were two of the many gifts and tributes made to Admiral Lord Duncan to mark his victory over the Dutch fleet at Camperdown in 1797.

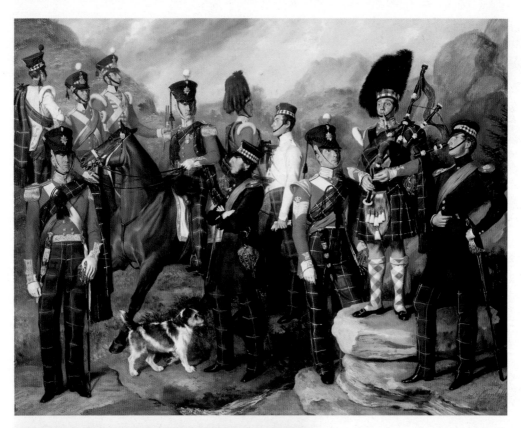

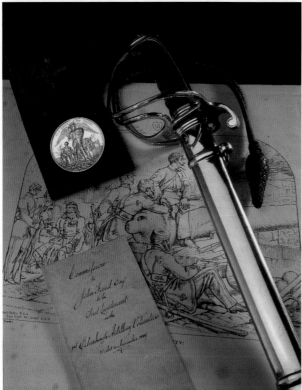

Plate 1.5 Daniel Cunliffe's painting of men of the 74th Highlanders was commissioned in 1846 to celebrate the regiment's return to highland dress. Thirty-seven years earlier, the 74th had been forced to give up its highland status in order to attract recruits from elsewhere. By the 1840s enthusiasm for the highland image overrode such concerns.

Plate 1.6 The artist and antiquarian Sir Joseph Noel Paton carried this sword in the early 1860s as commander of an 'Artists Battery' of the 1st Edinburgh City Artillery Volunteers. His first lieutenant was the painter John Faed. Paton later designed the medal struck for the 21st anniversary of the volunteer movement.

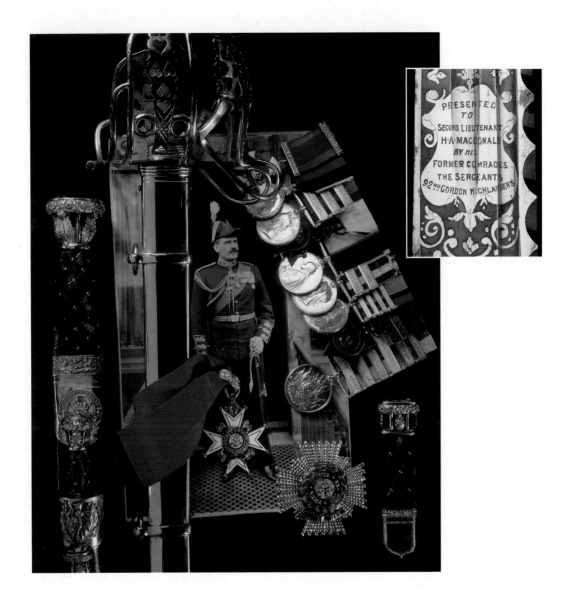

PRESENTED
TO
SECOND LIEUTENANT
H·A·MACDONALD
BY HIS
FORMER COMRADES
THE SERGEANTS
92ND GORDON HIGHLANDERS

Plate 1.7 (and detail) Mementoes of General Sir Hector MacDonald trace his spectacular rise from the ranks of the 92nd Highlanders to high command. The dirk and sgian dhu were farewell gifts from his comrades, the sword a welcome from the officers, as he crossed the social divide to become an officer in his own regiment. Before the shadow of scandal pushed him to suicide, this crofter's son was an imperial celebrity, the epitome of the highland military hero.

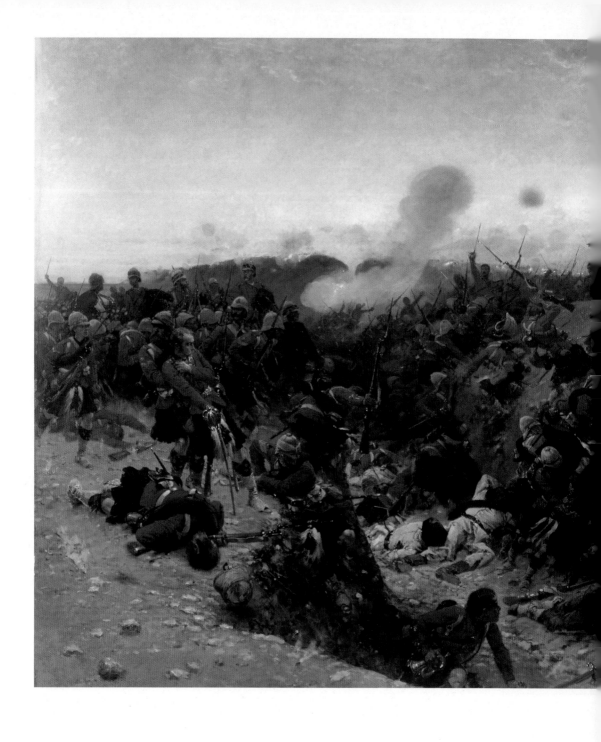

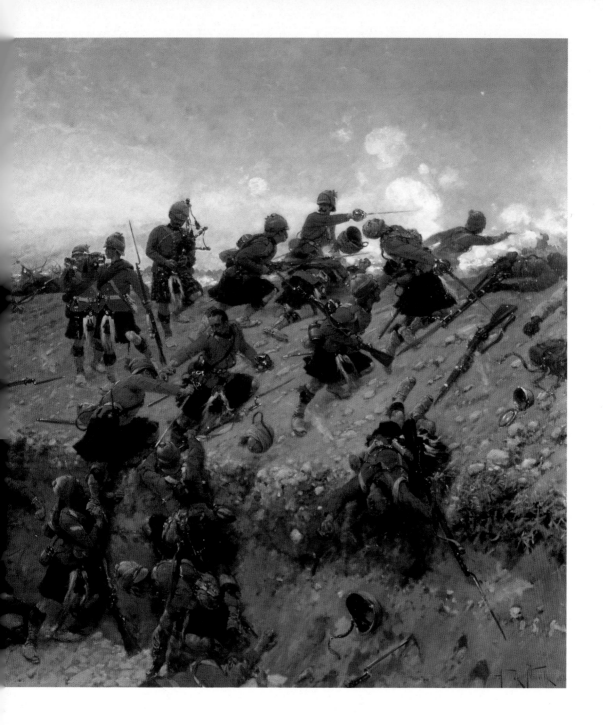

Plate 1.8 The dawn attack of the Highland Brigade at the battle of Tel-el Kebir in 1882 offered a dramatic subject for the French painter Alphonse Marie de Neuville. French admiration for highland regiments flourished as this British military intervention in Egypt brought down a nationalist regime to secure British and French control of the Suez Canal.

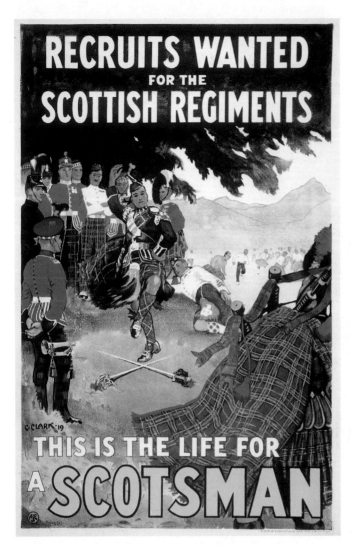

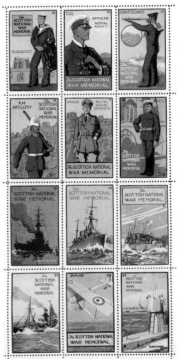

Plate 1.9 This 1919 recruiting poster uses the traditional imagery of the Scottish regiments. Such a colourful and patriotic approach was intended to appeal in a time of war-weariness and economic slump. For the regiments, this was an expression of a return to the conditions of pre-1914 soldiering.

Plate 1.10 Special stamps were sold to raise funds for the Scottish National War Memorial. As well as the Royal Navy, other sheets commemorated the RAF, the contribution of women, and 'The Twelve Famous Scottish Regiments'. The Memorial shown in the stamps was an early design, later altered to reduce the impact on the Castle skyline.

instituted a territorial system whereby infantry regiments were formally linked to geographical areas giving each a permanent local base and concentrating its recruiting activities. The new regiments were accorded formal names in place of the old numbers by which they had previously been officially identified, usually confirming the familiar names by which they had long been known. For many English regiments, one result was to validate their county identity. In Scotland the new names had a decidedly national ring. The words 'Scottish', 'Scots', 'Highland' or 'Highlanders' were the important ones.

The 1881 restructuring of the army in many ways culminated the process whereby the Scottish regiments established their cultural hegemony. In principle, however, the organisational reforms had nothing to do with their reputations or traditions. The purpose was to create a more flexible army that could balance imperial military requirements with a capability to mobilise for home defence in the event of conflict in Europe. In the eyes of the reformers, who tried different approaches, the old system based on the single battalion regiments of the line was too rigid a structure to distribute troops efficiently across the empire; a modern army was deemed to require larger units of organisation. The 1881 outcome, the Childers Reforms, in fact represented a compromise between the reformers (of whom the most prominent had been the Liberal Secretary of State for War Edward Cardwell) and those voices who spoke up for the importance of the regimental ethos and its suitability for the purposes of imperial defence. The new territorial units, essentially brigades comprising two battalions of regular soldiers with supporting battalions of militia and part-time volunteers, remained regiments in name, with identities, traditions and loyalties much like the old ones. Across the country pairs of single battalion regiments were amalgamated together.

So much for tradition, but in the Scottish context the result was indicative of the power of sentiment and reputation. Where Scottish battalions were amalgamated, it was the identity of the regiments with the public profiles, with the reputation for picturesque heroism that best survived the change. The five kilted single-battalion regiments that went into the melting pot of amalgamation in 1881 came out as four kilted two-battalion regiments and one kilted single-battalion regiment untouched altogether. In the process, other Scottish regiments with less exalted profiles found themselves effectively absorbed. One or two actually lost their Scottish designations altogether. The pairing of 141 infantry battalions across the British army also left an odd man out; few can have been surprised that the sole single-battalion regiment allowed to remain was a kilted one – the 79th or Queen's Own Cameron Highlanders – enjoying the particular favour of Queen Victoria and her highland fixation.[15]

It was the Scottish regiments emerging from the 1881 upheavals that consolidated their place in Scottish iconolatry. The territorial system also saw the regiments complete their absorption of the Victorian volunteer movement, the units of part-time amateur soldiers that had sprung up across the United Kingdom in the early 1860s. This was a Victorian revival of the volunteering phenomenon of the Napoleonic Wars and emerged similarly in response to growing French naval power and a consequent fear of invasion, albeit with the two countries actually at peace on this occasion.

The original ethos of many of these units had been distinctively local, rooted in ideas of an active, enlightened civil society that appealed to the Liberal middle classes and self-improving working classes – the last of which, at the beginning of the volunteer movement, did not have the benefit of political expression through the vote. To some degree, the volunteers had emerged as a counter to perceived moral inadequacy, complacency and the dead hand of aristocratic privilege in the traditional system of imperial defence. But in Scotland it was hardly the case that the most visible Scottish manifestation of the military establishment – the Scottish regiments – was widely seen in such critical light. Archibald Murray wrote his aforementioned 1862 eulogy to the regiments as an officer in the 97th Lanarkshire Volunteer Guards, a Glasgow volunteer unit with rather grand pretensions. Any association between the new volunteer units and the mighty Scottish regiments would have been taken as a high compliment by Scottish volunteers like Murray. The Scottish volunteer movement flourished in particular in cities and industrial lowland areas like Lanarkshire, but even there the simple grey uniforms characteristic of the volunteers throughout Britain were enlivened by tartan flourishes, and by the presence of designated 'highland companies' wearing full highland military dress and consisting of a core of volunteers who ostensibly considered themselves to be of highland origin.

Just as the volunteers of the Napoleonic Wars had attracted such patriotic Scots as Sir Walter Scott, leading lights of the new volunteer movement included such proponents of Scottish cultural nationalism as the aforementioned James Grant, and the artist Joseph Noel Paton. In the same year that Paton was organising a battery of Edinburgh Artillery Volunteers from amongst his artistic acquaintances, he was submitting designs to competitions for monuments to William Wallace at Stirling and a related National Memorial of the War of Independence in Edinburgh. Paton's grandiose schemes were both rejected. The work in Stirling went elsewhere, and the plan for the colossal monument Paton proposed for Edinburgh's Princes Street lapsed when it outstripped the funds available. As with the incomplete National Monument on Calton Hill, the eye of this brand of Scottish patriotism appears to have been larger than the pocket. Nevertheless, the design competition itself says

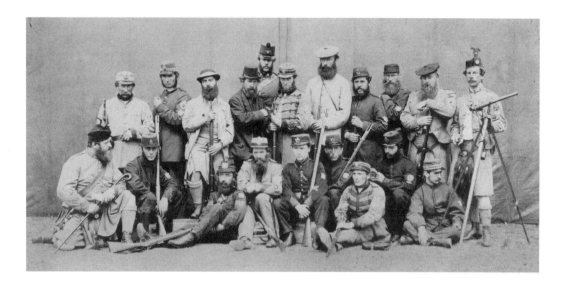

something of the relationship between sentimental Scottish nationalism
and the British imperial context in which it flourished. The scheme for
which Noel Paton the Scottish artillery volunteer had such grand
designs was (under) funded by a bequest left to the city of Edinburgh by
a patriotic Scottish proprietor of East India Company stock, whose path
to prosperity had begun with service as an officer in a Native Infantry
regiment of the East India Company's army.[16]

The connections between the Scottish volunteer movement and the
commemoration of Wallace do not end there. One of the celebrity supporters of the National Wallace Monument at Stirling was the Italian
nationalist leader and soldier Giuseppe Garibaldi. Garibaldi's cause of
Italian liberation and unity was popular in Victorian Scotland where
he was dubbed 'the Wallace of Italy'. Of the idealistic young men of
Edinburgh and Glasgow who in 1860 volunteered for a Scotch Company
to serve in Garibaldi's army in Italy, and who set off adorned with tartan
shirts and scarves, a number at least had some elementary experience of
drill as members of city volunteer units. Their departure from Granton
Pier was accompanied by enthusiastic crowds and the band of the Leith
Volunteer Rifles.

Although Scottish volunteer units clung to their independent local
identities, their integration into the reformed regular army structure in
1881 made formal a connection between the Scottish volunteers and the
Scottish regiments that had always been complimentary, because both
were held to represent all that was implied by the Scottish military tradition. Meantime, the regular regiments had gone about planting their
roots ever deeper in the Scottish psyche. A monument commemorating
the raising of the Black Watch was erected at Aberfeldy, Perthshire in
1887. Two years later the officers of the Cameronians, a regiment that

had very much rediscovered its Scottish presbyterian historical origins, placed a statue of the Earl of Angus at Douglas, Lanarkshire where he had raised the regiment to defend the Protestant succession in 1689. In keeping with their national status, the heritage of the regiments was also visibly displayed in the Scottish capital. A conspicuous memorial to the 78th Highlanders killed in the Indian Mutiny had been raised on Edinburgh Castle esplanade in 1862. Over the years this was joined by several others and, after the turn of the century, South African War Memorials to the Royal Scots Greys, the King's Own Scottish Borderers and the Black Watch became city centre landmarks.

This manner of public expression should not, of course, be taken to indicate unanimous approval among the Scottish people for the military successes of the British empire and Scotland's part in them. The wars against the Boers of South Africa caused particular trouble for the dominant Liberal Party in Scotland, whose radical wing represented a strong body of anti-imperialist opinion. Nevertheless, popular imperialism was a potent force. Divisions between the radical and imperialist wings of the Liberal Party at a time of popular support for the war in South Africa contributed to the Conservative victory in Scotland in the general election of 1900, the first Liberal defeat in nearly seventy years.

The South African War of 1899-1902, with the strategic difficulties it threw up and the large numbers of troops it required, also offered a first opportunity for members of the volunteer movement to participate in an overseas war. From the volunteer battalions service companies of war volunteers came forward for active service in South Africa. The British need for greater numbers of mounted troops to counter the mobile Boer forces brought volunteers from the yeomanry regiments into the conflict also. Service company and yeomanry volunteers alike were fêted by their local communities on their return from a war in which early British calamities had been overturned and in which Scottish civilians had played their part.

The Scottish contribution had also been of a peculiarly imperial character. One of the Scottish units raised to meet the need for mounted troops in South Africa – the Scottish Horse – was recruited not in Scotland but, on the initial suggestion of the Caledonian Society of Johannesburg, among those of Scottish descent in South Africa itself. To these men, mostly of Natal and the Cape, were added contingents from Australia and from home. Command of the Scottish Horse was given to Captain the Marquess of Tullibardine, then serving as a cavalry staff officer in Natal. Years later Lord Tullibardine was Colonel of three regiments of Scottish Horse that served in the First World War. From 1917, succeeding as the Duke of Atholl, he worked to create the Scottish National War Memorial and Museum in Edinburgh Castle. His natural instinct was to include in the rolls of Scottish sacrifice not only those of

Scottish domicile, but also those overseas Scots of the British empire who, like the men of the original Scottish Horse, were Scottish born or of Scottish descent. Atholl's conception of the Scottish National War Memorial, and its museum, was a monument to an imperial Scotland.

The late nineteenth-century conflict between the British empire and the Boer republics of southern Africa affords further insight into the resilience of the Scottish military reputation, offering as it does two pointed examples of that apparent rarity, the highland regiments in defeat. The destruction of a British force at the battle of Majuba Hill in Natal in 1881, though a small engagement, was a humiliation for the British army, a great propaganda victory for the Boer cause, and a fillip for all those who wished the British empire ill. Scotland's honour was implicated, since a third of the defeated force was made up by companies of the 92nd Highlanders. In putting these to flight, the Gordon Highlanders, battle-hardened men fresh from victories in Afghanistan, the Boers had it seemed vanquished and embarrassed the cream of British military might. Reeling from the blow, it took the Scottish propagandists (meantime distracted by timely highland glory won in Egypt in 1882) some time to prepare their answer, but, after the initial bewilderment subsided, it proved possible to find positive reassurance in the gallant conduct of the highlanders at Majuba. Thus defeat could be dressed for popular consumption as highland heroism in adversity, as in the pamphlet *The Majuba Disaster*, published in 1891 from the pen of James Cromb, author of *The Highland Brigade: its Battles and its Heroes*, *The Highlands and Highlanders of Scotland etc., etc.*.[17]

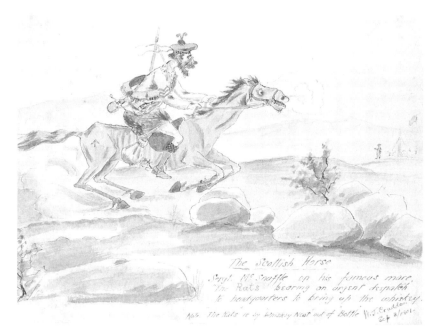

A Harry Lauder-like take on Scottish military identity, as seen through the eyes of an amateur cartoonist serving with the Scottish Horse in South Africa, 1901.

37

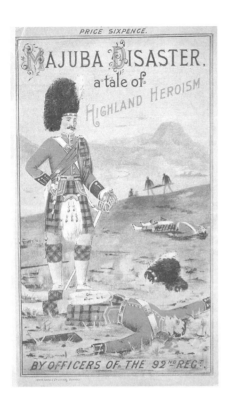

PRICE SIXPENCE.

MAJUBA DISASTER.
a tale of
HIGHLAND HEROISM

BY OFFICERS OF THE 92ND REG^{T}.

James Cromb's
patriotic pamphlet,
1891.

The real counter to Majuba came only when war with the Boers broke out again in 1899. Reports of Gordon Highlanders crying 'Remember Majuba' as they charged the enemy in the British victory at Elandslaagte balanced the books of national honour, and anticipation of just such victory provided an eager market for an enlarged version of Cromb's Majuba pamphlet reprinted in 1899.

The second South African War ended in victory for the British empire, but was not without its British military calamities. In one of these, the battle of Magersfontein, highland battalions again suffered serious loss of life and loss of face. Casualties were on a scale great enough to occasion public mourning in the Scottish highlands, but with overall victory in the war secured, and with the example of Majuba still fresh in the mind, the defeated highlanders were again cast in the role of tragic heroes. The monument to the Highland Brigade erected at Magersfontein, subscribed for by readers of the *Glasgow Herald*, proudly proclaimed, 'Scotland is poorer in men but richer in heroes'.

In 1908, following a long fund-raising campaign, a rather different memorial to the Scottish dead of the South African War opened at Dunblane, Stirlingshire. The Queen Victoria School and Memorial was instituted to maintain and provide an elementary education for the sons of Scotsmen in naval or army service, and the sons of soldiers of any nationality serving in the Scottish regiments. The School's printed brochure, explaining the origins of the institution, noted that while similar schools existed south of the border and in Dublin, the want of one was felt by the Scottish regiments.[18] The long list of subscribers to the school fund shows that individual Scots, Scottish counties and burghs all felt the scheme a worthy national cause. At the end of their schooling from years 9 to 14, the finished pupils were to be placed as apprentices, for training as army schoolmasters or – allowing their free consent – in the navy or army. With its miniature kilted uniform, its pipes and drums, and its Colours presented by King Edward VII 'to the School erected by the Scottish Nation', one can imagine its young graduates absorbed the full measure of the Scottish regimental tradition. For some of these young men who went on to military service, it would be possible to spend an entire life in its embrace. In 1910, troubled by the living conditions of some retired servicemen, two Seaforth Highlander officers began an appeal to create a Scottish residence for veteran sailors and soldiers, a (smaller) Scottish equivalent to London's Chelsea Hospital. The Scottish

Veterans' Residence at Whitefoord House in Edinburgh's Old Town was the first such Scottish institution, and is still in operation today. It was founded with the help of a significant charitable contribution from a Scottish mother who had lost a son in the South African War.

Perhaps the strongest statement of the relationship between the regiments and Scottish nationhood had earlier been enshrined in St Giles', Edinburgh – the nearest thing to a national mother church in presbyterian Scotland. Following the 1881 army reorganisation, it was decided that regiments would no longer carry Colours on active service. These hallowed flags, consecrated and imbued with heavy symbolism of regimental honour, were originally used as conspicuous rallying points in battle; they had no place in modern war. The decision prompted concern in Scotland that historic sets of regimental Colours, by custom laid up in churches or left in the possession of regimental colonels when new sets were issued, were being scattered and lost. It was proposed that they should be collected together in a place of national reverence, by tradition a church setting. In language that foreshadowed the later proposals for a Scottish National War Memorial up the hill in Edinburgh Castle, the *Edinburgh Courant* of 24 April 1882 opined:

> There are few stirring scenes in Scottish history with which St Giles Church is not in some way associated, and what resting-place more meet than under its ancient arches for the hallowed emblems of Scottish history.[19]

Again, as with the later Memorial, it was a small group of prominent Scots who took up the cause. The Old Colours Committee enlisted the support of their fellow noblemen, general officers and gentlemen to lobby the regiments and other distinguished custodians of Colours, persuading many to place them in St Giles'. Those received were installed with due pomp by Field Marshal His Royal Highness the Duke of Cambridge on 14th November 1883. On the occasion, the Minister of St Giles', the Reverend Doctor James Cameron Lees, observed:

> Scotland is a poor country compared with the neighbour with whom it is happily united; but it possesses a distinct national life of its own, which all true Scotsmen would not willingly let die, but would rather seek to cherish to the last – for individuality is as precious to a people as it is to a man. We are proud of the few distinct national possessions that are left us. We cling to them more fondly perhaps, because they are few. We are proud of our Scottish regiments. We feel they, of the whole army, specially belong to ourselves; and they, too, as they have swept on to battle with the cry 'Old Scotland for ever!' feel, we believe, that they specially belong to us.[20]

Such was the view from the pulpit of St Giles'. Above it, the skeletal remains of the Old Scottish Colours hung for a century.

At the outbreak of the First World War, the regiments enjoyed an unchallenged prominence in Scottish society as symbols of national self-image. Approval was widespread, as was acceptance of a British imperial military role for Scotland among Scots of all classes and almost all political persuasions, including the bulk of the growing Labour movement in the early twentieth century. Those few whose political principles led them to oppose the war and (at cost to themselves) to resist conscripted military service, did so largely from the standpoint of ideals of anti-imperialist international socialism rather than anti-imperialist separatist nationalism. At this period the idea that British military service, particularly in a Scottish unit of the British army, might have been 'un-Scottish', or in any way a betrayal of Scotland, would have seemed absurd to most. Even in Ireland, where separatist nationalism and republicanism were much more potent forces, the question of the war proved vexing for the nationalist cause and British military service remained a significant, if dwindling, source of employment and pride for Irishmen in the 1920s and '30s.

Outside Scotland one might expect to find a more dispassionate reaction to the Scottish military tradition. Its potency among the colonies and dominions of the British empire was apparent, and naturally strongest among those populations of Scottish descent, but fascination with high-landers in particular could extend to neutrals and even to enemies. That said, it is hard to imagine that peoples on the frontiers of the empire

Pipers of the 12th Indian Pioneers pose with their instructor, Pipe Major Duff of the 2nd Battalion Royal Scots, c.1904.

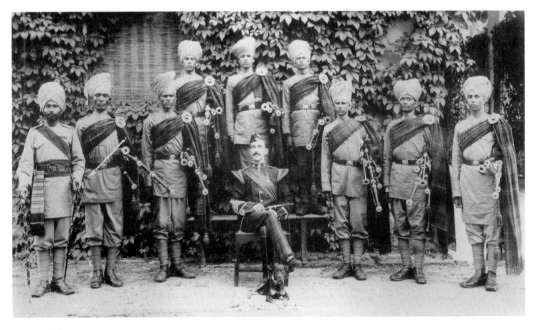

placed any great stock in the cultural differences among the multifarious British imperial forces that bore upon them. It cannot, for example, have been a matter of great import to the Afridi people of Tirah on the North-West Frontier of India whether it was Scottish highlanders, Englishmen or Sikhs who finally forced them from their hill-top positions at Dargai in 1897, though the praises of the Scots were sung around the empire for the feat. But in the context of European warfare, highlanders were distinct enough in origin and appearance to attract attention from the beginning. Scottish soldiers were known to the peoples of seventeenth century Europe from their service in the great continental armies of the Thirty Years' War. From the first overseas deployment of highland regiments of the British army, during the War of the Austrian Succession in the 1740s, German prints testify to the curiosity aroused among the local populations by the highlanders' appearance as they passed through. Britain's use of highlanders in the eighteenth century had parallels elsewhere in Europe, as supposedly warlike peoples from the fringes of the major powers were recruited for military service. Thus images of Scottish highlanders appeared in print alongside such outlandish groups as 'Pandours or Croats, Waradins or Sclavonians, Ulans and Hanaks'.[21]

France had a long, turbulent history of military involvement with Scotland, but at the battle of Fontenoy in 1745, facing highlanders as enemies in the British service for the first time, little sentiment can have been felt by French troops towards the 'Highland furies, who rushed upon us with more violence than ever sea did when driven by tempest'.[22] Nevertheless, for all that, on and off until 1815, French contact with Scots in a military context was most likely to be as between enemies, the development of French interest in the kilt-wearing, bagpipe carrying tradition through the nineteenth century was not greatly hindered. Instead it flourished as Britain and France became allies first against Russia in the Crimean War and then against Germany in the years

German print depicting the novel and curious sight of highlanders on the march at Mainz in 1743.

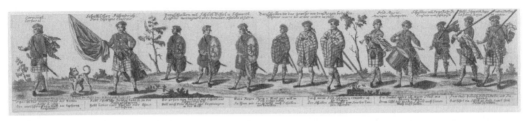

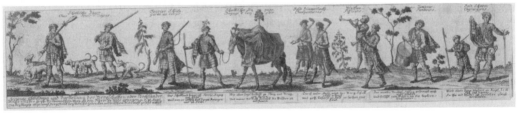

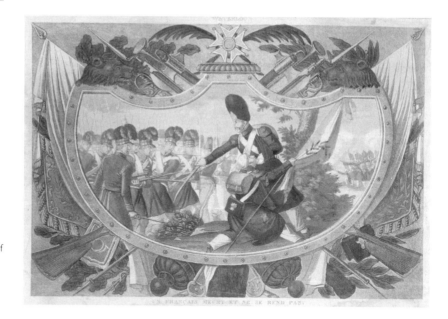

Highlanders are the foil for the heroism of Napoleon's Imperial Guard in this French print published after Waterloo.

leading up to the First World War. Through German eyes, there was no such scope in practical co-operation for curiosity to develop into sympathy and affection. The Scottish military image was certainly noticed, but in that it was encountered most immediately warring on opposing sides of the Western Front in the First World War it was hardly received with enthusiasm. In 1918 it was widely reported that German military intelligence had placed the 51st (Highland) Division at the head of its list of British divisions to be feared as *berühmte* – renowned. There might have been an element of wish-fulfilment in the dissemination of this information, but German propaganda testifies to the fact that the kilted battalions had made an impression, be it through first-hand experience, distinctive appearance or a combination of the two.

Whatever their feelings, twentieth century opponents of the British army cannot have seen Scottish soldiers as anything other than fully paid-up members of the British imperial endeavour. This had not always been the case, as remembered in French involvement with Jacobite military activity against the Hanoverian British state in the eighteenth century. Later conflicts could also raise questions about Scottish loyalties, though the hopes of Britain's enemies were usually disappointed in this regard.

During the American War of Independence, some Scottish settlers did side with the Revolutionaries, but Scots were far more conspicuous on the other side. American distrust of the Scottish highlanders in their midst borrowed something from the mother country. In the 1770s anti-Scottish feelings were still prevalent among the English 'Whig' political tendency in London, whose memories of armed Jacobitism and concern over ongoing Scottish infiltration of the British Tory establishment led them to identify Scots as the servile and mercenary agents of arbitrary power and similar perceptions among what became the Revolutionary party in North American were reinforced by direct experience when the time came to choose sides. Recent highland emigrants to North Carolina stood out in American eyes as an identifiable and reprehensible group of adherents to British rule after efforts on the part of Scottish settlers to woo them to the cause of American liberty failed. Their formation instead of a loyalist highland battalion on the traditional lines, with officers drawn from the highland emigrant gentry, and all gathered to the Royal Standard by the music of the pipes, resulted in the destruction of some and the imprisonment of many North Carolina highlanders at the battle of Moore's Creek Bridge in 1776. In post-war Georgia, in 1782, the state legislature passed a law forbidding Scots from settling in the state unless they had fought on the American side. Since Scots had formed the nucleus of Georgia's original settlement, the latter reflected a particular sense of distaste and betrayal felt towards the Scottish loyalists; it may also have proceeded from unhappy memories of the 1778 campaign waged in Georgia by the 71st (Fraser's) Highlanders.

The figure of Death is a Scottish piper in this German medal of 1915, possibly a response to the battle of Loos.

If a call to Scottish kin away from British allegiance was to be heard anywhere, then Ireland was the likeliest place. Yet even in Ireland the sentiment was a rarity, and the military authorities felt no uneasiness in sending Scottish regiments there. Indeed, when trouble threatened in the 1790s, it was war-service Fencible regiments, many of them raised in Scotland, that were sent to Ireland in preference to regular army regiments, partly for fear over the reliability of the many Irishmen who filled the ranks of the latter. A sense of Celtic betrayal survived in the folk memory of the 1798 Rebellion where the attempts of the Glengarry Fencibles, a Scottish highland regiment, to capture the outlaw Michael Dwyer in the Wicklow mountains, were rued in song:

> But kilted foes around them set,
> And fired the house of Connell;
> Those hungry Scots, the hounds of death,
> Ah, shame on you Macdonell!
> Spirits of the dead, the butchered of Glencoe,
> Look down with vengeful ire
> On you degenerate sons, the murdering crew,
> That sought the life of Dwyer,
> Of the freedom-loving Dwyer.[23]

The Glengarry Fencibles, recruited among the MacDonalds or *Macdonells* of Glengarry, was a unit composed largely, and openly, of Roman Catholics, raised on the urgings of a priest, and so was unusual among the Scottish fencible regiments sent to Ireland in the 1790s, many of whose men were likely to have sympathy with the Protestant cause. But if the Wicklow rebels expected any special sympathy from the Glengarry men, and it seems unlikely that they did, then they were on a hiding to nothing. The unit's dogged though unsuccessful pursuit of Dwyer and his comrades earned it the sobriquet 'the Devil's Bloodhounds'. As we have seen, by the late eighteenth century, Scots could happily square a sentimental highland inheritance identifying with, for example, the MacDonald victims of the government-ordered Glencoe massacre alluded to in the song, with the fulfilment of their duty and national destiny on behalf of, and at one with, the British state that paid them.

Friend or foe, those who encountered the British empire in all its forms recognised and understood the Scots in their military role. For Scots, the military tradition carried by the Scottish regiments expressed something of themselves that they wished to preserve and to celebrate. The power of the image was strong enough for the bulk of the Scottish people to regard it as something to cling to as they came to terms with the scale of the destruction and change that the First World War had wrought upon them. The manner in which the tradition was put to work and adapted to fit the changing military situation in the following century, through the Second World War and the British withdrawal from empire, is the subject of a later chapter. But throughout the period with which this book is concerned, the Scottish military tradition evolved as a cultural response to a rather more stark set of practical imperatives and opportunities. The strategic, industrial and manpower requirements of state and empire left room for tradition where it did not impede and fostered tradition where it was useful. But it was these bare military demands, sketched out in the following chapter, which actively directed the course of Scottish history and with it the lives of countless Scots.

---

1 Estimates of the Scottish dead varied according to definitions of 'Scottish' and were to grow as omissions were noted. See I Hay, *Their Name Liveth, The Book of the Scottish National War Memorial* (Edinburgh: Trustees of the Scottish National War Memorial, 1985), second edition, p.114. The present calculation stands at a little over 148,000.

2 *Memorandum on a Scottish National War Museum, Home of Record, and Monument* (1917). (National War Museum of Scotland, M.1993.50).

3 Robert Munro, Secretary of State, to the Duke of Atholl, 28th January 1920 (Scottish National War Memorial Papers, Bundle 10).

4 Report by the Propaganda Committee of the Scottish National War Memorial, 30 January 1923 (Scottish National War Memorial Papers, Bundle 45).

5 Authors' correspondence with Mr B Rough, of Brisbane, 1996.

6 J E Cookson, *The British Armed Nation, 1793-1815* (Oxford: Clarendon Press, 1997), p.141.

7   W Scott, *Minstrelsy of the Scottish Border: consisting of historical and romantic ballads, collected in the Southern Counties of Scotland; with a few of modern date, founded upon local tradition*, second edition (Edinburgh, 1803).

8   Cookson, op. cit., pp. 126-7.

9   H J Hanham, 'Religion and Nationality in the mid-Victorian Army', in M R D Foot (ed), *War and Society* (London: Elek, 1973). Quoted in H Strachan, *The Politics of the British Army* (Oxford: Clarendon Press, 1997), pp 205-6.

10 Major-General D Stewart, *Sketches of the character, manners and present state of the high-landers of Scotland with details of the military service of the highland regiments*, third edition (Edinburgh: Archibald Constable & Co, 1825).

11 The Right Honourable Sir John Sinclair (of Ulbster, Baronet), *An Account of the Highland Society of London, from its establishment in May 1778, to the Commencement of the Year 1813* (London, 1813). The Society's efforts were otherwise dedicated to the restoration and preservation of highland dress, music, Gaelic language and literature, the maintenance of such institutions as the Gaelic Schools and the Caledonian asylum for the children of Scottish veterans, the relief of distressed highlanders, and the promotion of improvements in agriculture and fisheries.

12 Lieutenant-Colonel C Greenhill Gardyne, *The Life of a Regiment*, volume I (London: The Medici Society, 1929), p.46.

13 Arch. K Murray, *History of the Scottish Regiments in the British Army* (Glasgow: Thomas Murray and Son, 1862), p.79.

14 P Abercromby, *The Martial Achievements of the Scots Nation* (Edinburgh: Robert Freebairn, 1715).

15 See H Strachan, op. cit., pp. 199-206.

16 The bequest of Captain Hugh Reid towards a monument to Wallace and Bruce had lain with the City of Edinburgh gathering interest since 1832. It was finally put to use in 1927 to erect the statues of the two heroes that stand in niches on either side of the main entrance to Edinburgh Castle.

17 J Cromb, *The Majuba Disaster, a story of Highland heroism told by officers of the 92nd Regiment* (Dundee: John Leng & Co, 1891).

18 *The Queen Victoria School, Dunblane, opened by His Majesty King Edward ... 1902-15* (1915).

19 Quoted in Andrew Ross, *Old Scottish Regimental Colours* (Edinburgh: William Blackwood & Sons, 1885).

20 Ibid., p.140.

21 A depiction of Scottish highlanders featured among these other exotics of the War of the Austrian Succession in G Meyer, *Portraits of the Hungarians, Hussars, Pandours or Croats, Waradins or Sclavonians, Ulans, and Hanaks who are in the service of their Majesties the Queen of Hungary and the King of Prussia. Design'd after the life, by persons of distinction. To which are added, exact descriptions of the countries, manners, habits and arms of the people*, second edition (London, 1743).

22 A French account of Fontenoy, published at Paris, 26th May 1745, quoted in F H Skrine, *Fontenoy And Great Britain's Share in the War of the Austrian Succession 1741-48* (Edinburgh and London: William Blackwood & Sons), 1906, p.168.

23 Quoted in B W Kelly, *The Fate of Glengarry, or the expatriation of the Macdonells: a historico-biographical study* (Dublin: James Duffy & Co Ltd), 1905, p.42.

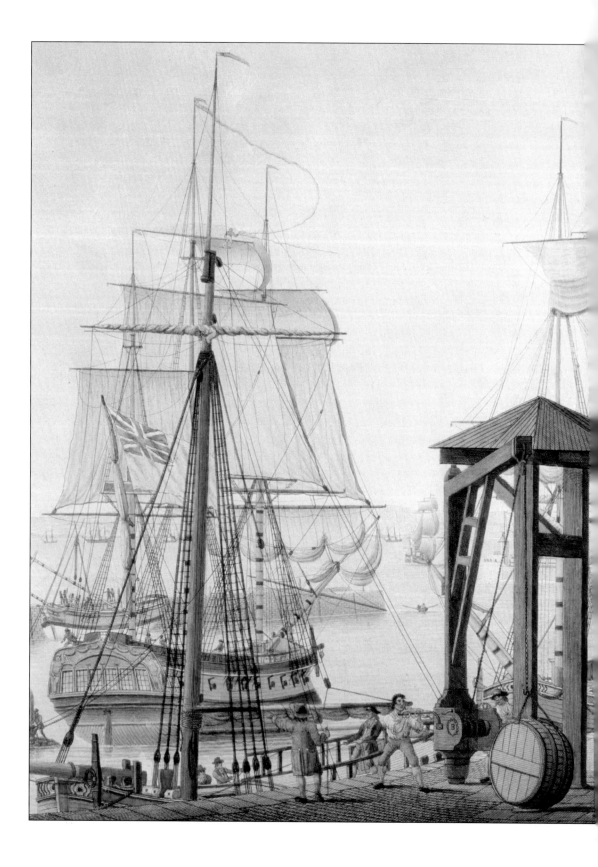

Stands Scotland where it did?[1]

IF A NATION'S HISTORY CAN EVER BE SAID TO BE DETERMINED BY anything more substantial than the confluence of actors and events, then that nation's position on the map of the world must be an essential shaping factor. Just as the matter of location is something fixed, by and large, so too is the nature of the land itself. The Scottish topography of mountain and water, the physical division between highland and lowland, all ringed by a long and sometimes complex coastline, has set a pattern for the experience of the Scottish people. Like any nation, Scotland's strategic importance, its military significance, has waxed and waned according to the relative power and interests of the nations that surround it. Scotland's position on the north-west fringe of Europe has oft-times rendered it remote and peripheral, at others vitally central in the competition of great military powers. Crucially, Scotland's proximity to other nations larger and usually stronger than itself – England in particular – and Scotland's military capability relative to those other nations, has worked to direct the flow of Scottish history.

An abiding theme of that history has been the desire to understand how Scotland came to its modern existence as a nation within a nation. Scots today are quick to remember that in the late thirteenth and early fourteenth century their sovereign nationhood was honed and preserved on the field of battle. They would perhaps be less ready to allow that by dint of war and military power (and not just by happy bargain or by treachery) that same national sovereignty was later lost. The principal events of the latter process are known well enough – in 1603 the Crowns of Scotland and England were united in the person of King James, VI of Scotland and I of Great Britain, and in 1707 Scottish government was wound up and absorbed into a single machine of British state in London. Today, devolution notwithstanding, Scotland remains an integral part of that unitary British nation state. Neither of the two salient events in the historic process of union was of itself sullied by the shedding of blood, a surprising, and creditable, aspect of a union between nations that had been warring on and off since the late thirteenth century. Yet in all the manoeuvring, accommodation and historical accident that surrounded these political watersheds, considerations of war and military security

Leith harbour, engraving by J Wadell, 1797.

were always in play. Anglo-Scottish relations were also subject to powerful interest from beyond the respective kingdoms. Threads of strategy and military power were woven through European dynastic and political relationships and rivalries, stretching across the seas that separated the British Isles from the military powers of the European continent.

A feel for the fragile nature of Scottish sovereignty in the sixteenth century might be found in a glance at those military forces present in the Scottish realm in 1548. This was the year after the defeat of a large Scottish host at the battle of Pinkie by an English force aggressively pressing a marriage alliance between the English and Scottish royal houses. The proposed nuptial union between Prince Edward of England and the young Mary Queen of Scots appeared to spell absorption for the independent Scottish monarchy and little other than the extension of the English patrimony. From this design, known to history as 'the Rough Wooings', only the presence of French garrisons around the Firth of Forth, and the French naval power that brought them, could keep Scotland secure. That security, which even at its firmest could barely eject English garrisons from their military strongholds in Scotland, entailed the presence of some 10,000 foreign troops on Scottish soil, defending Scottish interests – in so far as they were interpreted to suit the needs of a French monarchy pursuing its own violent rivalry with England. Its logical extension, absorption in another form, was the marriage between Mary of Scots and the French Dauphin Francis. This was celebrated in Paris in 1548 during the temporary ascendancy of the pro-French faction in Scottish politics and curtailed only by Francis' early death. Scotland's best interests could be interpreted in different ways, but for the Scottish political élite in the mid-sixteenth century, this essentially meant leaning towards dominance by either England or France, or continually attempting to play one off against the other. Experience told that the latter course offered little prospect of lasting peace and prosperity.

Through the sixteenth century, the vagaries of relationships between the ruling dynasties of England, France and Scotland, were shaped and re-shaped, but Scotland's predicament remained in essence the same. Without the means to support and maintain armies and navies that could match those of the English and the French, Scotland stood vulnerable to raid, invasion and compulsion from its powerful land neighbour to the south and, at the same time, beholden to the demands of its overseas ally for costly wars with England to suit French priorities.

It had not always been so. In the fourteenth century Robert Bruce's successful rebuttal of English dominance had involved more than the famous victory at Bannockburn. With a naval force of war galleys, Bruce had temporarily made himself master of the Irish Sea and a persistent threat to English trade. Bruce's second great triumph, the taking of Berwick in 1318, was achieved with the aid of an effective naval blockade. Two centuries later, King James IV of Scotland built warships, the greatest of them the famous *Great Michael*, that, ship for ship, could rival anything on the seas. Yet James' death, political turmoil, and the drain of such ambition on the Scottish exchequer, put paid to any lasting prospect of a Scottish fleet that could protect and project Scottish influence and trade on the world stage.

This is not to suggest that by the sixteenth century Scotland was entirely helpless, prostrate before the designs of others. English armies could inflict heavy defeats on the Scots, but they did not, as yet, have the military capacity or will to conquer outright. Scotland's hostile terrain, its places of natural and manufactured strength, its ability to raise armies and procure artillery, kept it from dominance. By the same token, it was Scotland's very military capability, its ability to strike at England and tie up English armies and expenditure, that made Scotland so very useful to the French. Nevertheless, by the second half of the sixteenth century Scottish scope for independent military action and influence was diminished. The land, its people and its trade had been ravaged by war to a degree not seen since the Wars of Independence. While England and France concerned themselves with internal religious convulsions and opposition to Spain, Scotland busily exhausted itself in Reformation, and its own occasionally violent, ever debilitating power struggles. The technology of warfare had advanced, and with it the cost. Scotland lacked not only a fleet; the expensive tools and techniques of modern fortification and artillery were moving beyond the Scottish wherewithal.

In the circumstances the 1603 Union of the Crowns of Scotland and England, a union of the two nations under a Scottish king, might have seemed more than the Scots could have hoped for in the preceding decades. It appeared to hold up the tantalising prospect of peace without English domination in a union of two by-then Protestant nations, and the rejection of interference, or assistance – depending on the point of view – from Catholic France. Though it came about essentially by dynastic accident, in the failure of Queen Elizabeth of England to produce an heir, the 1603 Union proceeded in no small part because it offered to bolster the military security of the English state. To the English political élite, the accession of the Protestant James Stewart, albeit he was a Scot, offered political stability, the defence of the new religious settlement, and the removal of Scotland as a political and military base through which the French or other potential enemies could strike. Though much upheaval was to occur in the century between, broadly similar considerations, considerations of military security, were to promote the full union of the English and Scottish states in 1707.

For Scotland a principal consequence of the 1603 Regal Union was of course the removal south of the Crown and Court, south out of Scotland. Thereafter, the strategic interest of the Scottish Crown equated with that of a power centre in London from which Scotland was remote. In the following 150 years that same remoteness from the nexus of what we might begin to call 'British' power, and the determination of that power centre to exert military control over the Scottish periphery of its domain, would bring war to Scotland with a force and calamity equal to anything that had been visited upon it before. Wars engulfed much of the European continent in the seventeenth century, and with it Scotland and the rest of the British Isles. These wars had their myriad causes in dynastic struggle, religion and money. But repeatedly they witnessed military resistance against the power of the British Crown and/or the English state by parties claiming to represent the Scottish nation in arms. Presented with the divisions within Scotland that these conflicts embraced, later generations have allotted them the character of civil wars, civil wars within the British Isles and within Scotland itself. Yet in the more straightforward terms of military strategy, as seen from the perspective of the security requirements of the centre of power in London, the combating and ultimate defeat of these Scottish forces, be they Covenanting anti-Royalist or Covenanting pro-Royalist Scottish armies, or, extending the pattern into the late seventeenth and early eighteenth centuries, pro-Jacobite Scottish armies, involved nothing less than the military pacification of the territory of Scotland itself. In other words, it meant the conquest of Scotland and the crushing of its independent military capability.

Most strikingly, the conquest of Scotland by English parliamentary armies in 1650-52 was total. Oliver Cromwell's victory over the Scottish army at Dunbar, Lambert's at Inverkeithing, and the destruction of a Scottish expedition into England at the battle of Worcester in 1651, led to the military subjugation and occupation of Scotland, rigidly maintained until 1660. Supported and supplied by an unopposed navy, English armies gradually forced their way up the Scottish east coast, down into the south-west and even into the highlands, a military achievement far beyond anything realistically aspired to by their sixteenth-century forebears. Castles great and small, Edinburgh and Stirling among them, fell or surrendered without a fight as Scottish disunity, war-exhaustion and weariness with Covenanter government took its toll. For its spirited resistance, Dundee, far to the north of border towns more familiar with English spoliation, was sacked. An English garrison, at its height near 36,000 strong, occupied and fortified Scotland building citadels – modern artillery forts – at Perth, Ayr, Inverness, Inverlochy and Leith. In what amounted to an unconditional surrender, representatives of the burghs and shires of Scotland consented, without any real choice in the matter, to a fully incorporating union with the English republic, effectively the termination of the Scottish state and an acceptance of English military government in Scotland.

The conquest of Scotland was achieved by an army that in military organisation, training, equipment and leadership was a cut above previous English invading forces. In the earlier war between Crown and Parliament, Cromwell had created Parliament's New Model Army, applying the most up-to-date continental techniques of disciplined professional soldiering and introducing the rudiments of logistic support. The army that forced its way into Scotland in 1650 counted solid campaigning experience along with these original assets. Yet in this it was not alone. In reaching such a state of modern military efficiency the English Parliament had in fact followed a lead set by the Scots.

If in the seventeenth century (as before and after), Scotland suffered a relative poverty of financial means, it was not short of another important military resource: military manpower. By the 1630s circumstances had arisen that allowed Scotland to draw upon a source of trained and experienced professional soldiers. In 1638 the Scottish Covenanters raised an army in defiance of King Charles I and his determination to impose English forms of worship upon his Scottish kingdom. To organise this army, the Covenanters called home experienced Scottish officers and soldiers who had been serving in the armies of continental powers.

As a later chapter will describe, the traditional overseas movement of Scottish soldiers of fortune to serve foreign masters reached new heights during the Thirty Years' War of 1618-48. Although connections can be made between the interests of the House of Stewart, the defence of Protestantism and Scottish service in the anti-Habsburg armies of Sweden, the United Provinces, Denmark-Norway and France, the presence of numbers of Scots in the Habsburg armies suggests the main incentive was pecuniary. Whatever their motive in departing Scotland, it was returning Scottish officers with continental war service, and with a commitment to the principles of the Covenant, that created a Scottish army to which King Charles I had no ready equivalent. These professional military men allowed the Covenanters to field a drilled army that represented a marked advance from the feudal hosts raised by the Scottish kings and nobles of the past. In the Bishops' Wars of 1638-39, Charles' less sophisticated armies backed off from

General Alexander Leslie returned from Sweden in 1638 to raise and train a Scottish army.

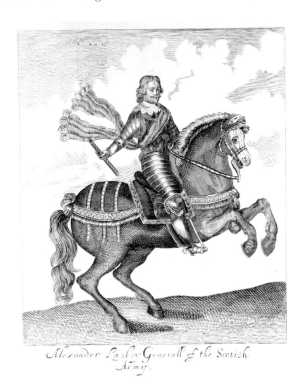

Alexander Lasley Generall of the Scotish Army.

51

this formidable Scottish array and his necessary capitulation to Scottish demands pushed him further down the road to armed confrontation with the English Parliament, and to ruin. Scottish military power in the 1640s extended south into England and, for the first time since the Bruce invasions of the early fourteenth century, across the North Channel to Ulster where a Scottish army intervened to defend Scottish settlers against Irish rebellion, albeit in a state of uneasy allegiance between Crown and Covenant.

The military superiority of the Scottish Covenanters was temporary. The English armies that fought for Crown or for Parliament in the 1640s drew on continental experience similar to that called on by the Scots, and on resources greater than anything the Scots could sustain. In the 1650s Cromwell was no more willing to tolerate Scottish self-determination where it affected the security of the English state – namely the proclamation of Charles II as King of Scots – than Cromwell's enemy King Charles I had been willing to countenance Scottish self-determination in religious matters in 1638. The difference was that Cromwell had the military means to impose his will. Strategically, Cromwell's position was also significantly stronger than that of the bellicose 'Rough Wooing' English statesmen of the previous century. Crucially, the threat of French or other foreign interference on Scotland's behalf, so potent in the sixteenth century, had since been curtailed by a dramatic expansion and improvement of the English navy. Under Cromwell, the English fleet grew to be one of the most powerful in Europe. It inflicted defeat on the Dutch and commanded from the Catholic monarchs of Spain and France recognition and a respectful wariness of the regicide English state. Sea power gave Cromwell a free hand in Scotland, and as his armies marched north up the Scottish east coast they were supplied and supported by warships against which the Scots had no means of resistance.

The English military occupation of Scotland ended in 1660 as Scotland's independent statehood was recovered on Cromwell's death and the restoration of the British monarchy in the person of King Charles II. Things were back to looking much as they had done in the 1630s and, as before, the paucity of Scottish naval power continued to be a factor undermining the viability of the Scottish state. The later Stewart monarchs followed Cromwell's example and spent heavily on their Royal Navy, but this was in every meaningful sense an English navy, projecting Crown policy that equated to English requirements. Scotland was required to assist with the levying of manpower for the Royal Navy, but was to see little concern for the protection of Scottish interests in return. Although Scottish privateer captains were able to take advantage of England's trade wars against the Dutch, Scottish maritime and mercantile interests were specifically excluded from the trade monopolies enjoyed by their English counterparts and protected by English naval power.

Restoration Scotland also saw the maintenance of a regular standing army for the first time. Although it was paid for from the Scottish exchequer, the Scottish standing army was a new and direct manifestation of royal power in Scotland, imposing the will of the London-based Stewart monarchs and protecting the Stewart dispensation in church and state from armed Covenanter resistance.

In 1688 the removal of the Stewart dynasty from the throne, and the accession of William of Orange as king, underlined further the true nature of the Scottish royal army. Using Scottish regular troops against his Jacobite opponents in Scotland itself, and, more significantly, recruiting large numbers of Scots into regiments that served in his continental wars against the French, William made no distinction between his English, Scottish or Irish regiments. The army that fought William and his successor's anti-French wars in Flanders was truly a British army, in essence the same institution that exists today. As we have seen, some of these regiments, together with standing regiments inherited by William from the pre-1688 period, stayed in business and came down to later centuries among the celebrated Scottish regiments of the British army. In the shorter term, the growing hostility and rivalry between the Crown and the increasingly powerful French monarchy was to have implications for Scotland that were of deeper significance.

The full Union between the English and Scottish states that was enacted in 1707 has been the subject of close scrutiny by Scottish historians in recent decades. In the machinations of the pro-Union and anti-Union factions in the Scottish Parliament, and in recognition of the financial prostration of Scottish government, the manner in which Union came about in Scotland has been closely tracked. Yet it is also recognised that these events make sense only against the backdrop of the military-strategic factors that underlay the agreement. A full understanding of why Scotland became part of a unitary British state in 1707 rests on the recognition that Union was pressed by the English ministry for reasons of political and military security. Union became a matter of urgency from the English perspective only when the Scottish parliament equivocated in conforming to English requirements in its choice of a successor to the heir-less Queen Anne. While England looked to the Protestant Elector of Hanover, the prospect of a separate Scottish succession and, in the person of James Stewart, a Roman Catholic, French-supported succession at that, was not to be countenanced by the English ministry any more than Oliver Cromwell had been prepared to let the Scots choose their own king fifty years earlier. Committed to the Protestant succession and the pursuit of commercial and military rivalry with France, England could not and would not allow the re-setting of a land border between England and Scotland above which French influence and military power could once again play. The extent to which conquest by an English army was threatened as an alternative to peaceful union has been the subject of recent interest among historians.[2] With Scotland's subjection to Cromwell's idea of union only four decades distant, the Scots would not have needed much reminding of potential English military capability in this direction.

The 1707 Treaty of Union appeared to guarantee the Crown and its ministry a greater degree of strategic security. In return, in addition to a hope of peace, it is generally understood that Scotland was offered a prospect of greater prosperity through free access to what had been exclusively English colonial trade. To a nation financially crippled by the expensive failure of its own colonial ambitions – the collapse of the nascent Scottish colony at Darien, Central America in 1700 – this was a Godsend, not least to those of political influence who had personally invested in the Company of Scotland and its Darien scheme. The Darien failure was a stark demonstration of Scotland's marginal position in the foreign policy considerations of its king; it also demonstrated Scotland's inability to compete on the world stage, not least because it lacked the naval power to support aggressive commercial activity.

Shy of muddying the water in his relations with Spain, and wary of upsetting the vested interests of the English East India Company, King William offered the Scottish colonists no support from his Royal Navy, much indeed as Scottish merchant ships had seen little protection from attacks by French privateers during William's wars with France. French depredations off the east coast had eventually caused the Scottish Parliament to vote funds for a tiny Scottish naval squadron, commissioned in 1696.[3] In the case of Darien, firmly in crisis by 1700, William even declined to direct that the three small frigates of the Scottish naval establishment, laid up at Burntisland in 1697, should go to the aid of the few armed merchant vessels of the Company of Scotland. When the Darien settlement fell prey to disease, military pressure and direct attack from Spanish colonial forces, when its supply ships were scattered, when King William specifically ordered that no English trade or help of any kind was to be offered to the Scottish colony, there was no Scottish fleet to offer succour and protection. Overseas empire without naval power was not viable. For this the Scots relied on the favour of their king and the English resources in his gift; the Darien debacle demonstrated that they could put little faith in that. When in 1707 the Treaty of Union compensated the Darien investors, it also added the entire might of the Scottish navy to the Royal Navy – those same three modest men-of-war that had remained at Burntisland throughout the Darien venture.[4]

The Union brought neither the peace and security nor the prosperity sought after by its respective English and Scottish proponents, at least not for the following fifty years, thanks to the fault-line in the royal succession. The armed risings in support of the Jacobite cause, originating and

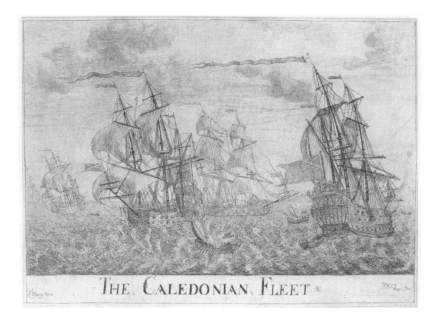

THE CALEDONIAN FLEET *

The size of the Scottish navy is exaggerated in this undated print, possibly published as a piece of anti-Union propaganda.

(largely) fought out in Scotland, and ending in abject defeat at Culloden in 1746, are among the best-known episodes in Scottish history.

The epic and tragic qualities of the Jacobite cause, packaged in the romantic reinvention of the highlands described in the previous chapter, tend to overshadow the strategic dimension in which armed Jacobitism was sustained. In 1690 a highland army had fought for James Stewart in Scotland, while the main, French-supported, campaign was fought and lost in Ireland. After the 1707 Union, the Jacobite thorn in the side of the new British state flourished in the highlands of Scotland. There, physical barriers of mountains and water still preserved cultural traits of a marginal highland society in which Jacobite sympathies converged with traditional social structures of personal loyalty, prowess in arms, and remoteness from the structures of wealth and influence proffered by the state. Unlike Ireland, the other seat of Jacobite hopes, the Scottish highlands, and the military manpower that could be raised there, were not separated by a sea barrier from the prize in London.

The highland terrain made Scotland harder to garrison than Ireland, where the Jacobite-leaning population was more easily disarmed and watched. But armed Jacobitism did not function in Scotland by virtue of highland society alone. Particularly in the years immediately following the 1707 Treaty, popular anti-Union sentiment was prevalent throughout Scotland and the exiled Stewarts were not slow to catch on by offering to reverse the Treaty. For both these reasons, Scotland was once again a strategic counter that the French monarchy (and others) could play against its rival and some-time enemy in London. In 1745 the bulk of the Jacobite army was highland, certainly, but it included a number of units raised in other parts of Scotland. As they strove to create a military force as close as could be achieved to a conventional, modern field army, the Jacobite leadership deliberately adopted the idea of a highland uniform of tartan for all of its units, regardless of origin. This Jacobite attempt at tartan uniformity pre-dated the rise of the fashion for tartan described in the previous chapter, and so is noteworthy all the more as perhaps the first example of a conscious use of the highland military dress to delineate a Scottish national army. When the French held out some genuine expectation of Jacobite military power projecting from the north, their commitment to deploy in Scotland was considerable. In 1708, with Scottish anti-Union sentiment running high, a French naval expedition arrived off the Fife coast carrying some 6000 French troops. French vacillation and the approach of a Royal Navy squadron saw them off before the troops could be landed, but it was potentially a serious invasion and a pertinent danger to the nascent British state.

Although plans for a full-scale invasion of Scotland were never to get any closer than this, Jacobite support in the Scottish highlands offered an ongoing means for French interference in the British political situation by means of intrigue. The remote sea lochs of the Scottish west coast were hard approaches to cover for the patrols of the Royal Navy and it was there that the French could help to land agents, money, munitions – and pretenders to the throne. France was generally hesitant in doing much more, but with the inadequate military garrisoning of Scotland by the British army, this was quite enough to get things going. In 1745 the benefit to France proved to lie less in the prospects for an overthrow of the British ruling dynasty than in the annoyance caused to its rival. The main French effort against the British mainland had come in 1743 and was aimed further south, directly against the centre of British power. A French fleet sailed into the English Channel to cover the crossing of an invasion force of French regular troops under Marshal de Saxe, bound for the Thames and carrying the Jacobite Pretender Charles Edward Stewart. This was a serious attempt to defeat the Royal Navy's Channel Fleet and overthrow the British regime by the force of French arms, but French hopes were extinguished in the destruction wrought by a storm in the Channel and the moment of opportunity passed. Instead, as the war between Great Britain and France continued into 1745, sponsorship of the Jacobite rising in Scotland was a cheap and risk-free means of harassing the enemy. The initial Jacobite successes in Scotland worked in France's interest as the need to bring troops home to counter the threat from the north meant withdrawal of British army regiments away from the campaign against the French army in Flanders.

The nature of the Jacobite rebellions as a feature of broader European dynastic conflict, strategic and commercial rivalry, is demonstrated by the roll call of troops that were involved. Between 1689 and 1746 troops from France, Spain and Ireland came to Scotland in aid of the Jacobite cause. With the possible exception of the Irish, their purpose lay as much in creating trouble and diversion for their British rivals as in any genuine enthusiasm for, and confidence in, the prospect of a Stewart restoration. The Swedish monarchy, at war with Hanover, also engaged in intrigue with Jacobite agents towards possible military support. On the opposing side, to prop up William of Orange and his Hanoverian successors, came regiments from Germany and the Low Countries as well as English and Scottish regiments of the British army.

As is well known, and still painfully remembered, active Jacobitism was finally and effectively snuffed out by the military suppression of the highlands in the years after Culloden. However, the most significant defence against the Jacobites and their allies was undoubtedly the Royal Navy. In the face of considerable armies raised for the Jacobite cause in Scotland, and the temporary loss of British military control in Scotland, naval power kept the Jacobites isolated. The naval blockade of French ports, aided by the uncertainties of weather, kept the prospect of serious invasion at bay and the import of soldiers, cash and supplies for the Scottish Jacobites to a trickle. In 1745 Royal Navy ships swiftly landed the regiments from Flanders that were to defeat them in the field.

From the strategic perspective of Crown and state, the anti-Jacobite campaigns hardly broke new ground, at least in aspirations and objectives. The challenges of exerting military authority in the remote fastnesses of the highlands of Scotland pre-dated the accession of William of Orange in 1688. During the Wars of the Covenant in the 1640s, the celebrated Royalist general James Graham, Marquis of Montrose, set the pattern for using highland and Irish troops to threaten the security of lowland-based government. Indeed, even before the 1603 Union of the Crowns, much the same problem was faced by the Scottish Stewart kings whose authority and power was based in the eastern lowlands. The unruliness of the highlands attracted the particular attention of James VI before his accession to the English throne, although James's political and military efforts towards highland pacification met only with limited, temporary success. The eighteenth-century solutions to the problem were far from unprecedented. The network of highland military roads, bridges, forts and barracks constructed under the direction of Field Marshal George Wade and Major William Caulfield took up where Oliver Cromwell's mid-seventeenth century infrastructure of military pacification left off. Fort William, a key army garrison in the highlands, was built in 1690 on the foundations of Cromwell's 1654 citadel at Inverlochy. Inverness too had seen the construction of a Cromwellian citadel, the site of which was considered suitable for rebuilding in 1746 until the decision was taken to build the greatest British fortress in the highlands, the second Fort George, at nearby Ardersier.

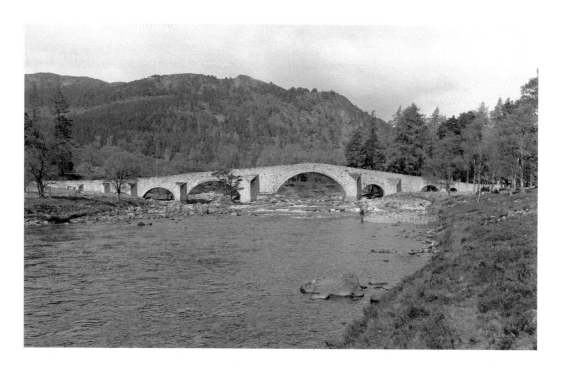

Bridge over the River Dee at Invercauld near Braemar, built in 1753 under the direction of Major Caulfield.

As Scots can be quick to aver, the defeat of the highland Jacobite armies was not of course a straightforward matter of English military triumph over Scotland. That 'there were Scots on both sides at Culloden' is a refrain often heard. Yet for all that the support for, or at least the passive acceptance of, the Williamite and Hanoverian regimes in Scotland was widespread, the campaigns against the Jacobite armies were pursued with little reference to such political niceties. The British army in Scotland was engaged in the pacification of hostile territory. In 1745 Edinburgh itself had welcomed the highland army, advertising the precariousness of the British military hold on Scotland. Thereafter, a concerted effort was made to bring the Scottish highlands, and by extension Scotland itself, finally and fully under British military control, and beyond the reach of French military interference.

The manner in which this was gradually achieved, between 1688 and the 1750s, involves some notable parallels with later patterns of British military imperial expansion overseas. Like the peoples of India, North America and Africa, Scots were offered the benefits of British trade. British military protection from French-backed recalcitrants was offered to those who hoped to prosper. Economic benefits came directly to landed and commercial interests in the remoter regions with the establishment of forts and roads in the highlands, exposing and connecting remoter areas of Scotland to expanding maritime trade and economic activity in the lowlands that was to develop into solid growth by mid century. Along with the soldiers and road-builders came mapmakers (the military survey of Scotland was begun in 1747), providing the means of opening up country previously seen as dangerous and impenetrable to outsiders.

And, throughout the period, with the offer of the carrot came the application of the stick. Overt demonstrations of potential military strength were used to encourage the hesitant and punish the recalcitrant. As well as the notorious Glencoe Massacre of 1692, King William practised gunboat diplomacy on Scotland, sending warships up the west coast to urge the loyalty of highland chiefs. Later, after Culloden, the notorious burning and pillaging of the western glens and islands was a deliberate display of terror, intended to teach a general lesson about the consequences of resistance to British power to those as yet unconvinced of its benefits.

The most telling similarity, one that resounds through the Scottish military experience of the ensuing two centuries, was the recruitment of numbers of the male population of the pacified territory into the British forces. The incorporation of peripheral peoples deemed 'warlike' into the large imperial armies of European powers, often after their military defeat by those same armies, was a common feature of eighteenth and nineteenth century warfare and was a practice with a heritage dating back to the recruitment of auxiliaries into the armies of imperial Rome. Recognition of the supposed military attributes and cultural identities of such peoples often saw them clothed and equipped in traditional, or quasi-traditional style, distinguishing them from regular troops. The fact that British military service was quickly identified as an important source of livelihood, cash and status by the Scottish highlanders themselves, be they British army recruits or highland landowners turned British army recruiters, does not, in this context, differentiate them from the Mahrattas, Sikhs, Gurkhas, who later were encountered and co-opted by the forces of the British empire.

Such features of conquest and co-option notwithstanding, the situation of Scotland in the aftermath of final Jacobite defeat was not entirely analogous to that of a conquered colonial possession nor indeed to that of Scotland as it lay defeated in 1652. To a large degree the military defeat of Jacobitism in 1745-46 finished off a spent force, a cause that was well on the way to becoming an irrelevance as increasing numbers of Scots identified with, and began to prosper under, the British state which protected their religion, their trade and offered them new markets within its empire. To many Scots the highlanders were an enemy of long standing, against whom common cause and protection had been found in union with England.

Nevertheless, it was only from the 1750s that Scotland, its loyalties, its difficult topography and its location remote from the centre of government ceased to be a problem in strategic terms for that same British state. Increasingly integrated in political and economic terms, Scotland

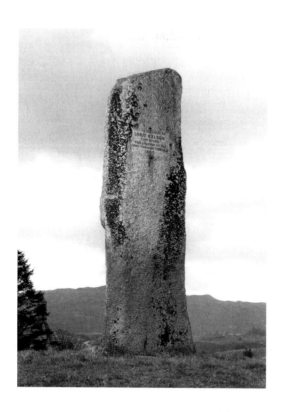

In 1805 ironworkers at Bonawe reacted to news of Trafalgar by erecting this monument.

as a whole became British military home ground. The economic promise of the Union had taken time to materialise, but the benefits were there, in burgeoning Atlantic trades – like tobacco – aided by British overseas conquest, and in textile industries enjoying new markets in the empire, not least the clothing of its soldiers, and the equipping of its ships.

Scotland's utility meanwhile, in strategic terms, was to be as a military and industrial resource, available to be drawn upon for British defence and the advancement of British imperial military power. Scotland had natural resources, and a growing ability to harness them, that could meet some of the military requirements of the British empire. Timber was in abundant supply in the highlands, and as a source of charcoal was the vital ingredient of iron smelting. With the network of military roads in the highlands, timber and the other necessary components could be transported economically. Thus at Bonawe in Lorn and other sites in the west highlands, often using ore from central Scotland, blast furnaces made pig iron and cannonballs for the Board of Ordnance supplying the army and the Royal Navy. The mark of this industrial extraction of timber remains on the highland landscape today. In the lowlands, coke smelting at the much larger Stirlingshire iron works of the Carron Company, founded in 1759, developed to make Scotland a centre for the production of field and naval guns, including the company's successful designs of the short, large-calibre gun, the Carronade.

The principal strategic asset that the absorption of Scotland put on offer was nevertheless a supply of affordable military manpower. Through the eighteenth and nineteenth centuries, the British imperial military service persisted as an established and popular source of employment and advancement for Scots. Some of the opportunities, hardships and variety of experiences that such employment entailed, taking Scots in number far from their home shores, are explored in the next chapter; the resonance of British military service in nineteenth and early twentieth century Scottish culture has already been touched upon. The British state sought and found its military recruits throughout Great Britain and Ireland and, to a large degree, had little concern as to where they came from. The socio-economic forces shaping patterns of recruitment – industrialisation, agricultural consolidation, population movement and war – were largely common to all parts of the realm, albeit at different rates and with different concentrations. However, in the case of Scotland, economic factors met political and cultural distinctions in a particular way.

The upsurge in British military recruitment in Scotland at first centred on the highlands. British governments, including their principal agents in Scotland, believed they had found a peculiar asset in an apparently huge resource of available military manpower among the 'clansmen' of the highlands. The employment of highlanders in British military service was also seen to have the convenient benefit of further negating the possibility of future highland threats to British military security. This was the view famously expressed in 1751 by General James Wolfe, victor (with the help of highland soldiers) at Quebec in 1759 and a veteran of Culloden, in his memorably stark assessment of the suitability of highland troops for service in North America: 'they are hardy and intrepid, accustomed to a rough country, and no great mischief if they fall. How can you better employ a secret enemy than by making his end conducive to the common good?'[5] If comments such as this reflected the state's attitude towards its new highland recruits, it is worth recognising that there was no huge difference between this and the attitude of government and its officers towards its military servants in general.

Equally, the fact that highland recruits poured into British military service in the second half of the eighteenth century should neither be taken to mean that they were forced against their will into the service of an alien power, nor, conversely, that they were transformed en masse into patriotic agents of the British state. Recruitment was facilitated by highland landlords seeking recognition, political influence and material gain in return for meeting the state's needs. Their tenants and dependents were brought into the ranks partly through the connections and obligations of kinship and clanship in which the threat of eviction could be present and the element of choice consequently absent. Certainly, mutinies amongst newly recruited highlanders were one unforeseen feature of the recruitment drive, the result of a clash of expectations and cultures between the British army, highland recruiters and the men who felt they had been duped or brow-beaten into long periods of overseas service against their will.[6]

Nevertheless, the men and families of the highland tenantry were entirely capable of making the best for themselves from the official and proprietorial need for their military labour. Successful recruitment in the highlands became a matter of offering incentives in land and, increasingly, in good rates of hard cash. The market for highland military manpower became integrated with recruiting efforts centred in the growing towns of the Scottish lowlands, towards which economic

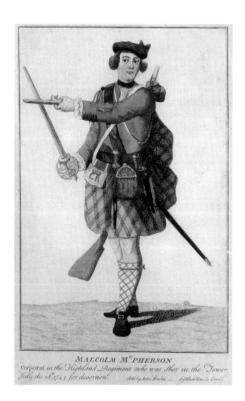

MALCOLM M'PHERSON
corporal in the Highland Regiment who was Shot in the Tower
July the 18 1743 for desertion. Sold by John Bowles at ye Black Horse in Corn

Prints produced in London reflected public interest and sympathy for highland soldiers executed for mutiny in 1743.

pressure was already pushing young male labour from the highlands. Enlistment was frequently a matter of economic necessity, and occasionally a matter of bare survival, but in this it did not differ essentially from many other sources of employment.

Locked into a succession of anti-French wars on a world-wide scale, the eighteenth century British state leant heavily on Scottish military manpower, highland and lowland, to help fill its armed forces. This was a matter of strategic necessity, and one that applied not only to recruiting for imperial service in North America and India, but one that also became relevant to the defence of Scotland itself as the Jacobite challenge finally disappeared. For as long as France continued to be the main commercial rival and military threat to British power, the geographical position of Scotland placed the land itself remote from the preoccupations of British and imperial strategic defence, which naturally centred around the south coast of England and extended far from Scotland.

The fear of French invasion was real enough, but it was government policy that the power of the British fleet, and not a scattering of coastal defences and coastal naval protection, was the main bulwark against it. For this reason, in the later eighteenth century, and indeed for much of the nineteenth century, Scotland saw comparatively little of the Royal Navy. The absence of naval protection close at hand was a cause of disquiet for coastal populations during the American War of Independence, such as those in Kirkcudbrightshire who in 1778 were subjected to a raid by the (Kirkcudbrightshire-born) Captain John Paul Jones of the American Continental Navy. The next year Jones was able to place even the port of Leith temporarily in his thrall, underlining its vulnerability and so that of Scotland's capital. With British troops heavily committed against the colonists in North America, and with France and Spain having entered the war on the American side, these attacks created localised panic and a general unease among Scottish commercial and political interests.

The scares fuelled demands, articulated by some leading figures from among the Scottish intelligentsia, that a national militia should be constituted in Scotland. In their desires for a force of home defence troops drawn and trained from across the civilian population by ballot, the supporters of the militia idea saw not only a bulwark against French incursion and invasion that seemed to threaten Scottish lives and livelihoods, but also a salve to the patriotic dignity of a nation whose inhabitants were not being permitted to defend themselves. To those agitating for its creation, the absence of a Scottish militia appeared a poor reflection on Scotland and its status in the Union when compared to the fact that a county militia had existed throughout England and Wales since 1757.

At that time the British state had not seen fit to arm and train the population of a nation that had only recently been the source of armed Jacobite rebellion. That argument against a Scottish militia had lost currency by the 1770s, but in the interim a useful method of providing for British home defence had been adopted, with particular success in Scotland. When the regular army was committed to wars in foreign theatres, 'fencible' regiments were raised for the duration of the conflicts. These were intended for home defence only, but otherwise were recruited much as were regular army regiments, through the agency of trusted Scottish aristocrats and highland proprietors as colonels and recruiters. Such was the success of the fencible idea, the government in Scotland had no wish to interfere with the process of recruitment by creating the competing draw on manpower of a Scottish militia.

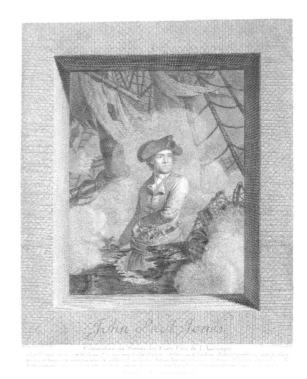

French sympathies in the American War of Independence are evident in this print celebrating the exploits of Captain John Paul Jones.

The question of Scotland's defence became more critical at the century's end when, during the wars with Revolutionary and Napoleonic France, the threat of a French invasion of the British Isles became pertinent. Ireland was seen as the most likely target for French incursion however, and Scotland was not the first priority. The protection afforded by the Royal Navy's North Sea Fleet extended, in theory, north to Scotland as well as south to the English Channel; a more immediate Royal Navy presence off the Scottish coast was afforded only by a small squadron of the North Sea Fleet kept in the Leith Roads, principally for the purpose of convoy escort. For Scotland, in common with the rest of the British east coast, the crisis of vulnerability to invasion receded with Admiral Adam Duncan's victory over the Dutch fleet, allied with France, at the battle of Camperdown in 1797, but only temporarily. In response to revived fears of French invasion in 1803, an extensive system of Martello towers (independent coastal gun emplacements) began construction at strategic points along the British coastline, but this eventually extended to Scotland only in the form of one tower protecting the naval supply yard at Leith. Two further towers, built in the Orkney Islands, were constructed only in 1814-15 – after the French threat had passed and, again, for the purposes of convoy protection, protecting the Baltic trade from United States privateers.[7] Such limited preparations hardly rendered Scotland impregnable, nor greatly reassured its population. A further layer of concern was added by fear of revolution, a threat that exercised the imagination of the Scottish property-owning classes every bit as much as their fears of the sight of French ships and troops.

The war against Revolutionary France drained available Scottish military manpower into the regular army and the fencible regiments to such an extent that in order to defend Scotland to its satisfaction the government had to look again at the idea of a Scottish militia. Many fencible regiments were actually extracted from Scotland as a means of controlling a deteriorating situation in Ireland. There, faced with armed resistance from among its Irish subjects, the government in Ireland had little trust in its own militia, as little faith in the competence of its yeomanry, and was worried at the increasingly Irish character of recruitment in British regular infantry regiments. Instead, some ninety-three fencible regiments had their terms of service extended to Ireland and were brought in to suppress the 1798 Rebellion. Of these, no less than forty-six were Scottish.[8]

The transfer of the bulk of the Scottish fencibles to Ireland was feasible only on the grounds that the gap in Scottish defence could be filled. The market price of even fencible recruits was becoming more than the state could bear; the volunteer infantry and yeomanry units of patriotic civilians that had organised themselves for local defence were not quite the competent and controllable force the government felt was needed. A conscripted force was seen as the answer, and in 1797 the agitators for a Scottish militia finally had their wish. Ultimately it was bare necessity that overrode the casuistry of the debate about the desirability and ideal form of a Scottish militia that had been conducted in Scottish intellectual circles since before the Union. The state now needed a Scottish militia and so one was created.[9]

On the militia's inception, voices of protest were heard from different quarters: from the Scottish landowning interest whose fears over the spread of French Revolutionary ideas had decidedly put them off any idea of an armed and trained working populace, and from among the people on whom the actual burden of compulsory militia service was about to fall. Sporadic but serious anti-conscription rioting broke out in parishes across Scotland, apparently realising the fears of those who felt a militia politically unwise. These sometimes violent demonstrations of popular

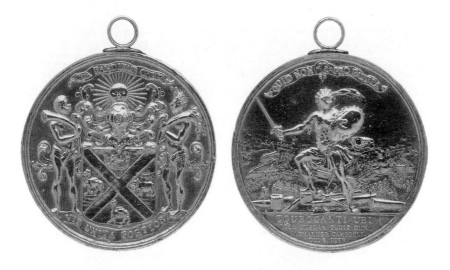

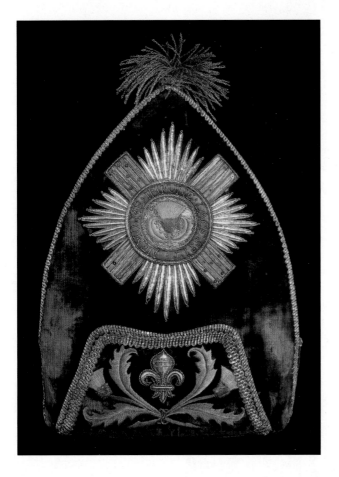

Plate 2.1 (above, two views) Medals were struck to celebrate the Darien colonists' successful attack on Spanish entrenchments at Toubocanti in 1700. This minor military success could not prevent the collapse of the isolated Scottish colony, bereft of adequate naval support.

Plate 2.2 (left) Scottish and French national symbols adorn the cap worn by a grenadier officer of the Royal Ecossais. Sending this Scottish regiment of the French army was one means by which France sought to support the Jacobite cause. The cap was taken in 1745 from a ship carrying officers and men from France, captured by the Royal Navy before it reached Scotland.

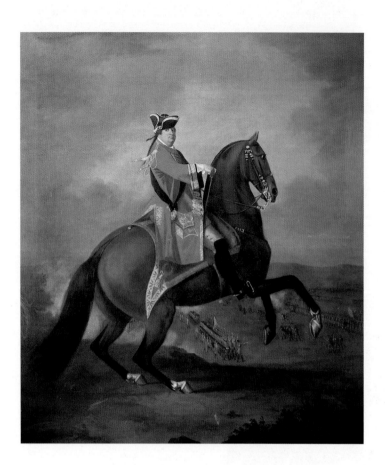

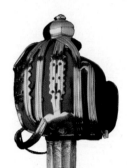

Plate 2.3 The Duke of Cumberland is shown triumphant at Culloden in 1746 by the painter David Morier. Scotland's instability represented a mortal threat to his family's position both in Britain and in the wider arena of European power.

Plate 2.4 (right, and details) Inscriptions on the blade of this highland basket-hilted sword proclaim the Jacobite and anti-Union politics of its owner. Such convictions, backed by military capability, made the highlands a potent threat to the new British state.

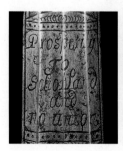

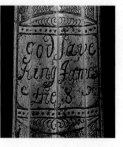

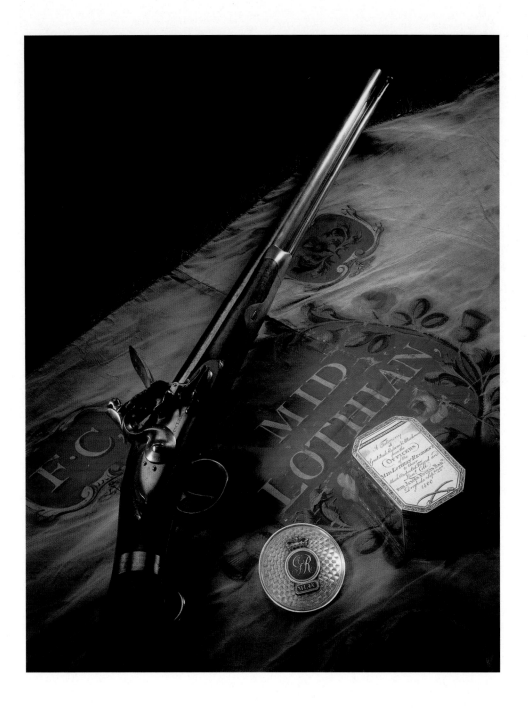

Plate 2.5 The Midlothian Fencibles spent three years in Ireland and saw active service during the 1798 Rebellion. The experimental carbine developed by its colonel, the Earl of Ancrum, was one manifestation of the regiment's professional approach to its duties.

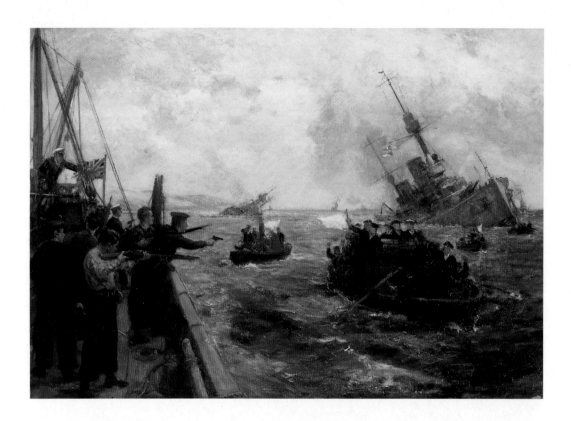

Plate 2.6 The naval artist Bernard Gribble was sketching at Scapa Flow, Orkney in June 1919 when he witnessed German crews abandoning their sinking ships. The scuttling of the fleet was a breach of the Armistice and Gribble shows the crew of a Royal Navy ship preparing to open fire in an initial attempt to force the Germans back to their ships.

Plate 2.7 (opposite) *Seven Cranes on the Clyde* represents the Clyde shipbuilding industry in a print of 1918 by the official war artist Sir Muirhead Bone. The government-backed artistic record of the conflict included strategic industry and the contribution of the civilian workforce to the war effort.

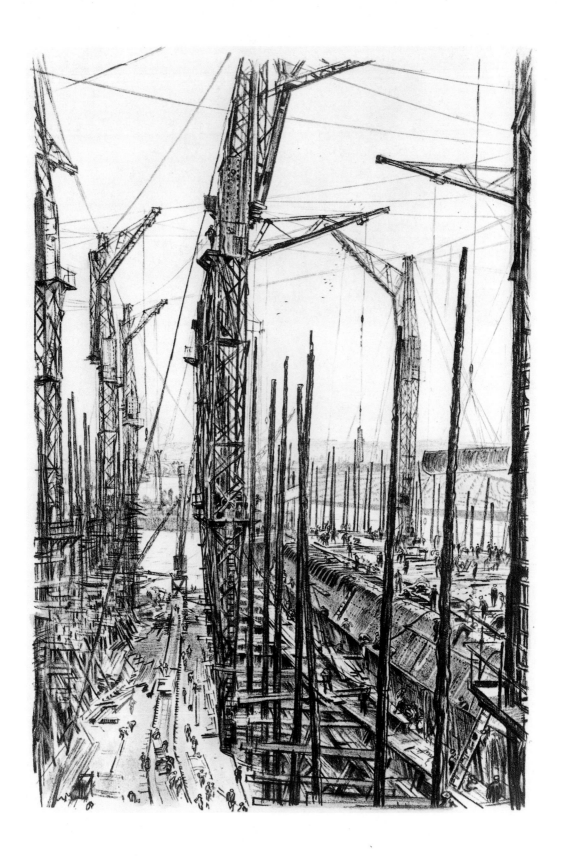

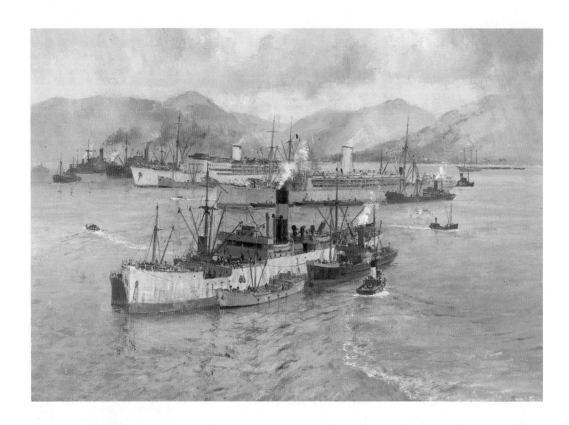

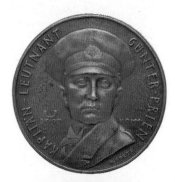

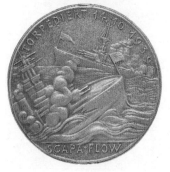

Plate 2.8 Convoy vessels are unloaded in the Holy Loch in this Second World War painting by Arthur W Burgess. The Holy Loch was one of the four anchorages behind the Firth of Clyde anti-submarine defences. Arriving convoy ships were unloaded by small coaster vessels, keeping up the vital supply of food, war materials and manpower.

Plate 2.9 (left, two views) This German medal celebrates the sinking by a U-Boat of the battleship HMS *Royal Oak* inside the fleet anchorage at Scapa Flow in October 1939. U-Boat commander Günter Prien was wrongly credited with the destruction of two ships, but the loss of the *Royal Oak* was a shocking demonstration of British naval vulnerability to submarine attack.

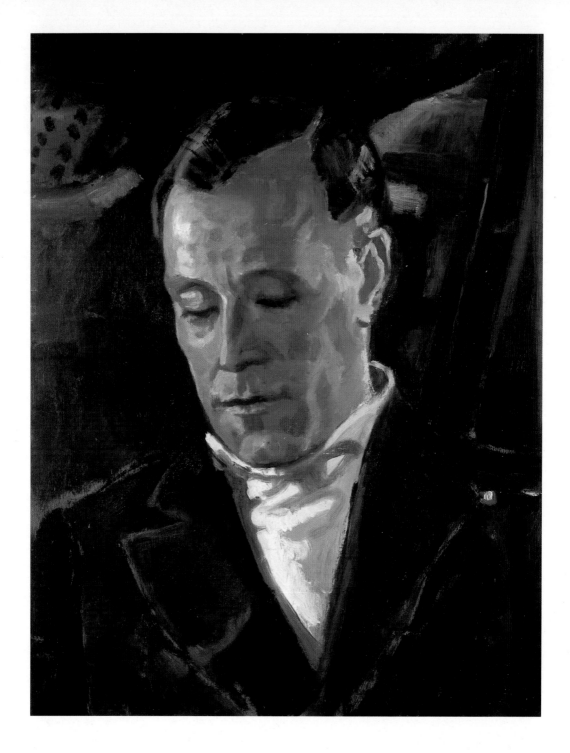

Plate 2.10 The renowned Royal Navy submarine commander Captain Ben Bryant was painted by the Scottish artist Robert Sivell in 1945. After successfully preying on enemy shipping in the Mediterranean, Bryant had been promoted to command HMS *Forth*, a submarine depot ship in the Holy Loch.

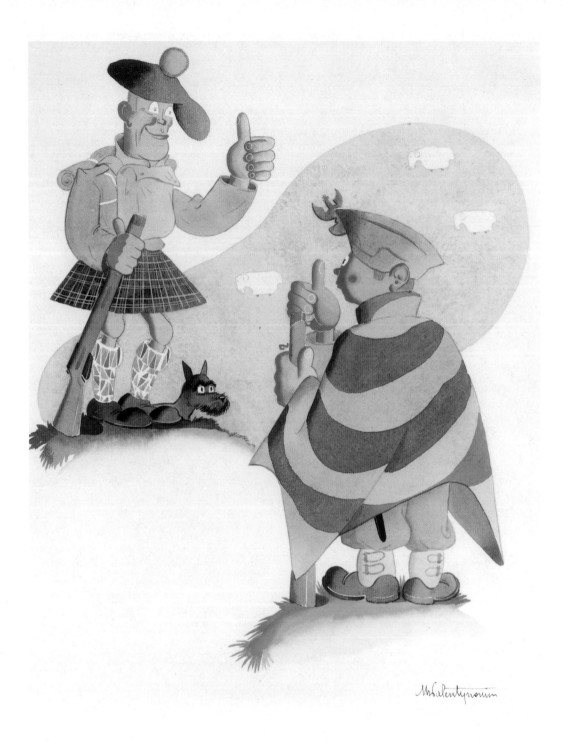

Plate 2.11 Friendship between Scottish and Polish soldiers is the subject for a cartoon by Marian Walentynowicz, an artist serving with the Polish forces in Scotland. It was part of a set of drawings and paintings presented in 1941 by the Polish army to the Lord Provost of Glasgow, in recognition of the hospitality the Poles had received.

opposition were also taken by the authorities as evidence of dangerous radical political activity and suppressed by military means; once, at Tranent, East Lothian, with a surfeit of force and ineptitude that left twelve dead.[10] However, the government in Scotland had actually anticipated the likely concerns of the population over compulsory service and had carefully limited service effectively to young, unmarried men while building in to the system legal routes of evasion to those with a little means, principally by the paying of willing substitutes. When the terms of the militia act became widely known, the protests petered out.

One of the tasks of the militia was to guard the prisoners of war who were incarcerated in Scotland. In previous conflicts the number of prisoners held in Scotland, mostly French sailors and the crews of French and American privateer vessels, had been modest enough to allow for their secure accommodation in such gloomy residences as the vaults of Edinburgh Castle. The wars against Napoleon's France were of a different order, particularly after British troops came into direct and sustained conflict with French armies in Spain; in 1814 some 72,000 prisoners were being held in Britain. In Scotland, as elsewhere, new prison depots had to be built to supplement the existing gaols. Three of these were constructed around Penicuik in Midlothian. The largest, at Valleyfield, held around 7500 prisoners. Some of the war prisons built at this time were substantial structures, more permanent than any of the prison camps operating in Scotland during the two world wars of the twentieth century. Perth Prison, completed in 1812, was constructed to hold around 7000 French internees. In 1839 it became Scotland's general central prison, and remains in use as a prison today. The accommodation of prisoners was of course more than a matter of keeping them together in body and soul; they actually had to be guarded. In such concentrations, French prisoners represented a potential security threat less in the likelihood of individual escapes, which were frequent, but rather in the possibility of a mass break-out should an invasion come, or revolution be attempted. This in itself was one cogent argument for a Scottish militia.[11]

Another complication in the militia system was the immunity from service acquired by those who were serving in the part-time volunteers. The government was happy enough to encourage the local yeomanry regiments – mounted volunteers officered by the landed gentry and manned by farmers and their tenants – since these had a utility in the swift policing of civil unrest, but the military efficiency of the volunteer infantry was a matter of doubt in official quarters. Autonomous local volunteer units found their government subsidy removed in 1808 when legislation created a new Local Militia throughout Britain. Part-time military service was brought firmly under central control, and so subject to the dictates of overall strategic priorities. Only those volunteer units with the financial means to be self-sufficient kept their semi-independent status. Included among these was the Edinburgh Volunteers, a unit that numbered members of the Scottish political and legal establishment in its ranks.

The fear of revolution endured as a security concern in the years following the final defeat of Napoleon's France in 1815. Political unrest, fuelled in part by post-war unemployment, gave the state an interest in retaining the services of the yeomanry units in peacetime. None of the Scottish yeomanry regiments ever charged in anger in wartime, but after 1815 yeomanry units from Glasgow, Ayrshire and Stirlingshire were used by the authorities to break up political demonstrations in nearby industrial areas. The defence of property and privilege was the normal business of these volunteers, but on at least one occasion they were called on to counter what appeared to the authorities to be a more substantial and immediate military threat. During the disturbances of 1820 known as the Radical War, a troop of the Stirlingshire Yeomanry attacked and dispersed a group of agitators who were believed to be marching on the Carron Ironworks in order to arm their Radical brethren. The small group that hoped to seize the works, its cannon, arms and ammunition, included a number of former soldiers discharged at the end of the French wars.

By the mid-nineteenth century economic success and a first measure of democratic reform had quietened internal political unrest. While Scotland's contribution to British imperial military manpower remained disproportionately strong in relation to its population, it had been outstripped by that of Ireland. The strategic rivalry between Britain and France had not, however, been concluded. Into the age of the steam-powered ironclad warship, the navies of Britain and France continued to eye each other warily and the respective governments spent heavily to promote the supremacy of their fleets. In the midst of this naval arms race, serious concerns again emerged about the state of Britain's defences.

A substantial (voluntary) militia was reorganised in 1852, housed in militia barracks and armouries that were constructed in several Scottish towns. This was not enough to satisfy the popular disquiet about perceived British vulnerability to attack; the volunteer movement revived in 1859 with great success in Scotland and, as has already been touched upon, endured to form the basis of a permanent army reserve in the following decades.

Of more immediate application to the strategic concerns of state was the 1859 creation of the Royal Naval Reserve, intended to supplement the Royal Navy in wartime with a supply of experienced seamen, trained for a national emergency. In Scotland many of these reservists were found in the fishing communities of the west highlands and islands.

A new programme of British coastal fortification building began, but the defensive measures taken were again designed less to meet a French invasion than to prevent a naval defeat that could lead to such an invasion. The new forts and batteries were therefore concentrated on the Royal Navy's strategically important ports and dockyards along the English south and south-east coast. As there was no naval base in Scotland, the measures taken were limited to protecting commercial ports from possible French naval bombardment, with artillery militia units manning the guns. The principal works undertaken in Scotland were the construction of batteries on Inchkeith Island in the Forth, and on the Fife coast opposite at Kinghorn. Historical continuities in considerations of strategic defence emerge in the fact that Inchkeith had previously been fortified against naval attacks on the Forth – for the purpose of the Franco-Scottish alliance against England in the 1550s.

The use of existing, sometimes ancient, places of fortification was also a practice of the army. Military accommodation was neglected after the defeat of Napoleon, at least until the Cardwell/Childers army reforms of the 1870s and '80s led to the expansion and construction of local bases as permanent infantry depots. Nevertheless, into the twentieth century, some Scottish garrisons continued to live in fortifications built

1st Battalion Argyll and Sutherland Highlanders parade on Edinburgh Castle esplanade, 1892.

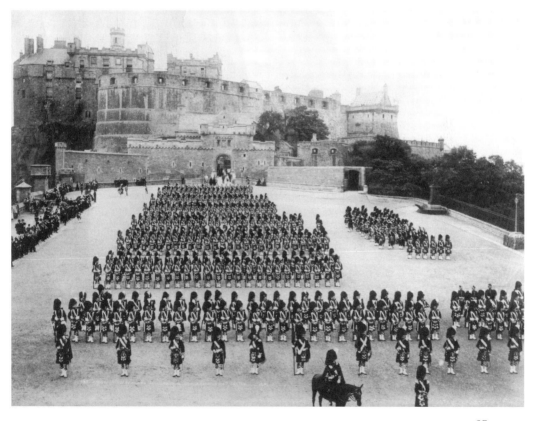

for an antique strategic purpose. The later history and physical character of Scottish ancient monuments, such as the castles at Stirling and Edinburgh, is much shaped by the army's utilitarian requirement for accommodation. Today, although new barracks constructed in the early twentieth century took the main garrison away from Edinburgh Castle, the army maintains a working presence within its walls. At the time of writing, Fort George near Inverness, a state of the art fortification completed in 1769 to guard against the Jacobite threat, is still a barrack home to Scottish infantry battalions.

At the end of the nineteenth century one element of strategic continuity was about to be broken, with immense consequences for the place and function of Scotland in British imperial defence imperatives. In the early twentieth century the rapid rise of imperial Germany as a naval power brought entente between Britain and France and, as the strategic map of Europe was re-drawn, the focus of British strategic defence moved north. From being an afterthought, a peripheral source of men and materials, Scotland was suddenly pushed to the forefront in strategies of containment and confrontation between Britain and Germany, now Britain's most likely adversary.

The naval arms race with Germany first impacted on the shipbuilding industry in the Clyde. In the 1890s the sudden need for new warships was more than the Admiralty's own Royal Dockyards could supply. When major orders began to be placed with private shipyards, the Clyde firms were well placed to compete. Strategic considerations made the Scottish west coast shipbuilding industry an attractive choice for the Admiralty since the Clyde yards were located beyond the reach of the marauding German surface ships known as raiders and of German airship attack. The need to keep ahead of the German navy made the Clyde shipyards the major centre of warship construction up to and through the First World War. When Britain began to re-arm against Germany in the 1930s, the Clyde retained the capacity to be the Admiralty's main supplier. From 1889 to 1939, more than 40 per cent of British warships constructed outside the Royal Dockyards were Clyde built. [12]

But the confrontation in the North Sea with a northern European naval power meant that naval strategy demanded more from Scotland than a source of ships. For the first time, the Royal Navy had to move to major strategic fleet bases far to the north of its traditional berths along the English south coast. The result was the creation of a new naval dockyard at Rosyth in the Firth of Forth, and the identification of Scapa Flow, Orkney as the main war-time anchorage for the British Grand Fleet. To similar purpose, a lesser base was developed at Invergordon in the Cromarty Firth.

The popular memory of the First World War is characterised by the imagery of trench warfare in France and Flanders. The contribution of

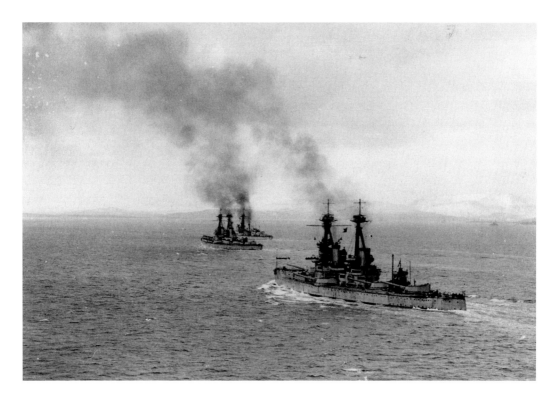

Royal Navy battle-
ships at gunnery
practice at Scapa
Flow during the
winter of 1916-17.

Scottish military manpower to the war, in the form of volunteers and,
later, conscripts, was overwhelmingly directed towards the army. Nevertheless, to a large degree, Britain was in the war because of the German
threat to the supremacy of the Royal Navy and so to the existence of the
British empire. To the British public, as well as to the war planners, the
naval conflict was anything but a sideshow. The arrival of the fleet in
Scotland in 1914 was a manifestation of British imperial power the like
of which Scotland had not seen before. From its new Scottish anchorages,
the Grand Fleet kept the German High Seas Fleet blockaded in its North
Sea bases and allowed armed merchant cruisers to effect a blockade,
stretching from Scottish waters to Norway and Iceland, against merchant
shipping bound for the Baltic. From Scapa Flow the Grand Fleet sailed
out to its single great encounter with its German counterpart, the battle
of Jutland off Denmark in May 1916, a battle that kept the German
surface fleet from the high seas for the rest of the war.

Ultimately, Scottish waters were to be the scene of the momentous
spectacle of final British victory. It was into the Firth of Forth that the
defeated German High Seas Fleet sailed into internment under the
terms of the Armistice of 11th November 1918. Although this was not,
or not as yet, technically, a surrender, the passing of the German fleet into
the control of the British Admiral Sir David Beatty at Rosyth was a
symbolic acknowledgement of defeat on a scale unparalleled in modern

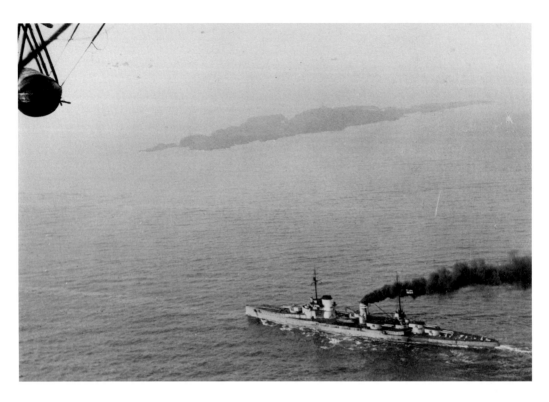

The German battle cruiser SMS *Seydlitz* approaches the Firth of Forth, November 1918, photographed from a patrolling airship.

naval history. The weight of the event was not lost on those who witnessed it, like one midshipman of the Royal Naval Volunteer Reserve:

> We were number two in our division, we were second boat to *Wolfhound* and then through the mist came this amazing spectacle. First of all you got the loom of some smoke and then the first of these big ships. One of the most wonderful things in the world because you realised that whatever was going to happen, this was one of the greatest naval occasions that ever occurred. [13]

As the German ships approached Scotland, the Royal Navy escort was on its guard against a last act of defiance. In the event this came six months later at Scapa Flow, where the interned German fleet had been transferred to await the deliberations of the Peace Conference at Versailles. When British attention was diverted by a naval exercise, the German skeleton crews left on the interned ships received orders to scuttle them rather than hand them over permanently as the Allies were demanding. The grotesque spectacle of the sinking German warships marked the bitter end of the First World War. The wrecks of German naval power still litter the bottom of Scapa Flow.

Scotland's emergence as a feature in naval strategy coincided with the emergence of a new powerful factor in naval warfare. The war economies of Great Britain and her European allies were heavily reliant on overseas supply and the submarine campaign waged against merchant shipping from 1915 made the U-Boat Germany's most effective, most dangerous weapon. It was on the sea lanes, and not the Western Front, that the British empire perhaps ran the greatest peril. Efforts to block off the Straits of Dover with mines having had some effect, it was by way of rounding the north of Scotland that German U-Boats could most easily get out into the Atlantic to prey on shipping in the Western Approaches. Patrol work off the Scottish coast was an essential weapon first against German surface 'raiders' and then in the long struggle against the submarine blockade, one which drew Scottish fishing fleets into the conflict armed and equipped for coastal patrol and mine-sweeping. But despite concerted offensive efforts against submarine traffic in the seas to the north of Scotland, the only truly effective anti-submarine technique developed was the essentially defensive convoy system for directly escorting merchant shipping at sea. Endeavours to address the problem closer to source, and keep the U-Boats out of the Atlantic, continued and, with the assistance of Great Britain's powerful new ally the United States, grew more ambitious and expensive. By the end of the war a colossal mine barrier, the Northern Barrage, had been laid in the North Sea stretching from the Orkney Islands to Norwegian waters. The efficacy of the Barrage in actually destroying and deterring submarines was much questioned, however (Admiral Beatty was one of the doubters, with further concerns that it impeded his own scope for operations), and by the time of its completion the war was all but at an end.[14]

Scotland's proximity to the passage of U-Boats in the North Sea had caused another modern weapon to be deployed – the aircraft. Seaplanes and land-based patrol planes were used for intensive anti-submarine searches, operating from Royal Naval Air Stations at Lerwick, Scapa Flow, Strathbeg and the major station at Dundee. East Fortune in East Lothian (now the National Museums of Scotland's Museum of Flight) was a strategic airfield close to the mouth of the Firth of Forth from which coastal airships and aircraft of the Royal Naval Air Service patrolled in defence of the fleet base at Rosyth. East Fortune aircraft were also put to development work with the fleet as aircraft carrier capability and the techniques of torpedo-bombing from the air were tested. At the war's end it was from the strategically placed East Fortune that the Royal Air Force sent its most up-to-date airship, the R.34, on an armed patrol over the German coast – a conspicuous threat intended to concentrate the minds of German negotiators as peace talks dragged on at Versailles.

The presence of the precursors of the Royal Air Force in Scotland from the outset of the First World War represented the northernmost extension of British east coast air defences against German submarines and Zeppelin raids. Scottish industry also contributed substantially to the wartime manufacture of military aircraft. Yet this was only the very beginning of air warfare as an element in the dictates of strategy. Between the two world wars, the imperatives of air defence were hugely extended by the development of long-range aerial bombing. The re-emergence of the German threat, this time in the form of rearmament under the National Socialist government, brought the possibility of mass bombing of the British mainland. The development of warship building, armaments production and heavy engineering on the Clyde had made central Scotland a potential target, along with other industrialised areas of Great Britain.

However, as was the case in the First World War, it was Scotland's physical proximity to northern Europe, and its harbouring of British naval might, that had immediate implications for Scotland's air strategic value and vulnerability. During the First World War, German airships had attempted raids on the naval installations in the Firth of Forth, but these machines lacked the power to find and damage their strategic targets. When war came again in 1939, German bombers were a more substantial proposition. The first German air attacks on the British coast came over the east of Scotland, on Rosyth and Scapa Flow, flown from airfields in northern Germany. The raids on the Forth were resisted by the Glasgow and Edinburgh squadrons of the Auxiliary Air Force formed in the 1920s, operating from airfields in East Lothian. It was these pre-war squadrons of part-time Scottish airmen that recorded the first destruction of German aircraft over sea and land in September 1939. With the war in its infancy, and air combat itself still a novelty, the fate of the German aircrews killed or captured drew national attention, and

German Heinkel 111 bomber shot down at Humbie, East Lothian on 28th October 1939, the first enemy aircraft brought down on British soil.

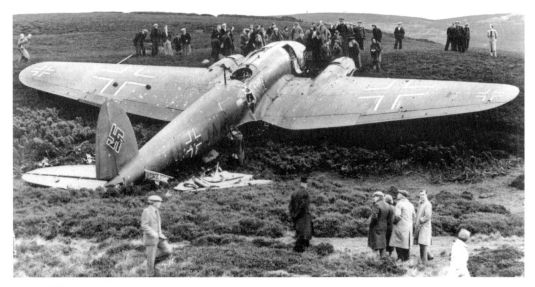

souvenirs of the downed aircraft were avidly collected by local people in East Lothian. Many have since found a home as museum pieces in the national collection.

The fall of France to German invasion in June 1940 shifted the focus of the air war south. If France had been held, and with Germany in occupation of Norway, Scotland's strategic place in the war might have been very much greater. As it was, even the Scottish auxiliary air squadrons were called south to play their part in the Battle of Britain campaign that lifted the immediate threat of a German invasion across the English Channel. Although it was the south of England, London and the industrialised English midlands that were most heavily exposed to German bombing thereafter, Scotland was far from untouched. The devastating Clydebank Blitz air raids of March 1941 were testimony to the importance of Scottish industrial production to the British war effort. With an intensity which, for a short time, matched destruction wrought by German air attack anywhere in the country, over 1000 bombs were dropped on the town on 13th and 14th March, killing over 500 civilians and leaving barely a building in the town intact.[15] With John Brown's shipyard and the Singer engineering factory presumably identified as strategic targets, Clydebank had the misfortune to attract this concentration of enemy attention, but the whole of Clydeside and west central Scotland was a target for German bombers.

The aftermath of the air attack on Clydebank.

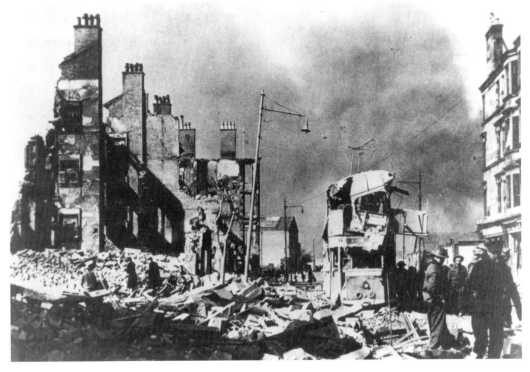

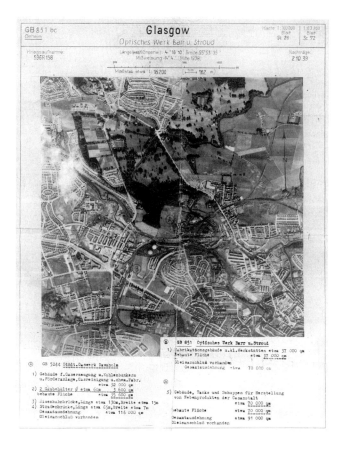

German aerial reconnaissance photograph of the Barr & Stroud optical engineering works, 1939.

In May 1941 Greenock received similar treatment to Clydebank. As well as warships, merchant ships and submarines, the centres of Scottish industry produced aircraft and aircraft engines, explosives, specialised optical equipment and all manner of ordnance. Steel and coal, railway engineering and lighter industry, including clothing manufacture and sugar refining, were also worthwhile and concentrated destinations for German aerial bombs. Other Scottish cities and towns, in particular Aberdeen, were subjected to less focussed raids, damaging nevertheless.

If German air attacks were sporadic in comparison to those launched against the south, Scotland's position was again pivotal in relation to the re-emergence of the German submarine threat. A shocking demonstration of the renewed potency of the U-Boat was given in the early weeks of the war when a German submarine succeeded in entering Scapa Flow itself and sank the battleship HMS *Royal Oak*. Soon, allied and neutral merchant ships were being sunk with regularity off the north and north-east of Scotland. The danger was increased as the German occupation of Denmark and Norway was achieved, overcoming attempted British naval intervention launched from Scapa Flow and Rosyth. When the Allied position deteriorated still further with German victory in France, the submarine problem changed markedly from that faced in the First World War. With submarine bases on the French coast, German U-Boats had a direct outlet into the Atlantic and into British trade heading to and from the major southern English ports. This situation heightened the strategic importance of the Clyde which, along with Liverpool and Belfast, became a vital conduit for supplies of food, war materials and, after the entry of the United States into the war, military personnel. Towards this traffic the enemy inevitably came hunting and an extensive infrastructure of support for the Atlantic convoy system, including defended anchorages, submarine bases and escort training was developed around the Firth of Clyde, the Cowal sea lochs and along the west coast, with another important centre at Loch Ryan, Galloway. A crucial element in this Scottish end of the battle of the Atlantic was the convoy air escort and anti-submarine patrol conducted by Royal Air Force squadrons of Coastal Command. It was in the combination of air escort and refinements of the convoy escort system that the effective counter to enemy submarine capability was found, and had to be found as the situation became critical. Incoming air traffic from North America also became a feature of the transatlantic strategic utility of the Scottish west coast. RAF Prestwick in Ayrshire was developed to take delivery of thousands of military aircraft manufactured in the United States and routed to Great Britain via Canada.

Wartime sea traffic around Scotland was not only concerned with inbound British supply. German domination of northern Europe also brought Scotland a role in outward bound supply and offensive operations. With the German invasion of the Soviet Union in 1941, a new strategic imperative emerged in the need to supply Britain's new Soviet ally with the war materials it required to keep the fight going in the east. In September 1941 the first of the Arctic convoys sailed for the northern Russian ports of Murmansk and Archangel. In the years following, the point of assembly and departure for many of these convoys was Loch Ewe in Wester Ross. As with the Atlantic traffic, the dangers faced by those who manned the Arctic convoys were extreme. To the U-Boat factor was added a vulnerability to German surface ships and aircraft that could prey upon them from bases in Norway. Counter-measures were launched from Scotland, most famously against the German battleship *Tirpitz* whose very presence had consistently hampered the convoy effort. Damage was inflicted repeatedly on the ship by midget submarines (trained up off Rothesay, Bute), Fleet Air Arm aircraft flown from carriers, and bombers flown from northern Russia, but the apparently indestructible *Tirpitz* was finally sunk in Kjaa Fjord near Tromsö, Norway by Lancaster bombers flown from RAF Lossiemouth on the Moray coast. Less spectacularly, but consistently, RAF squadrons operating from bases along the north-east Scottish coastline struck at enemy shipping in the North Sea and the Norwegian fjords in the later years of the war.

Not for the first time, the remote and mountainous terrain of Scotland also found a strategic application during the Second World War. The rather perilous state of opposition to German domination of Europe by late 1940 brought forth one response in the assertion of ideas about irregular warfare training. These emerged with one eye towards a possible successful German invasion of Britain and, more optimistically, with a desire to strike at the enemy in occupied Europe in advance of more conventional offensive action. With the blessing of the British

Prime Minister Winston Churchill, these ideas were advanced using Scotland as a testing and training ground. Around Loch Fyne, Argyll, the Firth of Clyde and the western sea lochs, a variety of Combined Operations training establishments evolved and rehearsed the crucial techniques of amphibious landings that were to be mounted against the coasts of North Africa, Italy and, ultimately, Normandy. At Lochailort, Inverness-shire, the first special service troops and commandos were trained in fieldcraft, close-quarter fighting and demolitions in preparation for raids on German-held territory.

From 1942 the function of the Special Training Centre at Lochailort was picked up by the Commando Basic Training Centre at Achnacarry, Inverness-shire, seat of Cameron of Lochiel. In this area, marked now by the Commando Memorial above Spean Bridge, growing numbers of recruits were exposed to the rigours of the Scottish hills and climate as the Commandos evolved into a more conventional, though still highly trained, large-scale offensive force. The training possibilities offered by Scotland were enhanced not only by the difficulties of its highland terrain, but also by the relative remoteness and inaccessibility of sparsely populated western coastal areas, distant from the reaches of enemy intelligence. The highland topography of inland lochs allowed an imaginary line to be drawn along the Great Glen, to the north-west of which was designated the Protected Area. It was in this large area of the country, subject to special security restrictions against unauthorised access, that

Soldiers were prepared for officer training by the tough regime of the Highland Fieldcraft Training Centre, 1943-44.

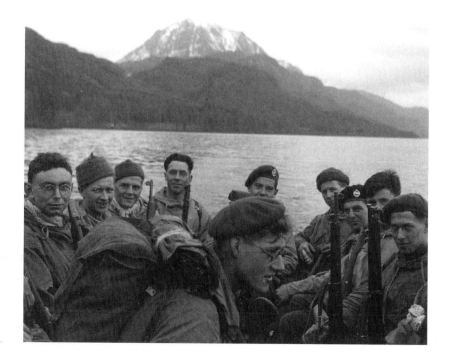

the Lochailort and Achnacarry centres were sited. Nearby, at training schools of the Special Operations Executive in remote quarters of Arisaig, Morar and Knoydart, resistance volunteers from a variety of enemy-occupied nations secretly received instruction along the lines of that inculcated at Lochailort, before being dropped back into their own countries.

While the Commandos and would-be resistance fighters ranged over the terrain to the west, the Cairngorm mountains to the east also filled with soldiers. The 52nd (Lowland) Division was trained in the occasionally Arctic conditions of the Cairngorm plateau as a fully-fledged mountain warfare force. This was a contingency for a possible invasion of German-occupied Norway, which remained a serious strategic option at least until the end of 1943 and retained throughout the added attraction of conveying to enemy intelligence that a Norwegian invasion objective was at any rate intended, thereby keeping enemy troops and resources from the French coast. To preparations for the Normandy landings Scotland contributed training beaches and such out-of-the-way installations as the artificial harbour development centre on Wigtown Bay in the far south-west.

But meanwhile it remained a specific objective of British military intelligence to keep Scotland's proximity to Norway at the forefront of the enemy's mind. As part of an elaborate UK-wide scheme of strategic deception, the Fortitude North intelligence operation in Scotland created an elaborate network of dummy aircraft, bogus radio traffic, fictional troop formations and movements that succeeded in convincing German intelligence that an invasion force was gathering in Scotland, bound for an amphibious landing in southern Norway to support an invasion of France targeted not on Normandy but on the pas de Calais. In the event, having been a 'real' element in the Fortitude North intelligence deception, and kept ready to pre-empt any Soviet attempt to occupy northern Norway in the event of a German collapse, the Scottish mountain-trained 52nd (Lowland) Division, complete with its Norwegian contingent, was diverted to the main theatre of operations in western Europe and fought through the notably mountain-free terrain of the Netherlands and northern Germany.

Elements of the 52nd (Lowland) Division aside, Scotland played host to a large contingent of Norwegian forces for much of the war, as parts of the country became harbouring and preparation areas for allied forces forced into exile in the early stages of the war. On the collapse of the British intervention in Norway in 1940, many Norwegians escaped the German occupation by coming to Scotland directly. A small number were soon in a position to strike straight back. Norwegian commandos trained in the highlands to carry out raids against the German occupa-tion forces, including the celebrated disruption to the feared German

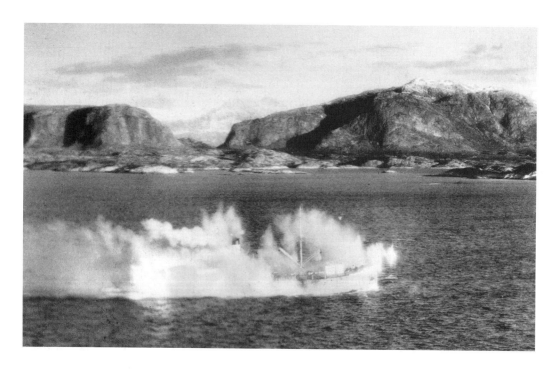

German shipping off Norway under attack by Mosquito bombers from the Banff Strike Wing, 1945.

nuclear programme achieved by the sabotage of the Norsk-Hydro heavy water factory at Vermok in the Telemark district. Support for the Norwegian Resistance, and facilitation of such raids, was launched from the Shetland Islands – the 'Shetland Bus' traffic of Norwegian fishing vessels that infiltrated and extracted sabotage teams, instructors and materials across the North Sea – and, less well-known, from Peterhead, where naval intelligence agents were similarly transported by Norwegian refugee vessels. Norwegian airmen also had the opportunity to take the fight from Scotland directly home. In 1944-45 the Banff and Dallachy Strike Wings of RAF Coastal Command had the asset of local knowledge among Norwegian aircrew in launching an air offensive from the Scottish north-east coast against German shipping off south-west Norway. But for the bulk of the Norwegian contingent based in Scotland, the fight for home was subsumed into the bigger picture, with the Navy or with the merchant fleet in the Atlantic, or was a matter of waiting. After four years of preparation and frustration in bases around Dumfries and in Easter Ross, the Norwegian Army Brigade was finally deployed in the uncontested liberation of Norway in May 1945.

No such relief was to fall to a second, and numerically far stronger, wartime foreign presence in Scotland – the Poles. Polish forces came to Scotland by a long and traumatic route, first regrouping in France after their homeland was carved up between Germany and the Soviet Union, then experiencing defeat for a second time as the battle for France was lost. Some 17,000 Poles evacuated from France to British ports were

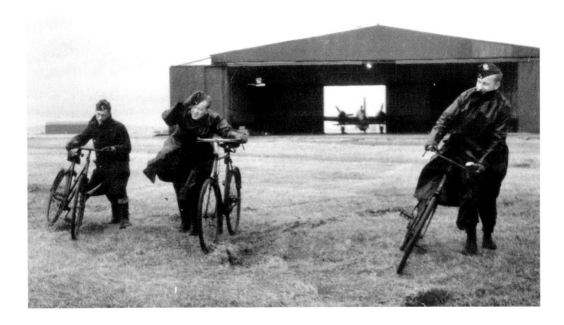

sent by rail to Scotland, concentrated first in Glasgow and then in areas of open country requisitioned in Lanarkshire.[16] Unlike the Norwegians, there was little scope for Polish forces to strike back at the occupiers of their own country. Instead, Polish troops were moved east and strengthened to defend the Fife and Angus coasts from invasion, a convenient replacement for Scottish territorial troops needed to fill in for the 51st (Highland) Division lost to captivity in France. Polish armoured and airborne units were soon formed and began the long preparations for the invasion of north-west Europe in June 1944, their numbers boosted by new arrivals from the Middle East following the forced evacuation of Polish forces from the Soviet Union. By the time Polish troops were back on mainland Europe, it was clear that Soviet, and not Polish, troops would have the task of ending the German occupation of Poland, and apparent that they would not be leaving. For the Poles, overall German defeat brought no redeeming campaign of liberation. After the disbandment of Polish troops under British command, the majority could not return to a country still under foreign occupation. Instead, many chose to make Scotland their home.

Among the foreign nationals that gathered in wartime Scotland were those whose job was not to fight, but to work. One task to which they were set was the extraction of timber. It is not the purpose of this survey to assess the overall impact of war on the Scottish economy, but in the midst of the U-Boat blockade, areas of industry and agriculture became essential to Britain's capacity to continue the war. One such

Polish air squadrons also served in Scotland. Based at Benbecula in the winter of 1944-45, 304 Squadron had to contend with the elements as well as German submarines.

strategic economic resource was timber, for which military demands –
for temporary accommodation, crating for transportation, for manufacture of rifle stocks and tools and high explosives – were added to the
needs of industry. Much of the home timber available to be felled was
in Scottish forests. Reliance on imported timber had been recognised as
a critical weakness during the submarine blockade of the First World
War; native timber sources were much reduced since the days of the wars
against France. In late 1916, in the midst of the first U-Boat crisis,
Canadian Forestry workers had arrived in Scotland to assist with the
felling of home timber requisitioned by the government. At the war's
end the government drew some lessons and retained an involvement in
the strategic provision of timber stocks. The Forestry Commission was
created with a remit to acquire and plant land, and to support private
endeavour through grants. When war with Germany recommenced in
1939, the government plantations were not sufficiently mature to supply
the needs of home industry and the armed forces, and privately owned
Scottish forests were again turned to meeting the needs of the state. With
the home labour force denuded by conscription, the Canadians were
called on again. Some 7000 men of the Canadian Forestry Corps cleared
230,000 acres of Scottish forest by the war's end, an impact that was
to be redressed after the war by widespread state plantation schemes.[17]
The Canadians were joined in the Scottish forests by around 750 men
of the British Honduran Forestry Unit, many of them experienced
mahogany-cutters capable of rapidly processing the significantly
smaller, softer Scottish product. The third main source of labour in the
timber extraction was female. Just short of 4000 Scottish women chose
service in the Scottish Women's Timber Corps as an option of National
Service that kept them in Scotland and in a more agreeable environment
than munitions work.[18]

Much as it might have been wished for, the defeat and military
enfeeblement of Germany in 1945 brought little reduction in Scotland's
strategic significance and proximity to the likely passages of war. In
the post-war era, British defence policy continued to rest on the need
to counter a naval threat from the north, with the Soviet Union donning
the mantle previously worn by Germany in the latter role. One factor in
British strategic calculations had however gained far greater weight –
cost. The economic strictures bearing upon Britain as a result of two
financially crippling war efforts in the space of three decades demanded
realistic assessment of military priorities.

In the first instance it was recognised that British military reliance on
the United States, as manifested in the Second World War, was not going
to go away. In 1948 the Royal Navy, the ballast of British world power,
acknowledged that in a major war it could only defend and supply Britain
by operating in alliance with the US Navy. British military hardware

constructed in wartime soon passed into obsolescence and the retention of a British military presence 'east of Suez' proved financially debilitating. The result was that successive British governments concentrated defence spending on Britain's role in co-ordinated, American-led war planning under the control of the North Atlantic Treaty Organisation.

From the outset in the early 1950s, NATO strategy for a war against the Soviet Union encompassed American-led naval offensive operations in the Norwegian Sea, maintaining a role for Royal Navy submarines operating from Scottish bases together with all the naval and air support required for a campaign to the north. By the early 1960s, NATO strategy carried consequences for Scotland of even greater weight. First, operating from a depot in the Holy Loch were submarines that were not British but American. Second, these submarines, together with Royal Navy submarines operating from the base at Faslane in the Gare Loch, were armed with Polaris nuclear missiles. The positioning of these formidable weapons undoubtedly had much to do with the same strategic considerations that had placed submarines and other naval installations along the Scottish west coast in the Second World War – remoteness and seclusion relative to the potential enemy, a choice of routes into the Arctic and Atlantic, and a reliable supply of Scottish west coast weather as cover for activity. Yet the suspicion was aroused that, with a view to accident as well as attack, these bases took advantage of naval infrastructure more remote from population centres than would be possible with equivalent installations to the south. For the populations that were in proximity, this was not a comforting assessment. Whatever the reasoning, unease about and ongoing active protest against the siting of Polaris and its Trident successor in Scotland was generally more concerned with moral principle and with the attendant dangers of the

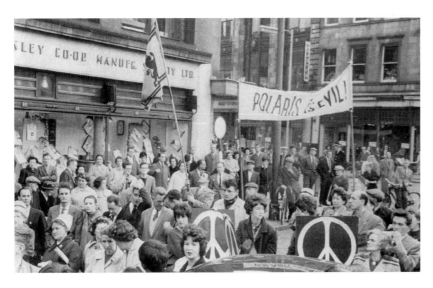

A demonstration in Paisley against the arrival of US *Polaris* submarines in the Holy Loch combined anti-nuclear protest with nationalist feeling, May 1961.

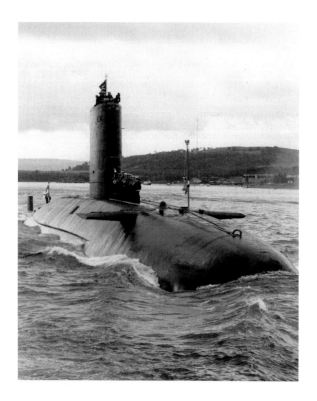

Conventionally armed submarine HMS *Conqueror* returns to Faslane after sinking the Argentine cruiser *General Belgrano*, during the Falklands War, 1982.

nuclear arsenal than with the placing of significant weapons in Scotland outside the sole control of the British state.

At the height of the Cold War in the early 1980s, when the limited tactical use of nuclear weapons was envisaged in combination with conventional operations in western Europe and the northern Atlantic, Scotland, and especially some of its remote northern coastal quarters, fairly bristled with Royal Air Force radar stations, command and control installations, naval depots and war-ready airfields. Established RAF stations on the Moray Firth at Kinloss and Lossiemouth had largely been used during the Second World War to train bomber air crews, but these airfields were well placed for squadrons to monitor (and, if it had become necessary, strike against) Soviet submarine and surface naval activity emanating from the Barents Sea. At RAF Leuchars in Fife, one of the principal air bases in the United Kingdom, fighter squadrons were ready to intercept Soviet long-range incursion into British air space, and to support NATO fleets in the north Atlantic. In the event of war, the strategy of the Soviet Union and her Warsaw Pact allies involved a large scale air attack on western Europe, including Great Britain, in preparation for a ground advance west, and Scottish strategic air installations would have been targeted by Soviet bombers. War between NATO and the Warsaw Pact would have come home to Scotland very quickly. Meanwhile, in preparation, the complex coastal and mountain terrain of north-west Scotland continued to have a strategic application. The considerable sound of military low-flying training, particularly the distinctive scream of Buccaneers from RAF Lossiemouth, became a regular reminder to highland populations that the remote and dramatic Scottish landscape was anything but peripheral in military planning terms.

Today, elements of this Cold War array remain, most significantly the Royal Navy's nuclear submarine base at Faslane. Yet the collapse of the Soviet Union in the early 1990s effected a steep decline in Scotland's direct involvement in the strategic concerns of NATO and the western world. By 1992 American nuclear submarines had departed from the

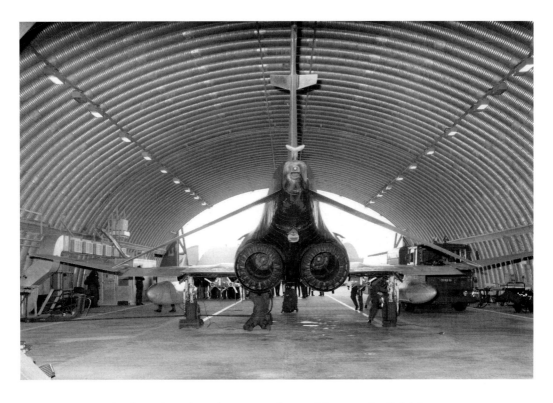

Holy Loch. This changing situation was mirrored by cuts in British military spending which have seen the armed services contract and reorganise for new roles. Essentially, the extension northwards of conventional British military power that began in the early twentieth century has gone into reverse. The Scapa Flow naval base closed in 1957. Submarines, maritime air power and missile technology having ended the era of the grand fleets; a new role in refitting nuclear submarines kept the Rosyth dockyard alive for a time, but both this work, and Rosyth's strategic value as a base, are now gone. If the current strategic picture endures, the prospect of a long-term future for Rosyth appears uncertain. Faslane remains, but the shore installations of the Royal Navy are concentrating again around the traditional home of the service along the English south coast. Less forcefully as yet, a similar trend can be followed in relation to the Royal Air Force presence in Scotland with the down-sizing and closure of important Cold War stations like the radar defence centres at RAF Saxe Vord, Shetland and RAF Buchan.

The passing of Britain's imperial power status has also reduced the need for military manpower, both in regular and reserve forces. The following chapters will explore the manner in which the loss of the imperial role in the later twentieth century has re-shaped Scottish involvement in the British armed forces and, with it, the position of the military influence in Scottish society. But in organisational terms, with

Hardened aircraft shelters protected the F4 *Phantom* interceptor fighters stationed at RAF Leuchars, Fife, during the 1980s.

the absorption of Scottish Division into 2nd Division in 1999, Scotland no longer even has existence as an army district, a status that Scotland (or, for a time, 'North Britain') had previously maintained since the earliest organisation of the British standing army.

In the context of Scotland's military history since the creation of the British armed forces, perhaps the significant shift of the last fifty years has been the subsuming of Britain's conventional military capability into the shared control of larger alliances and organisations: NATO, the United Nations, United States-led coalitions not under the aegis of these two, and, as would appear to be emerging, the European Union. Since the end of the Cold War the absence of a consistent northern threat to any of these has neutralised Scotland's strategic position somewhat. And yet, the operation of a British independent nuclear capability on a strategic scale is the concentrated modern equivalent of the deterrent power that once resided in the great fleets of the Royal Navy. In the existence of the Trident submarine fleet, Britain retains its theoretical autonomy as a significant military power and, as such, it is maintained as a guarantor of British inviolability in the future. The location of the nuclear fleet base at Faslane and Coulport on the Scottish west coast is something inherited from the strategic requirements of a past era, but the fact remains that the British state still relies on Scotland's strategic utility to operate the military means it needs to secure its chosen place in the world.

---

1   William Shakespeare, *Macbeth*, act IV, scene iii, line 64.

2   See especially J Robertson, 'An elusive sovereignty. The course of the Union debate in Scotland 1698-1707', in J Robertson (ed), *A Union for Empire. Political Thought and the British Union of 1707* (Cambridge: Cambridge University Press, 1995), and J R Young, 'The parliamentary incorporating Union of 1707: political management, anti-Unionism and foreign policy', in T M Devine and J R Young (eds), *Eighteenth Century Scotland: New Perspectives* (East Linton: Tuckwell Press, 1999).

3   A similar move to reactivate the Scottish navy in 1627, to protect Scottish shipping from Spanish privateers, had proved an unsustainable burden on Scottish revenues.

4   A detailed assessment of the consequences of Union on Scottish maritime trade and security is given in E Graham, *A Maritime History of Scotland 1650-1790* (East Linton: Tuckwell Press, 2002).

5   Wolfe's letter of 9th June 1751 to Captain William Rickson, in B Willson, *The Life and Letters of James Wolfe* (London: William Heinemann, 1909), pp.139-45.

6   A vivid account of mutinies in the early highland regiments is supplied by J Prebble, *Mutiny. Highland Regiments in revolt, 1743-1804* (London: Secker & Warburg, 1975).

7   The Hackness Martello Tower in Orkney survives today in the care of Historic Scotland. Martello towers were named after a corruption of Cape Mortella in Corsica where the enemy's effective use of such a round tower fortification frustrated a British naval attack in 1794.

8 A Carswell, 'The Scottish Fencible Regiments in Ireland', in *The Irish Sword*, volume XXI (no. 84), pp.155-9.

9 The militia debate is examined in J Robertson, *The Scottish Enlightenment and the Militia Issue* (Edinburgh: John Donald, 1985).

10 For analysis of the Militia riots, see K Logue, *Popular Disturbances in Scotland 1780-1815* (Edinburgh: John Donald, 1979), pp.75-115.

11 Figures from F Abell, *Prisoners of War in Britain 1756 to 1815. A Record of their Lives, their Romance and their Sufferings* (Oxford: Oxford University Press, 1914), and I MacDougall, *The Prisoners at Penicuik. French and other prisoners of war, 1803-1814* (Dalkeith: Midlothian District Council, 1989).

12 H Peebles, *Warshipbuilding on the Clyde. Naval Orders and the Prosperity of the Clyde Shipbuilding Industry, 1889-1939* (Edinburgh: John Donald, 1987), p.157.

13 'The Surrender of the German High Seas Fleet, an address by the Hon Lord Cameron, DSC LL.D, Senator of the College of Justice, to the Ship's Company of HMS *Claverhouse*, Forth Division Royal Naval Reserve, on Thursday, 21st November 1968, on the occasion of the fiftieth anniversary of the Surrender' (National War Museum of Scotland, M.1972.40).

14 The count of German submarines destroyed by mines in the Northern Barrage was believed to be a mere seven. See J Terraine, *Business in Great Waters. The U-Boat Wars 1916-1945* (London: Leo Copper Ltd, 1989), pp.114-15.

15 The Clydebank Blitz raid left some 1200 dead and 1100 seriously injured across Clydeside as a whole. The complexities and politics behind the compilation of the figures are discussed in I MacPhail, *The Clydebank Blitz* (Clydebank Town Council, 1974), p.66-9.

16 A Carswell, *For Your Freedom and Ours. Poland, Scotland and the Second World War* (Edinburgh: National Museums of Scotland, 1993), p.5.

17 W Wonders, *'The Sawdust Fusiliers', The Canadian Forestry Corps in the Scottish Highlands in World War Two* (Montreal: Canadian Pulp and Paper Association, 1991), pp.88-9.

18 Figures from A Ford, *Telling the Truth. The Life and Times of the British Honduran Forestry Unit in Scotland (1941-44)* (London: Karia Press, 1985), and A Gray, *Timber!* (East Linton: Tuckwell Press, 1998).

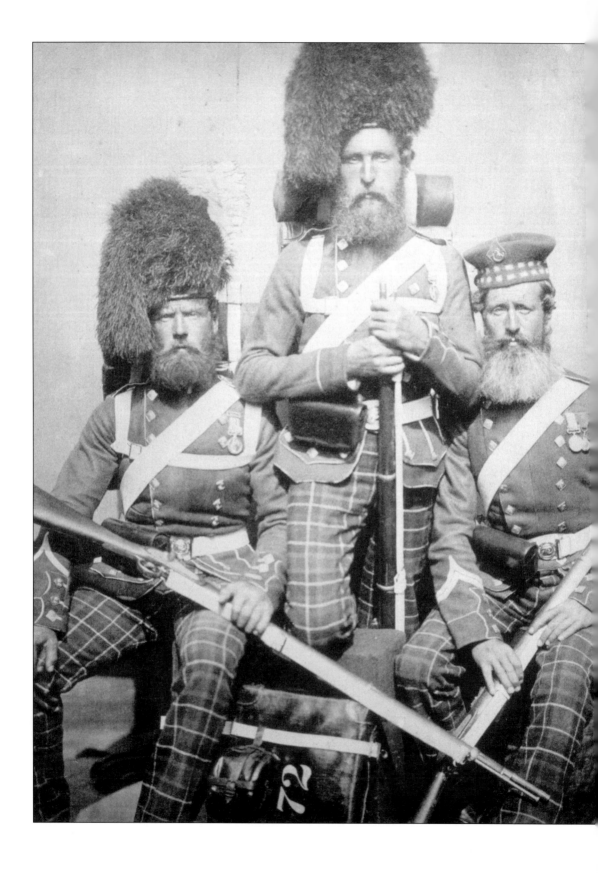

This is the life for a Scotsman

THE COLLECTIONS OF THE NATIONAL WAR MUSEUM OF SCOTLAND reflect and represent a great range of personal experience, individual lives shaped by time, place and circumstance. They demonstrate that, at the level of the individual, Scottish encounters with war and military service had much in common with those of the other British nationalities, and indeed with the general experience of those in military employment in other parts of the western world. Objects that speak of personal encounters with warfare, with its hardships, dangers and suffering, with its compensations in the sharing of common purpose, vitality and the resilience of human dignity, these have a power that transcends the Scottish context. A wallet of personal photographs pierced by a fatal shot, or a keepsake of loved ones separated by the great distances and duration of overseas service, such things do not require familiarity with the Scottish historical background to convey meaning. Yet for all that the collections suggest something of war, and of the military way of life, as might be said to be common to all or, at least, to be common to all those involved in the armed service of the British state and its empire, they can likewise suggest features of experience that were specific to Scotland or that had peculiarly Scottish manifestations. In this respect, they represent a material remnant of the connection between the sort of strategic realities considered in the previous chapter, and the economic, social and cultural trends of the Scottish society from which the people who served were drawn. If military service is viewed as a series of opportunities – for employment, for advancement, for gain, or merely for subsistence, the manner in which areas of opportunity opened for Scots in particular can be followed.

For the last three centuries, the Scottish military experience has largely been characterised by service in the British armed forces. Military professionals, full-time men-at-arms, have been a product of Scotland's society for centuries more. Scottish kings and lords customarily had only a small number of trained military professionals at their disposal, and fought their wars with temporary armies raised for the purpose, filled by the obligations of social contract where men owed military service for limited periods as part of the arrangement by which they held land.

Veterans of the 42nd Highlanders, from the *Crimean Heroes* series by J Cundall, 1856.

Yet the economics and social structure of pre-modern Scotland also produced men selling their military labour as a full-time means of livelihood – even when their homeland was, as much as then it ever was, at peace. Ireland was among the first of countries to see numbers of Scottish professional fighting men at work in its wars, wars that had nothing directly to do with them other than as a means of earning a living. By the thirteenth century, Gaelic Irish kings resisting Anglo-Norman military power, and warring among themselves, widely employed the *galloglass* class of armed men originally recruited from the western isles of Scotland. A statistical study of this type of military migration from Scotland is not possible, but it might be assumed that such factors as population pressure on limited resources of land, exacerbated by incidences of famine and disease, were significant.

The supply side of this export market would also have been affected by war at home, not just in the dislocation and poverty wrought in Scotland but also in the opportunity brought by war to acquire marketable fighting expertise. The long Wars of Independence in late thirteenth- and early fourteenth-century Scotland produced men who knew little better than how to fight, and who, when something like peace came to their own war-ravaged country, looked to sell their know-how abroad. Later, sporadic conflict between the kingdoms of Scotland and England during the Hundred Years' War kept up a supply of experienced men-at-arms that Scotland's ally France could lure with money and put to direct employment. In 1419, at the request of the French heir to the throne, a Scottish army was recruited to assist in the fight against the English in France. For centuries after this Scottish expeditionary force was defeated in 1424, the French royal army maintained a recognised Scottish element, including a Scottish company of the King's Bodyguard. Military migration continued from the Gaelic west in the sixteenth century as violent turmoil surrounding the collapse of the Lordship of the Isles bred a supply of skilled and available armed men in the Scottish islands and highlands. Great numbers of these transferred their skills to the theatre of war in Ireland, where the influx of the Scottish 'Redshanks' formed a substantial element in Irish armies until their decisive defeat by the English at Kinsale in 1603.

Although Scottish military employment overseas in the mediaeval and early modern period was driven by economic impetus, this need not rule out other motive forces. Strategic, political and cultural connections did help to channel Scottish soldiers into the service of foreign powers. Scottish highlanders fighting by the thousand in Ireland in the late sixteenth century no doubt felt some common cause with the Gaelic Irish who paid them, and probably a distinct enmity to the authority of the Scottish kings they defied in going there. At the times when Scotland and France shared in England a common enemy, the migration of the

Scottish kingdom's military surplus to the assistance of the French may be represented as a piece of state-craft, an inexpensive instrument of Scottish foreign policy. The same might be taken from the contentment with which post-Reformation Scottish governments let thousands of Scottish soldiers depart their country to assist Protestant causes such as the Dutch Revolt against Spain in the 1570s, and join the anti-Habsburg armies of the Thirty Years' War in the early seventeenth century. From the perspective of Scottish government, agreement to the departure of fighting men represented a happy meeting of Scottish strategic interests with a very welcome form of poor relief at home, since it was from among the ranks of the unemployed and often in the gaols that many of the men were to be found. The venturing of Scottish soldiers into foreign realms is best understood as but one among many forms of economic migration. The vagaries of the times, the conflicts within their own society, had rendered these men professional soldiers. At the level of the common fighting man, it was perhaps the bottom end of an opportunity-seeking exodus of skilled labour that over the centuries took Scottish traders and seamen, settlers, churchmen and scholars to the Low Countries, to Sweden and the Baltic, to Russia and Poland, and to Ireland.

The essentials of this type of migration lay not in the regulation of home or overseas governments but in the private means by which it was organised, in the entrepreneurial apparatus of recruitment. Troops raised in Scotland for overseas service were recruited by, or on behalf of, the Scottish officers who were going to lead them in the field. The officers were typically younger sons of landed families left looking for a living by consequence of the laws of primogeniture. In many cases these were men with long-standing personal or family connections to service on the European continent. They received their commissions directly, not at the behest of the Scottish Privy Council in Edinburgh, but from the powers in whose service they set about enlisting men. The Scots Brigade in Holland was one of the major employers of Scottish soldiers and endured in Dutch service until the late eighteenth century. Its administrative records provide numerous examples of succeeding generations of Scottish professional officers, descending from a nucleus of the sons of prominent Protestant lowland families who saw opportunity in the original appeal for military assistance made by the Dutch in the 1570s.[1] It was from the lands of Fife and the Lothians, the family home-lands of these officers, that many of the men of the brigade were drawn. Similarly, the great seventeenth-century Scottish enlistments into the armies of the Swedish empire were preceded by an earlier generation of Scottish officers who brought small companies of Scottish troops to the Swedish service in the 1570s. The loyal and successful service of some such officers had since brought them high-ranking status in the army of their adopted country, as landowners and noblemen. They could, in turn, use their powers of patronage and influence at the Swedish Court to bring relatives and clients from Scotland into low-ranking commissions in their own or other Swedish regiments.

The allegiances and interests of these Scottish officers in many respects determined the direction and form of the Scottish military migrations. This meant that before and during the Thirty Years' War the strong tendency for Scottish military service overseas was towards the Protestant powers of northern Europe. Nevertheless, gentlemen officers of different religious and political persuasions recruited Scotsmen for the service of the Catholic army of France and even into the service of the Catholic Habsburg power of imperial Spain, albeit in far smaller numbers. The presence of Scots in the Spanish service of the sixteenth and seventeenth centuries is a relatively under-researched area. Even after the Scottish Reformation, it is known that Scottish officers such as Colonel Aristotle Patton and Colonel William Semple, founder of the Roman Catholic Scots College at Madrid, defected from the Dutch service, supposedly taking Scottish regiments with them into the imperial Spanish army in the 1580s. Others were recruited directly. Scots were also noticeable, if less than prevalent, in Spanish service during the Thirty Years' War. General Robert Monro, a Protestant Scottish officer in the Swedish service, noted their presence amongst the enemy, but expressed satisfaction at their scarcity: 'Likewise we did see here, how few of our Nation are induced to serve those Catholique Potentates: and for my part, I finde the reson good: for if we have any enemies in Europe, it must be those ....'[2]

One power not prominent in the list of foreign employers drawing in Scottish military manpower at this period is England. This should not be taken to indicate that the service of Scotland's then traditional military enemy was beyond the stomach of Scottish professional soldiers; in the fifteenth and early sixteenth centuries some did indeed take employment in the English garrisons and armies in France manned by hired professionals. But beyond the expansionist efforts of Henry VIII, English desire and capacity to maintain large-scale standing military forces diminished; there were few long-term opportunities for Scots there. England itself was a substantial exporter of men to the armies of those same continental powers that drew in the Scots. When England's own sixteenth-century military adventures demanded trained men, experienced English soldiers were recalled from the continent in much the same way as the Scottish Covenanter government called home its Swedish military exiles in the 1630s.

This position changed in the middle of the seventeenth century when England's navies and armies began to expand under the Commonwealth and the later Stewarts. The permanent military forces of the Crown, the combined Crown of Scotland and England, added a new and easier-reached source of employment for the Scottish full-time soldier.

The Scottish standing army created in the 1660s was at first a modest affair, largely dedicated to protecting the Crown and state against armed insurgency at home. This was a volatile and divisive period in Scottish politics, and commissions in the army were the preserve of trusted supporters of the royal regime. The army began to expand and modernise under the reign of James VII, and some Scottish professional officers were lured home to serve, but it was after 1688, when the regime of James VII was overthrown, that new opportunities in the home service really opened up for Scottish military professionals. Once again, it was a Dutch employer who created a sudden upsurge in demand for Scottish soldiers. By this time however, said Dutchman, the head of the House of Orange, was also King of Great Britain and Ireland. William of Orange invaded England and abruptly ended James's rule with an army that included much of the Scots Brigade of the Dutch service, many of whose officers, by virtue of religion and politics, had been exiles of conscience. Under William, the armies of the Scottish, English and Irish military establishments were reorganised and enlarged for major European warfare – to fight the French in Flanders. The financial, strategic and manpower resources of the three kingdoms were to be put towards the Protestant cause in Europe; in a struggle between imperial powers, and in the force he created, lie the structural beginnings of what we recognise as the modern British army. William's new Scottish kingdom offered little in the way of treasure to support his European ambitions, but he could look to it as a supplier of military manpower to help maintain his continental campaigns. Thereafter, although overseas sources of military employment remained an alternative, the British service was firmly established as the main marketplace for Scottish military labour.

This applied as much to the scions of Scottish aristocratic families, the younger sons of lairds and lesser gentry, all searching out positions as officers, as it did to the class of land-less labourers seeking similarly stable, if less lucrative, sources of income. Scottish families were well versed in the pursuit of placement and profit from military careers in the service of different European powers. They were quick to establish similar networks of kinship, patronage and recruitment in the professional forces now being raised and maintained by their own king. Just as in the armies of Holland or Sweden, the prevalence and influence of Scots in the British service was cumulative. Those officers who made

Sir James Turner, a Scottish professional soldier who wrote in 1683 that a soldier need not worry in whose cause he served, so long as he served it well.

good positions for themselves could bring more of their own into the fold. The permeation of Scots through the officer class of the eighteenth-century British army was little short of saturation, and Scottish military employment was firmly tied to the fortunes of expanding British power.

The British service was not however palatable, or available, to all. To those who rejected William and his followers as usurpers, it was the motive to a new wave of military migration overseas – the Jacobite diaspora. The removal of James VII of Scotland from the throne in 1688, and his replacement with William and Mary, re-opened a fault line in Scottish society that, in the form of political intrigue and conflict on Scottish soil, was to dog the British state for sixty years. The Jacobite rebellions worked into the divide between highland and lowland society that had carried a military edge for centuries, and in raising highland armies for the cause the Jacobite leadership inherited practice established in the seventeenth century, most famously and successfully by the Marquess of Montrose, whose highland Scots and Irishmen pressed hard against the Covenanter Scottish government and its allies in the highlands. Montrose had relied heavily on the practitioners of Gaelic warfare to further his ends – his principal ally, Alistair MacColla, was a soldier whose skill and experience were grounded in the Gaelic world – but his own military training was done on the European continent where, at Angers in France, the young Montrose had studied the methods of Gustavus Adolphus. Another leading Scottish Royalist of the 1640s, the 1st Duke of Hamilton, had seen service as commander of a Swedish garrison – the importation of professional military skills was not solely the preserve of the Covenanters. The same pattern continued in the Jacobite conflicts of the late seventeenth and early eighteenth centuries where, as political fortunes changed, the officers of first one side then another went into exile and into military employment overseas.

With the Stewarts in exile after 1688, many of their adherents were barred by religious proscription as well as by inclination from the military service of the new regime, and so took their abilities elsewhere. Some made outstanding careers out of their predicament. James Keith, younger brother of the Jacobite leader the Earl Marischal, was one Scottish nobleman who found little joy in his efforts to restore the Stewarts by force of arms. He had greater return for his service to the powers of Spain, Russia and Prussia, becoming a Field Marshal in the Prussian army of Frederick the Great and governor of Berlin before falling in Frederick's service at the battle of Hochkirk in 1778. At a less elevated level, highland Catholic Scots, who had little hope of progressing in the British service, went instead to the French or even to the Dutch. The Scots Brigade in Holland, not long since a recipient of the opponents of the Stewart regime, actually became a refuge for Jacobite sympathisers and an employer of former Jacobite officers after Culloden. A more likely destination was one of the Irish regiments of the French army, their numbers boosted by successive failed Jacobite uprisings and intrigues which each added refugees from suspicion and retribution. With France openly at war with Great Britain, one French regiment, the Royal Ecossais, was recruited by Jacobite agents in the Scottish highlands and spirited across to France in the months before the 1745 Jacobite rebellion, a campaign in which, due to the intervention of the Royal Navy, it ultimately was to play only a small part. After their cause had died, some Scottish Jacobite émigrés were able to return home and enter the British service, often with the help of kin already holding military positions. Others lingered in foreign armies and became assimilated to their host countries. From this root sprung one of Napoleon's great marshals, the Duke of Taranto, Marchal Jacques-Etienne-Joseph-Alexandre MacDonald, whose father had joined one of the new Scottish regiments in France raised from the remnants of the Jacobite army defeated in 1746.

Covert French recruiting continued in the highlands for some years after the Jacobite defeat, but was to dwindle when the British army of the Hanoverian victors became a competitor for highland military labour. It is hopefully reasonable to assume that for the vast majority of Scots the sporadic wars between proponents of the different royal successions were an unwelcome impediment to the normal business of life and to the pursuit of wealth, the progress of which required the matter to be settled one way or another. In the late seventeenth century the general direction of Scottish economic activity had begun to swing away from traditional routes to the north and east and face boldly towards the New World in the west. The military trade followed a similar course. Merchant interest and permanent settlement in the American colonies had a strongly Scottish flavour from the first, but the military requirements of these vast colonial possessions increased the need for British troops in situ, and consequently the scope for Scottish enlistment. The most obvious manifestation of this demand was the creation of the early highland regiments of the British army and with it a remarkable level of military recruitment from the populations of highland estates. The precedent of recruiting specifically in the Scottish highlands for British military service overseas was established in the War of the Austrian Succession in Flanders in the 1740s, but it was the military confrontation between Britain and France in North America and India in the following decades that brought the practice into its own. As has already been considered, the recruitment of highland soldiers by an army that had only recently occupied and laid waste to parts of the highlands appears a logical step in a continuing policy of pacification. For the young men of the highland tenantry the meeting of interests between the state and their landlords could make military service as much an obligation as an opportunity. Yet in this

VICTORY

OR

DEATH!!!

AT a time when the proud Corfican Tyrant, the felf created Emperor of France, is daily Threatning this Country with Invafion, and Boafts that if he can effect a Landing upon our Coafts, he will make us his Slaves, it is the duty of every Good Man who wifhes to be Free Himfelf, and to preferve all that is Dear to Him, as a Man and a Chriftian, to facrifice his own Perfonal Good to the Public Welfare, (if he can do fo without injury to his Family,) and to come forward in active oppofition to the views of the Gallic Ufurper.— THE BRAVE VOLUNTEERS OF SCOTLAND, are in all refpects adequate to Meeting the Enemy, however numerous they may be, fhould they prove fo rafh as to venture upon our Shores : but a difpofeable Force is necef-fary, to prepare on all fides for the expected Foe.

His Majefty, Our Gracious King, has from a wifh to take every precaution for the Public defence, directed feveral new Regiments to be raifed : Among others, a Second Battalion to the Gallant 78th Regt. which has fo eminently diftinguifhed itfelf during the prefent War.—The men of the Corps are our Countrymen; and as much benefit is hoped to be derived, in cafe of need, from the Active Bravery of its Second Battalion at home, as has been experienced from the Noble Exertions of the 1ft Battalion abroad.

Step forward then, ye Young Heroes, without incumbrance, and prove that like your

Immortal Anceftors of Old,

You will defend a Country Dearer to you than Life to the Laft Drop of Your Blood.

You will be received with joy as a member of the 78th Regiment, by applying to   at the Sign of the   where the moft liberal encouragement will be given you.

The Government Bounty is Sixteen Guineas.

GOD SAVE THE KING.

Recruiting poster of the 2nd Battalion, 78th (Highland) Regiment, 1804, reflecting the end of highland recruitment through traditional 'clan levy' methods.

there was little difference from the pressure faced by those at the bottom of the highland social order when the ties of kinship and servitude were employed to create clan regiments for the Jacobite army a decade earlier. Those who made up the rank and file of highland regiments new and old did not have the luxury of political motivation in choosing who they fought for and against. As one factor in a range of economic influences acting to change the highlands, the British service gave employment, and the prospect of land (at home or abroad), to individuals whose recruitment required incentives as well as pressures. The creation of the highland regiments of the eighteenth and early nineteenth centuries has been portrayed on the one hand as a new outlet for the supposed warlike tendencies of the Gael or, on the other, as an early artifice in the clearing of the highland tenantry from the land by the forces of state and landlord. The reality was rather more complex, and for highland tenant families offering the military service of their sons seems to have been one way in which they could strengthen their hold on land. For the individual highlanders who joined up, the situation was more simple. If military service was the best way of bringing in ready money or improving the lot of their families, then those who could take it would take it. Where bargains made between recruiter and recruit connecting military service with issue of land were not kept, a particular bitterness and sense of betrayal was left.

The extent to which military recruitment speeded or impeded economic change and population movement in the highlands is arguable but, in the context of this present survey, it is useful to consider the correlation between the entry of these highland Scots into British military service in the eighteenth century and the overseas military service of Scots, highland and lowland, in previous centuries. Far from being isolated in some archaic world of clan warfare, highland fighting men in the sixteenth and seventeenth centuries had responded to continental demand for military labour in much the same pattern as had their lowland counterparts. There was a strong element of continuity in highland recruitment. Highland regiments were not the invention of the eighteenth-century British state designed to strip the highlands of its threatening (Jacobite) military potential, though for the interests of state this was a reassuring side effect. The role of the officer as recruiter, as intermediary between soldier and state, continued to be the moving force. In the eighteenth-century context, the action of highland land-owners (in their guise as clan chiefs) as recruiters of regiments from among their own tenantry, represents a conspicuous example of the gain that could be had from meeting state demands for military service. Officers' pay, including the half-pay that was on offer as a form of retainer for semi-retirement when a regiment was disbanded or reduced, helped to sustain the gentry status of a host of highland families. Certainly, these included families whose involvement in armed Jacobitism in 1745-46 had cost them their estates.

But for highland proprietors large and small, whether directly impli-cated in former Jacobite sympathy and military activity or not, family influence and career advancement through government patronage, as well as the shoring up of their local status, were the real prizes to be had in return for finding soldiers for Britain's army.[3] Thus in the British empire in North America in the eighteenth century we find not only former private soldiers of highland regiments settled in land holdings along the banks of the St Lawrence, but also men like John Campbell, Earl of Loudoun, Governor-in-Chief of Virginia and Commander-in-Chief of the British forces in America in the 1750s, whose status in the imperial machine rested as much on their endeavours as military recruiters and commanders as on the privileges of birth. To a class that earlier in the century had faced the undermining of its traditional status locally, and exclusion, on the grounds of suspect political loyalty, from membership of the British governing élite, these were rich prizes indeed.

For the rank and file, the prospect of owning land in North America was one incentive that drew Scots into the British army. Highland soldiers played a prominent part in the campaigns that wrested Canada from French control during the Seven Years' War of 1756-63 and the opportunity of remaining and settling in what had become British North America was given to the men of two highland regiments, the 77th (Montgomery's) and 78th (Fraser's), when they were disbanded at the war's end, together with men from the 42nd. With government land grants as reward for their successful military service, the pioneering settlements created by these veterans were at the vanguard of Scottish settlement in Canada. A similar prospect was held up in the following decade by recruiting parties in Scotland as they sought to fill new regiments being despatched to suppress resistance to British rule in the thirteen American colonies to the south. In 1776, a recruiting pamphlet for the 71st (Fraser's) Highland Regiment was explicit on the point:

> The advantages that will arise to those that enlist in this corps, are very great. They are to go to America, and by his Majesty's royal and most gracious proclamation, they will be entitled to a full discharge at the end of three years, that is in 1779, or of the present American rebellion. Now, considering that the British army will be from forty to fifty thousand men strong, there, in spring next, it cannot, in all human probability, fail to be entirely quelled, next summer. Then, gentlemen, will be your harvest, and the best one too you ever cropt. You will each one of you, by visiting this new world, become the founders of families. The land of the rebels will be divided amongst you, and every one of you will become lairds ....[4]

These tantalising prospects were never realised of course. The American War of Independence dragged on, the colonists prevailed, and the men who joined this highland regiment never had the chance to become 'lairds'. Most were instead taken prisoner in the British surrender at Yorktown, and were repatriated in 1783.

The British defeat in America nevertheless precipitated a second wave of Scottish settlement in Canada. The mass evacuation of British loyalist troops and civilian refugees north out of the United States included strongly Scottish units such as companies of the King's Royal Regiment of New York recruited among highland emigrants who had settled in the Mohawk Valley, and companies of the Royal Highland Emigrants formed from among the veteran military settlers in Canada as well as highlanders more recently arrived in New York and North Carolina. As they had done twenty years earlier, the evacuated and disbanded soldiers settled together on their government land grants in Canada.

Scottish settlement in Canada was to retain its military and community character, and in this it was supplemented directly from home. On return from service in Ireland in 1802, the Glengarry Fencible Regiment was disbanded in Glasgow. Recognising that there was little prospect of work for the discharged soldiers, the regiment's chaplain organised a scheme to settle the men in Canada. The subsequent arrival of more than half the Glengarry soldiers to new lives in what is now Ontario was an early example of the assisted migration schemes that were to remove

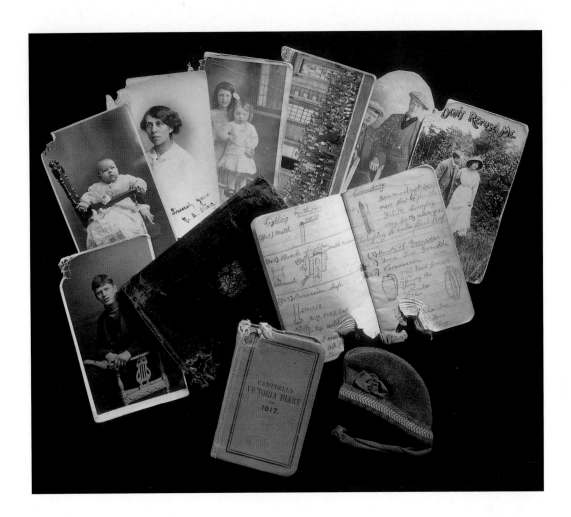

Plate 3.1 The personal effects carried on active service by Private Alexander Henderson, 16th Battalion Highland Light Infantry, include family photographs and a miniature glengarry bonnet carried for good luck. The damage to them was caused by the sniper's bullet that killed him on 15th April, 1917 at Fayet on the Western Front.

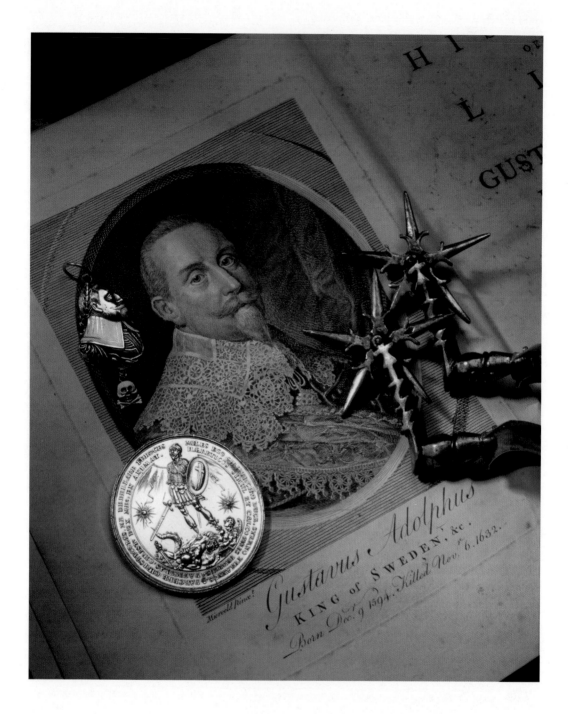

Plate 3.2 A medal and *memento mori* badge commemorate the death of King Gustavus Adolphus of Sweden at the battle of Lützen, 1632. Among thousands of Scots serving in his armies was his aide-de-camp at Lützen, Colonel Hugh Somerville, who kept these spurs taken from the King's body.

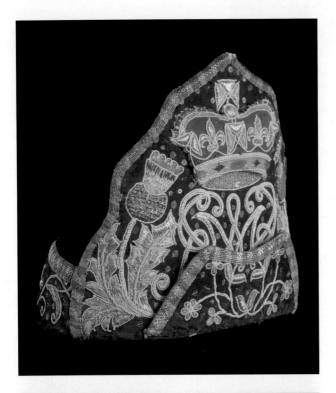

Plate 3.3 Embroidered thistles on either side of the royal cipher of William and Mary identify this officer's grenadier cap as belonging to a Scottish unit in the army of the 1690s. The continental wars waged against France by William of Orange opened up a huge new employment market for Scottish professional soldiers.

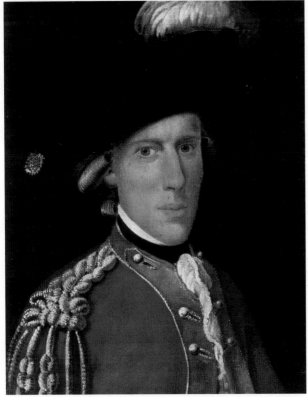

Plate 3.4 Lieutenant John Turnbull wears the uniform of Major-General Stuart's Regiment of the Scots Brigade in Holland. The portrait was painted in 1782, when war between Britain and the Netherlands meant Scots Brigade officers had to abjure their allegiance to the British Crown or leave the service.

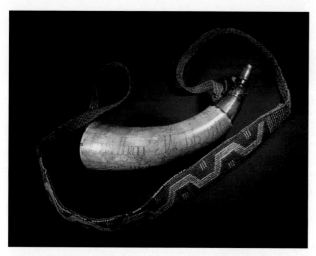

Plate 3.5 This powder horn was acquired by James Cameron of the 42nd (Royal Highland) Regiment during the war against the French in North America in the 1750s, probably from an American colonial soldier. The strap is believed to be of Iroquois or Huron manufacture, made from a woman's burden strap.

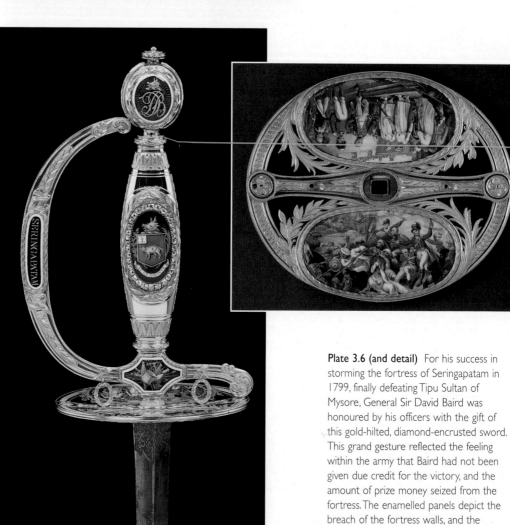

Plate 3.6 (and detail) For his success in storming the fortress of Seringapatam in 1799, finally defeating Tipu Sultan of Mysore, General Sir David Baird was honoured by his officers with the gift of this gold-hilted, diamond-encrusted sword. This grand gesture reflected the feeling within the army that Baird had not been given due credit for the victory, and the amount of prize money seized from the fortress. The enamelled panels depict the breach of the fortress walls, and the surrender of Tipu's sons to Baird.

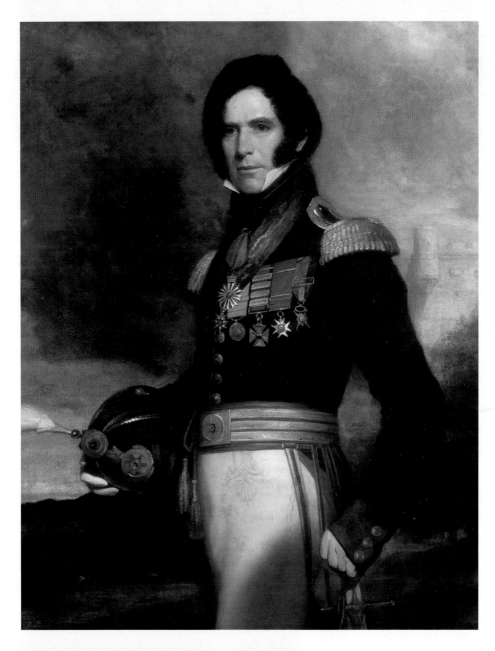

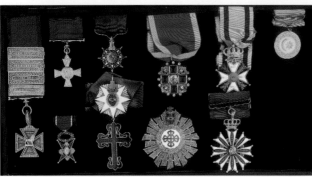

Plate 3.7a and b Former highland officer Colonel Sir Alexander Anderson transferred to the British-led Portuguese army in 1811. Despite years of distinguished service, he missed out on promotion in the British army. On his death in Edinburgh in 1842, the decorations awarded by Britain and her allies were all his family had to show for his career. The empty space in the box originally held the insignia of the Order of the Bath, returned on his death.

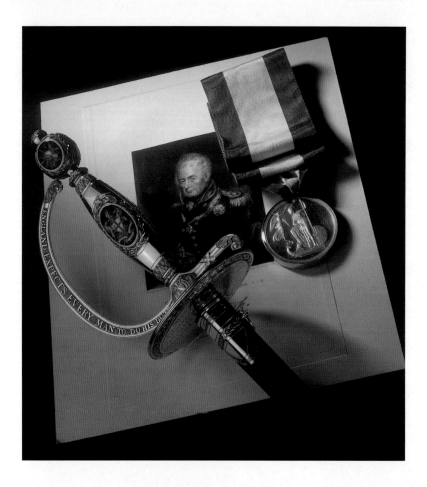

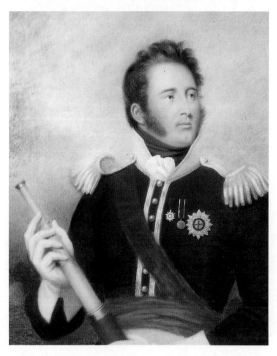

Plate 3.8 (above) At the battle of Trafalgar, 1805, the death of Lord Nelson left Admiral William Carnegie, Earl of Northesk, as second-in-command of the fleet. He was awarded the Gold Medal for Trafalgar and the City of London presented him with a 200 guinea sword. The design of the gold hilt incorporates the words of Nelson's famous signal to the fleet before the battle. As a senior officer in the British Royal Navy, Northesk would have had little difficulty with this appeal to English patriotism.

Plate 3.9 (left) Gregor MacGregor came from a highland military family. In 1811, after a brief career in the British and Portuguese armies, he sought his fortune in South America. Successful commands brought him a general's rank in the army of Venezuela fighting for independence from Spain. The failure of his later military and settlement schemes brought him notoriety as a fraud.

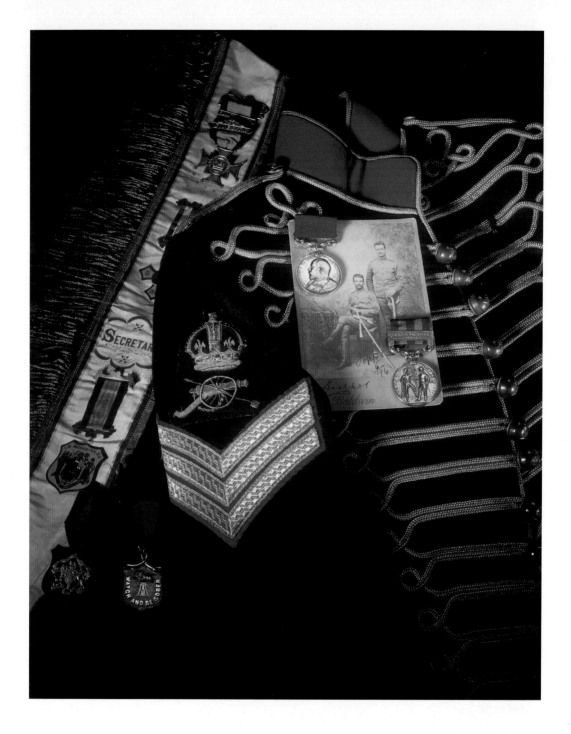

Plate 3.10 With a father established in an army administrative position, the Riddle brothers were born in India. Service in the Royal Horse Artillery gave them a secure and respectable career in India in the 1890s. Battery Sergeant-Major Fergus Riddle was prominent in the Army Temperance Association, freemasonry and the Independent Order of Rechabites, a society of total abstainers.

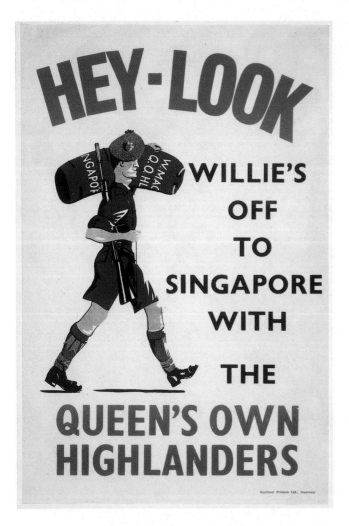

Plate 3.11 Recruiting for the Scottish regiments in the early 1960s did not reflect the army's drive for a modern technical image. The traditional appeal of adventure, foreign travel and local identity was employed by a regiment recently created by the amalgamation of the Seaforth and Cameron Highlanders.

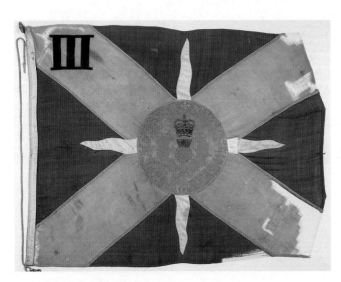

Plate 3.12 The flag flown by C Company of 1st Battalion Royal Highland Fusiliers on service in Northern Ireland during the 1970s was unchanged in design from those carried by the regiment's forebears in the late seventeenth century. The sense of continuity this reflected dated back beyond the 1707 Union between Scotland and England.

whole communities from the highlands as nineteenth-century emigration to Canada became a flood. The settlement of disbanded soldiers was but one small element in the removal of the marginalised and growing highland and urban populations from Scotland, but it did set a pattern for Scottish migration and created the basis of a lasting Scottish cultural presence in Canada. The military background of the early emigrants also continued to have application as a reuseable asset in British imperial defence. When war broke out again along the Canadian-American border in 1812, the burden of Canada's defence fell on locally raised fencible forces that included units raised from the military communities in 'Scottish' counties along the St Lawrence River. Amongst these were Glengarry Light Infantry, recruited from the settlements formed by the original Glengarry Fencibles.

Scottish interests in war in the American colonies were of course far from confined to the prospects of the highland gentry and their tenants. The highland regiments that fought there in the Seven Years' War against the French, and in the American War of Independence, also represented the commercial interests of the growing body of Scottish merchants at home or temporarily resident in colonial trading communities. New highland regiments contributed much to the expansion of the British army for service in the American War of Independence, but Scotland's two major cities, Edinburgh and Glasgow, also contributed regiments. For the merchants of Glasgow in particular, with its flourishing Atlantic tobacco trade, the stability and British control that were associated with their accumulation of wealth, and which equated with a rapid conclusion of the war, were considered things well worth fighting for, or at least worth encouraging others to fight for. In 1778, in order to raise the 83rd Regiment of Foot for the American War, the Provost and magistrates of Glasgow offered to each recruit the rights and privileges of a burgess in addition to the usual cash bounty. British military defeat in North America did not, in the event, close down the Glasgow tobacco trade as might have been feared, but the raising of the 83rd and the other Scottish regiments for America indicates that, in contributing military manpower to the British empire, there were rather more immediate Scottish interests at stake than that of national pride.

Those with perhaps the greatest stake in hopes of British victory in America were those long-standing American settler families whose status in colonial society rested on their position in the imperial establishment. These included men of Scottish descent like Samuel Auchmuty, whose grandfather had left Scotland to practice law in Boston and whose father was a prominent Anglican clergyman in New York. Like other young men of the loyalist colonial establishment, Auchmuty volunteered to fight with the British forces in America and obtained a commission and promotion in a British regiment. British defeat meant that America offered little future for families like Auchmuty's, but the British service did. Transferring to serve in India, Auchmuty had plenty of opportunity to demonstrate his abilities on active service. His long military career in British imperial campaigns around the world brought him a knighthood and a general's rank.

As a source of livelihood, status, and, in some cases, riches, India had become easier for Scots to get at, courtesy of Scotland's full incorporation into the new British nation state in 1707. Hitherto largely shut out by the English East India Company's monopoly, Scots in the eighteenth century were presented with new possibilities of commercial gain and placement in remunerative official positions. The continuing dominance of the Company in Indian trade and local administration meant that military service in the Company's own armies was one means whereby Scots could make a living and a career out of India. Among the first Scots there were surgeons in the employ of the Company's armies and navy and, as in North America, it was in the context of Great Britain's world-wide rivalry and military conflict with France in the mid- to late eighteenth century that the Scottish military presence in India grew in number and consequence. Not only did the Company's own Indian-manned armies expand, demanding professional officers from home to command them, but new British army regiments, many raised from the Scottish highlands, spent years in India defending and expanding Company interests. Scottish names such as Munro, Baird, Ochterlony and Campbell are conspicuous among the names synonymous with military success in the Company's wars against independent Indian states, French troops and French influence.

Scots were far from alone among the ranks of impecunious families of gentle birth who reacted to the prospect of independent livings in India. But, whereas the wealth of India was already filling the coffers of the English merchant interests that had the markets tied up and had their own established chains of patronage, it was for the Scots to use connections and education to muscle their way in by the best means available, a military career being one of these. The Scottish tradition of professional military service overseas eased Scots towards seeking such positions just as more immediate influences rendered it practicable. One such influence was Henry Dundas, the all-powerful Solicitor-General for Scotland and Senior Commissioner of the government board that oversaw the East India Company. In the closing decades of the eighteenth century, the personal patronage of Dundas commonly worked the securing of Indian administrative and military posts for young Scottish gentlemen.

At the top end of the market the military high road to great fortune was to become more difficult for Scots to negotiate. The long wars against Revolutionary and Napoleonic France continued to bring Scots to prominence in navy and army commands but, in the military establishment shaped under the hand of the Duke of Wellington, factors were combining to make access to military commissions a more complex matter for the sons of Scottish families. In his early career in India, Wellington (then Sir Arthur Wellesley) had already clashed with the Scottish cohort in senior military and administrative positions, notably in his uncomfortable relationship with General Sir David Baird, the Scottish hero of the 1799 storming of Seringapatam. Twenty years later, Wellington's military and political dominance was promoting a preference for Tory gentry backgrounds in young army officers while, on the urging of those of a like mind, the administration of British imperial concerns was becoming ever more a matter for the growing formal apparatus of government and less the preserve of commercial interests with the ad hoc backing of military power. Meanwhile, the tendency among Scottish élites towards English domicile and education and inter-marriage with English families gradually altered the profile of the officer class and placed the paths of military advancement at rather a remove from Scotland. As candidates for commissions and preferment began to coalesce around the public schools, formal instruction in military skills, and not just patronage and practice, was gaining credence as an appropriate and desirable preparation for a military career. In the early nineteenth century the principal military and naval colleges for English gentlemen were founded and revamped, extending their syllabi into general professional education beyond the specifics of navigation, engineering and gunnery with which such institutions had hitherto been largely concerned. Away from the great colleges, smaller schools also operated and one of these, the Scottish Naval and Military Academy, was founded in Edinburgh in 1825, enjoying the nominal patronage of King George IV and the Duke of Wellington. The Academy was principally concerned with preparing boys for cadetships in the East India Company's services and among the subjects taught were not only such soldierly disciplines as fortification, fencing and military drawing, but also the essential language skill 'Hindoostani'. Firmly geared to the imperial administrative system, and outside the charmed circle of the major public schools, the aspirations of the Academy's students were likely more modest and officially prescribed than the Indian riches and fame that their forebears might have dreamed of.

For potential entrants to the rank and file, service in India in the European (*ie* all white) Regiments of the East India Company still offered opportunities for vast advances in standards of living and prospects to those willing to leave their homes and families in Scotland

Academy pupil Simon Fraser was awarded this prize medal for Military Exercises in 1826 before going on to a successful career in the Royal Marines.

on something approaching a permanent basis and run the risk of having to adapt to a dangerous climate. The material rewards of this branch of service were greater than those on offer in the Crown forces. Private soldiers in the India service enjoyed better pay and pension provisions, and they and their families could find themselves living in their own houses in India, and with their own servants. This was an extraordinary leap in social position, equivalent to that achieved by senior Scottish officers whose success in India pushed them into the fold of the British establishment. Service in India could also provide a route for non-commissioned officers into secure and remunerative employment in the lower ranks of the military bureaucracy of British India, particularly for those men with a better standard of education. Edinburgh was one of the main centres of recruitment for the India regiments and attracted numbers among the numerate and literate, rather than the class of unskilled labourers more likely to join the Scottish regiments of the British army.

In one area of military service a Scottish education was pre-eminent. The eighteenth-century development of surgery and medicine in navy and army and East India Company service owed much to men with Scottish degrees. Their preponderance has been attributed to the broad-based nature of medical training in Scottish universities which combined medicine with surgery (the latter then being something of a poor relation elsewhere), giving Scottish graduates an interest and practical experience that applied well to the medical needs of expanding military power whose global interests made disease a more deadly threat than any enemy action.[5] Despite the indignity and expense of having to sit a London examination in order to obtain posts, Scottish graduates were conspicuous in the developing medical services, both in number and among its pioneering and innovative figures. Lind and McGrigor, the widely acknowledged 'fathers' of medicine in the Royal Navy and the army respectively, both took their degrees at Edinburgh. To these names might be added those whose observation and published treatises helped to alleviate suffering and improve the manpower efficiency of the British armed services, doctors like Sir John Pringle, Physician-General to Cumberland's army in Scotland and author of *Observations on the Diseases of the Army*, and Sir Gilbert Blane, who penned his influential *Observations on the Diseases Incident to Seamen* in the course of a career as a senior Royal Navy physician.[6]

The training of military surgeons was enhanced in 1806 by the creation of a Regius Chair of Military Surgery at Edinburgh University, for which the only equivalent was in Dublin, and which endured until 1855.[7] It is worth noting that, as with general military service, Scottish activity in the fields of naval and army medicine was not directed exclusively towards the British and East India Company services, and indeed pre-dated the existence of both. When Peter Lowe founded the Glasgow

Faculty of Physicians and Surgeons in 1599, he had seen two years of service as surgeon-major to a Spanish regiment and six years as an honorary surgeon in the military service of the king of France. But not all found the work to their liking. One famous Scots-trained naval surgeon found a rather different vocation. Celebrated novelist Tobias Smollett was a surgeon-apprentice in Glasgow and served aboard HMS *Chichester* in the West Indies before embarking on his literary career.

For those who could not offer such private training and specialist skills, the military career remained a risky one. Scottish regiments were among those that expanded and contracted as the size of the British service grew and shrank according to need. The popular fame of the Scottish soldier

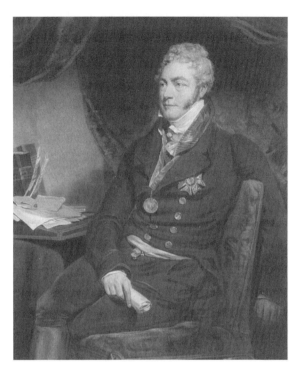

Sir James McGrigor, successful director-general of the army medical services for thirty-eight years.

was all very well, but it would not keep men in jobs if their maintenance on the public purse was not a military necessity. The final defeat of Napoleon in 1815 brought as much misery as reward to Scottish fighting men and their families since for many the subsequent reduction in the army meant that their livelihood was cut off. There were unemployed soldiers as well as unemployed weavers among the desperate and disenfranchised who agitated for political change in the following decades. Others, in common with their counterparts from elsewhere in the United Kingdom, took the time-honoured option of selling their military skills to overseas powers, for which a new market had opened up. During the war against the French in the Iberian peninsula, many British commissioned and non-commissioned officers had been transferred to bolster the armed strength of Britain's ally Portugal. After the expulsion of the French from Spain, numbers stayed on in the service of Viscount Beresford, the politically powerful (Anglo-Irish) Marshal of the Portuguese army. They were joined in the Portuguese ranks by new arrivals from home, their countrymen in search of work.

The convulsions of the Portuguese and Spanish monarchies, both in their own kingdoms and in their crumbling empires in Central and South America, were sufficient to keep experienced soldiers and sailors in employment, and to attract new recruits from Great Britain on and off for the next twenty-five years. Some of those who took part in these conflicts doubtless did so through motivations of principle as well as of pocket: the political character of fledgling nations struggling against conservative regimes and reactionary armies attracted idealists and soldiers of a liberal political persuasion to their cause. In this they foreshadowed the Scots whose support for liberal nationalism led them to join a Scottish volunteer company in the service of Garibaldi's Italian patriot armies in the 1860s, and indeed those whose socialist and communist convictions and opposition to fascism led them to participate in the Spanish Civil War in the 1930s. The idealists were not usually in the majority however. In 1835, a British Legion was recruited to fight in a civil war in Spain against the proponents of the ultra-conservative Don Carlos, and three regiments of the Legion were recruited in Scotland. Stirred by suggestions that this army was made up of the criminal and the dissolute, the celebrity Scottish radical, former Scottish soldier, and Spanish volunteer, Alexander Somerville, spoke up for the Legion's moral character, pointing to distressed conditions among English and Irish agricultural labourers that led men to enlist, and saying of the Scots:

> A great number of those composing the Scotch regiments were also of an unfortunate class; that is, the handloom weavers of the west of Scotland; so it was the force of circumstances, other than their moral character, that led many of them to go to Spain.[8]

That said, it is clear that at the outset the wars of Latin America in particular attracted mavericks and fortune seekers with the dream of riches that by then were available only on the very fringes of the British empire. Perhaps the most notorious of these was the self-styled Sir Gregor MacGregor, a former Royal Navy midshipman and British infantry officer who rose high in the revolutionary army of Venezuela, enjoying the patronage of Simón Bolívar himself. MacGregor attained something approaching hero status in his adopted country, but was rather less fondly regarded at home. His scheme to set up his very own colony on the coast of present-day Honduras attracted shiploads of Scottish colonists and huge loans from the City of London. To the distress of settlers and creditors, all that was built in the sand of the Caribbean coastline was MacGregor's dream of kingship. Financial and physical distress could also be the lot of those unemployed officers and soldiers who fell dupes to unscrupulous individuals posing as accredited recruiters to the services of the South American republics. One former Scottish Royal Artilleryman rued the day he set foot in South America, and recorded doleful recollections of the sick and destitute of the British Legion who arrived in Venezuela without means or valid commissions, 'found every other day lying like dogs along the beach, under any kind of shelter, boats or benches, where they had retired to die, unheeded and unknown'.[9]

The odour of financial scandal for a time attached itself to the most distinguished of Scottish participants in these foreign wars of independence. The naval and political career of Admiral Sir Thomas Cochrane, Lord Dundonald, was in many respects extraordinary. This British naval hero of the French wars was first lionised, then disgraced in a Stock Exchange fraud that was investigated in a snake-pit atmosphere of political and personal rivalry. And so he took his service with stunning personal success to the navies of Chile, Peru, Brazil and, finally, with less satisfying result, Greece, until he was rehabilitated to British public life, to popular acclaim, under a change of British government. In the previous century, a man of Dundonald's position and undoubted ability might not have found the British service so restrictive and irksome. Dundonald's career also stands as a reminder that, though most gravitated towards the army, Scots also made their way in the Royal Navy, the prestigious senior service of the British empire. To the prospect of a respectable occupation was added the alluring prospect of prize money from the capture of enemy ships in wartime, a more likely and potentially lucrative source of wealth than any equivalent in army service. While army commissions could be bought in hard cash, officer entry into the navy depended almost entirely on personal patronage and advancement on merit. Dundonald had both – outstanding ability as a naval tactician, and an uncle who was already a successful Royal Navy officer and who could nurture his nephew's career. The emergence into senior naval positions of the scions of Scottish landed families such as the Cochranes and the Carnegies was hard-earned, but also reflected Scottish inclusion in the mesh of a greater British aristocratic influence and connection, through alliances of marriage and political interest.

For seafaring Scots of more humble status, service in the Royal Navy was rather less of an attraction. Fishing and the merchant trade were usually enough to keep them in a living, and entry into the Royal Navy was more likely to occur in an involuntary manner. Manpower levies for the Royal Navy began to fall on Scottish sea-coast burghs as early as 1626, and the post-Union Royal Navy drew on seamen conscripted and impressed from Scottish ports in wartime, a practice that reached its height during the wars against Revolutionary and Napoleonic France. Finding themselves in the fighting fleets from the Mediterranean to the West Indies, and in the great sea battles such as Camperdown and Trafalgar, the seamen of the western and northern isles, and of the herring and trading ports of mainland Scotland, could doubtless have wished themselves more gainfully employed at home. Naval warfare could, however, present a greatly more enticing prospect for Scottish sea captains if they could obtain government 'letters of marque' – commission to operate as a privateer, preying on the shipping of Britain's enemies. Among the successful British exponents of this practice were

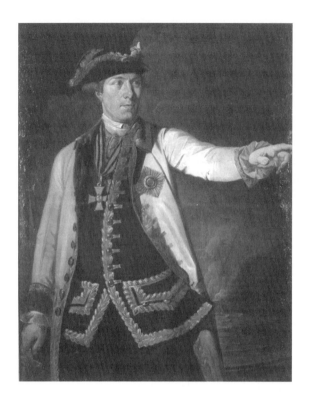

Sir Samuel Greig, Grand Admiral of Russia, by Ivan Petrovich Argunoff, 1773.

such Scots as Captain John MacIver and Captain William Gilmour who ran privateers out of Liverpool, and a clutch of privateer captains operating out of Greenock. As with their land-bound countrymen, Scottish naval professionals could also be found plying their trade much further afield than the British service. Dundonald is but one well-known example of the Scottish seafarer set by circumstance to seek out employment in the service of foreign powers. Many more were doing so in the previous two centuries. Among the mass military migrations from Scotland to the Baltic in the early seventeenth century were a relatively small number of sea captains and sea-men. A handful of the former reached Admiral's rank in the Swedish navy. A century later, the Russian navy built by Peter the Great required naval know-how from overseas and included Scots with marine experience, some of them exiled Jacobites dismissed from the Royal Navy after 1715. Scots also contributed to the later flourishing of Russian sea power under Catherine II. The Russian service offered a rapid pace of career advancement which prospects in the Royal Navy often could not match and many Scots answered the Russian recruiting drive that was directed towards the British service, none with greater success than Samuel Greig of Inverkeithing. With the relatively humble rank of master's mate, Greig quit the Royal Navy in 1763. His role in the reform of the Russian Baltic fleet and victories against the Turks in the Mediterranean brought him the highest honours and rank as Admiral of all the Russias. In a familiar pattern, the positions of favour he and other of his countrymen attained allowed them to recruit more Scots into Catherine's navy, through family and Royal Navy connections.

Without the demonstrably Scottish manifestations in appearance and organisation evinced by the army, Scottish naval service is easy to overlook. Indeed, it appears that in its exaggerated, anachronistic belief in the existence of a resource of 'clan warriors' to be found in the highlands, those in British naval and military establishment failed to recognise potential sources of skilled naval manpower created by the shift of highland populations to a coastal, fishing-based existence despite naval manpower being much needed in the wars against France.[10] Naval recruiting parties were nevertheless occasionally in evidence in those coastal areas of the highlands conveniently close to the frequent passage of Royal Navy vessels and major ports; the press gangs were liable to appear in Argyll and the northern isles. British naval service also emerged in a new form in the mid-nineteenth century, giving a useful and manageable economic opportunity that highland communities could take up with less drastic effect. The Royal Naval Reserve created in 1859 paid out enlistment bounties and wages for attendance at training days. Together with the alternative of part-time local service in the revamped army militia, this was a welcome source of income to crofting and maritime economies already heavily reliant on seasonal work.

In the meantime, emigration and migration to the industrial towns of the lowlands had left relatively little by way of potential full-time military manpower in the Scottish highlands for the regular army or navy. Highlanders increasingly joined their fellow Scots in concentrations of population in the expanding central towns, and recruiting there was subject to the same influences of short-term economic conditions and insecurities among transient, young labour as it was in urban areas across Britain. Deriving wealth from imperial labour and markets, the improving performance of other sectors of the Scottish economy slowly came to outshine the inducements of a military life, a recourse that always had some element of last resort about it, to all but those on the fragile periphery of fast-expanding urban society. Scottish regimental historians have occasionally been sensitive on the question of how far the early-Victorian ranks were filled instead by other (Irish and English) recruits, this in itself provoked by efforts to debunk the validity of the Scottish military reputation. To this subject an anonymous published pamphlet, based on official statistics, was specifically addressed in 1862, employing some determined number crunching

> ... to clear up a prevailing error to the disparagement of Scotsmen of the present century, as being devoid of martial spirit. But the warlike feelings that used to animate Scotsmen of old are not yet extinct: and in these pages it will be proved, by official figures, that even now the martial spirit exists in Scotland to a greater degree than either in England or Ireland.[11]

Recognising the fact that Scottish manning levels did recover some-what later in the century, there is no refuting that the heyday of Scottish regular enlistment had nevertheless passed by the middle of the century. For those who continued to sign up for regular military employment, the imperial character of the British service, and intermittent manpower shortages, often meant long periods of years serving overseas in imperial garrisons punctuated by active service in sporadic campaigns on the frontiers of empire. Conditions of service ameliorated somewhat as the nineteenth century progressed, with progress in official provision of the basics of medical care, education, pay and pensions on the one hand, and advancing notions of working-class respectability, literacy, self-help and temperance on the other. In long postings to India, where climate, tedium and the recourse to drink could be a problem, the alternatives of sport, religion and entertainment were organised, creating a community to which the rank and file could belong in the isolation of foreign garrisons. Service in the late-Victorian army and navy was of a rather less desperate character than the worst experiences that fell to such as those at the outset of the century sent to the doom-laden, diseased garrisons of the West Indies, and those men who laboured under the arbitrariness and occasional brutality of eighteenth- and early nineteenth-century military discipline. Victorian reforms in army organisation also placed the visible structures of permanent recruiting depots in localities throughout Scotland, helping to make the step into military life appear a more familiar, structured and respectable choice and less an act of waywardness or desperation.

From the 1860s, the patriotic, altruistic and more convivial aspects of the military life were also available to those who became involved in the revival of the volunteer movement. Scotland had produced a plethora of part-time volunteer regiments during the wars against Napoleonic France, but the Victorian volunteer movement developed from the patriotic local shooting clubs of the early 1860s into a constituted, permanent reserve for the army. It was as a part-time member of

The 2nd Battalion Highland Light Infantry pose as tourists while stationed at Cairo in 1882-83.

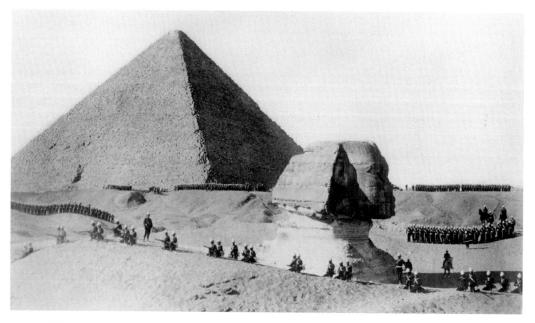

an extensively reformed, centralised military organisation that many a Scot was to encounter military service in the ensuing period. Although the emphasis of the reserve role was on home defence, the South African War of 1899-1902 saw volunteers from such units depart overseas on active service. Their involvement was a focus of local pride and national identification with the British empire in the crisis of war. Serious business this was, but a far cry from the departure beyond the pale, the great, often permanent undertaking of different lives in distant, little-known lands that the ancestors of such volunteers might have faced in donning British or Company uniform a century or so before. The development of the Victorian volunteer movement harnessed the contribution of the amateur, part-time soldier to the ongoing military planning of the state, and was to characterise the raising of Scottish military manpower in the twentieth century to meet the new threat to the British empire – that of an industrialised, militarised European power.

Mass volunteering and conscription in the two world wars against Germany meant that for the majority of Scots who experienced military service in the twentieth century the call was not one of economic opportunity, but of moral or legal obligation. It is clear nonetheless that in fighting for the defence of Britain and the empire against Germany and her allies, many Britons carried expectations of a better future that could include quite specific economic aspirations as features in a general desire for political and social change. In Scotland, and in the Scottish highlands in particular, land settlement was the outstanding aspiration for many of those who served as volunteers or conscripts in the First World War. The connection that was made between war service and a government-backed promise of access to land and security of tenure rested on assumptions drawn from memories of wartime recruiting practices in the highlands of a century and more before (another indication that military service could be associated with securing land, rather than being removed from it). In First World War highland recruitment, the promise of land was a spoken contract rather than a written one, and was inferred in the recruitment campaign rather more than it was declared. Yet its potency is suggested by the immediate post-war upsurge in 'land grabbing' protests in the highlands and islands, often involving returned servicemen, when the expectations raised failed to be realised.[12] In their illegal occupation of estate land, war veterans enjoyed popular public sympathy and support based on respect for their war service and a belief in the government's obligation to provide land in return, a support that helped make the land grab tactic temporarily successful.[13]

The social and economic dividend of war service was even less clear for the urban working classes. For some of the very poorest, war service actually proffered a higher standard of living and nutrition than had been their lot at home, and their return was often to more of the same

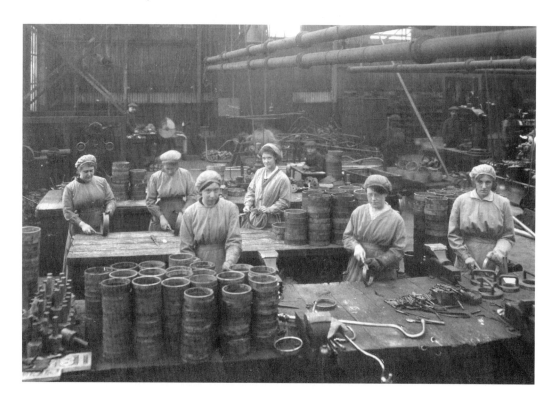

Female munition
workers finish drive
bands for howitzer
shells, Glasgow, 1918.

as the immediate post-war boom was quickly followed by economic crisis which brought unemployment and deprivation with a new vengeance to parts of industrial Scotland. In such areas industrial strife and political militancy had been features of the war years as war industry workers sought to gain from the state's need for their labour. By contrast, for those in military service, for all of its connotations of hierarchy and class structure, there was undoubtedly some sense of a task shared, of common sacrifice, of a nation in all its classes and backgrounds united against a common enemy. The degree to which this experience worked to push against the sturdy barriers of class and gender that had characterised pre-war Scotland is less than clear however.

For one major part of the Scottish population, the First World War appeared to hold forth a real prospect of advancement. While women had hardly been unaffected by war and military service in previous centuries, it was in the context of mass mobilisation for a twentieth-century national war effort that, for the first time, the contribution of female labour to the prosecution of war was heavily relied on by the state and acknowledged as significant to the outcome. As a centre of heavy industry, munitions and aircraft manufacture, west central Scotland in particular saw the emergence of women in new and essential wartime roles. Female substitution into traditionally male-dominated occupations became a feature of urban Scotland, and women from

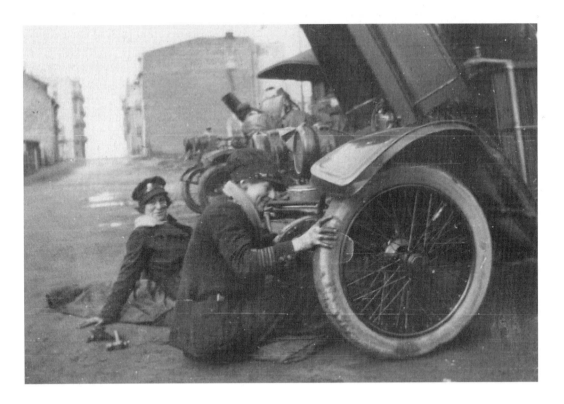

Miss Janet Cadell, a Voluntary Aid Detachment ambulance driver at the Allied hospital centre of Wimereux, France, 1918.

urban backgrounds were also recruited into food production in rural areas. The First World War origins of the Women's Land Army are easily lost behind the Second World War imagery with which the organisation is now associated in popular memory, but it was in the extremities of the U-Boat campaign of 1917, with the danger of defeat by starvation, that it came into being, complete with its own Scottish organisation. Employment in support of the war effort brought the prospect of higher wages, some greater degree of independence and mobility to many Scottish women. Yet for many the benefits – financial and social – were at best fleeting, and such change as was wrought by the war did not extend in any meaningful way beyond 1918. Precedents were nevertheless set, not least in the formation of women's uniformed services. Although these were organised for war service only, they were quickly reactivated at the outset of the Second World War and regular women's services existed on a permanent basis thereafter. In civilian occupations, it was taken as read that women would contribute national service as part of the mobilisation of the whole workforce when the country again entered into war in 1939.

The connection is often made between the roles taken up by British women during the First World War and the gaining of the vote for women aged over 30 in 1918. This connection was perhaps not so direct as has often been represented and assumed, but in the Scottish context

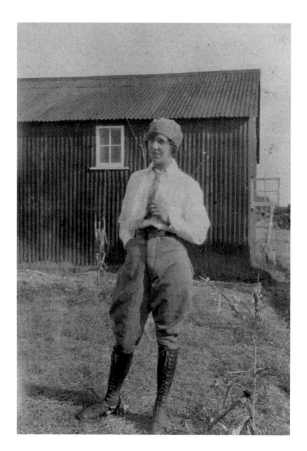

Miss Rose West, head of Motor Transport with a Scottish Women's Hospital unit, Macedonia, 1918.

there is one outstanding illustration of the links between the pre-war campaign for women's suffrage and the involvement of women in the war – the Scottish Women's Hospitals. Employment of women in various nursing services and nursing auxiliary organisations was the traditional route for female volunteer labour in wartime; the Scottish Women's Hospitals were rather different. The conception of Edinburgh doctor and women's suffrage campaigner Dr Elsie Inglis, these were fully-fledged hospital units entirely staffed, from doctors to drivers, by women. Such a radical idea, with its links to the National Union of Women's Suffrage Societies, was rather too much of a leap of thinking for the War Office and Inglis' initial offer of service to the British forces in France was declined. The Scottish Women's Hospitals instead took their skills and organisation to the aid of Britain's allies. Their success in running field hospitals and field ambulances in Serbia and France earned them admiration and recognition from their host governments. The gratitude they earned overseas was rather more lasting than any change to the status of women in Scotland to which their work might have contributed.

Perhaps inevitably, the women demonstrated their Scottish credentials with dress trappings drawn from the Scottish military tradition – hodden grey uniforms with tartan facings, and thistle badges. If the organisation of the Scottish Women's Hospitals was Scottish, around half of the women involved were not, leading one historian to wonder, 'Has there been any other organisation – bar the Scottish regiments – where the English have been content to be thought of as "Scottish"?'[14]

That traditional image of the Scottish regiments remained a powerful and enduring national symbol as the army grew and changed during the First World War. Initially part of the small British Expeditionary Force that halted the German advance in 1914, the Scottish regiments thereafter absorbed civilian volunteers and conscripts as the army expanded to the size that twentieth-century European warfare demanded. The phenomenon of mass volunteering brought so many from civilian life into the ranks, and into the officers' messes, of the traditional

Scottish regiments that both recruits and regiments could not help but be altered in the process. New battalions of the old regiments were raised under existing titles and traditions, but if the war service recruits gained temporary membership of a venerable Scottish military institution, they also brought something of their own skills and background with them. In regiments such as the Highland Light Infantry an urban character was reinforced by the raising of Glasgow city battalions like the 15th, formed among Glasgow's tramway workers, or the 16th, from among former members of the Christian youth organisation, the Boys' Brigade. Edinburgh equivalents included Colonel MacRae's 16th Royal Scots, which famously included a number of Edinburgh professional footballers. In a mass army, formations larger than the old regiments became the essential form of military organisation. The Scottish Territorial and New Army divisions – the 51st (Highland) Division, the 52nd (Lowland) Division, the 9th (Scottish) Division, and the 15th (Scottish) Division – promulgated their own overtly Scottish identity and a reputation that war service volunteers and conscripts could take a full share in, one which perhaps had greater meaning to them than the reputations of the regiments they had joined.

The reorganisation of the British army in the 1880s had deliberately linked regiments to local areas, and this bore fruit in the First World War mobilisations. If the Scottish regiments were still, culturally, 'national corps', the Territorial Force battalions and war service battalions that reinforced them were inheritors of the strongly local traditions of the Victorian volunteer movement. The background of the Territorial Force officers and non-commissioned officers was firmly rooted in the professional and rural gentry classes of their constituent local area – on joining a professional or commercial firm in civilian life, young men could find that service in the local Territorial Force unit was urged as part of the firm's tradition. In wartime, local communities endeavoured to maintain links with the volunteers from among them, particularly through the offices of the local church. The presence of a chaplain in war service units, usually supplied by the Church of Scotland, was one aspect

McCrae's Battalion
16th ROYAL SCOTS

MEN URGENTLY WANTED
DERBY MEN AND UNATTESTED MEN

YOU can by directly enlisting now in this Battalion secure a place amongst your companions and fellow townsmen instead of possibly being placed with strangers.

JAMES LEISHMAN
Chairman
Recruiting Committee

Recruiting Office
Palace Hotel, 1 Castle St., Edinburgh

The 16th Battalion Royal Scots was a city battalion raised in 1914 on the principle that men who enlisted together would serve together.

of this, the Scottish churches having long struggled to maintain their influence amidst a regular forces ministry that was inevitably of a strongly Anglican character. As their flocks volunteered for war, the Scottish clergy made a point of going with them, if not as chaplains then as combatants. In the highland battalions in particular, drawn as they were from communities where the church influence was strongest, ministers and sons of the manse were usually to be found among the officers. Dilution of the public school exclusivity of the army officer class by temporary officers was but one aspect of the change wrought by the creation of a mass volunteer army. For reasons of military necessity, the Scottish regiments of the First World War were more representative of the breadth of Scottish society than they had ever been. The military profession could not wage global war independently from civil society; the meeting of the two changed both. Active service in the First World War was hardly an agreeable undertaking overall, but it represented an opportunity for men of all backgrounds to take an honourable share in the national burden. To a considerable degree, service in the First World War was a realisation of the ideal of the Victorian volunteer movement – that the respectable civilian of any class should have a hand and a say in the defence of Britain and the empire. This acquisition of responsibility extended through those who could contribute essential civilian occupational skills – those of the naval reserves and the merchant marine for example – to those who participated in the new voluntary services and war industries.

Conscription was introduced in 1916, a fundamental change to the nature of military service, when the raising of volunteer New Armies in 1915 proved insufficient to meet the need for new recruits. It was in this compulsory form that Scots were most likely to experience the military life in the following five decades as the mechanism of conscription was revived at the outset of the Second World War and maintained thereafter. Technical and tactical change, the scale and complexity of war and the organisations that conducted it all brought a huge increase in the possibilities of service, varied by task, by training, by location, and by the fluidity of posting. Just as the encroachment of the state, of mass culture and communication into the lives of the people was rendering British society more homogenous, less distinctive by locality, region and constituent nationality, so amidst the multifarious units, theatres and campaigns of the Second World War it is harder than ever to point to a typically Scottish experience. For once, not even the Scottish regiments could dominate this aspect of Scottish life. Instead, the propaganda and popular culture of the war tended to emphasise modernism and technology, and to underline notions of a shared British, imperial and Allied experience. Alongside the glamorous image of aircrew, exotic foreign allies, enigmatic new forces like the Commandos, the growth of

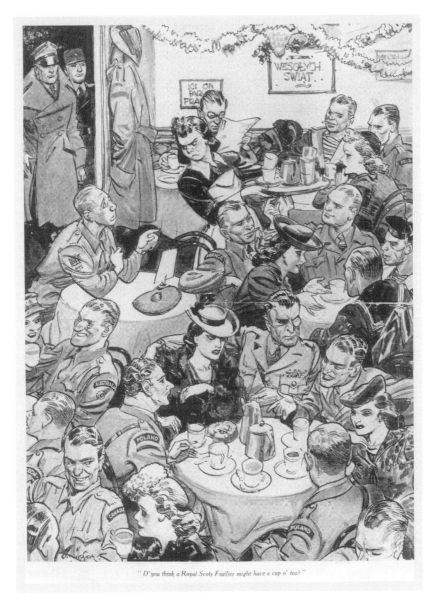

" D'you think a Royal Scots Fusilier might have a cup o' tea? "

A Scottish soldier is overlooked amongst charismatic foreign allies in this Christmas 1941 cartoon from *The Scottish Field.*

the women's uniformed services and such like, the traditional Scottish military image had much to compete with. This is not, however, to suggest that the national symbols of military heritage were forgotten. One manifestation was the overtly Scottish ethos and popular appeal of the 51st (Highland) Division, which of itself carried forth much of the essence of the Scottish military tradition. The 51st, with its pipers, became a popular symbol of British victory in North Africa and Italy. The wartime Scottish divisions (15th, 51st and 52nd) also incorporated units other than infantry – artillery, signals, engineers, *etc* – into the Scottish formation fold. Nevertheless, the Scottish experience of military service in the Second World War was essentially one of diversity; variety far greater even than that which the scale of the First World War had entailed. The demands of mass modern warfare involved a far greater concentration of manpower in logistical and support roles than in front-line combat units, a discomfiting realisation for many conventional senior officers. Against every company of infantry soldiers of a Scottish regiment one could point to multiples of drivers, mechanics, signallers, engineers, storemen, clerks, even sign-writers. Then there were Scots from the groundcrew and aircrew of the Royal Air Force, sailors of the Atlantic and Arctic convoys or of mine-sweeping and anti-submarine operations, anti-aircraft gunners and artillerymen, and a whole host of others, let alone the plethora of women's services and civilian war organisations. Scottish representation in the merchant navy, once again committed to the war effort in the convoy traffic through the western approaches, reinforced the position of this service, with its distinct culture of a civilian occupation, as an aspect of the Scottish experience of war. This diversity is marked in the Second World War collections of the National War Museum of Scotland. Post-war museum staff had some rethinking to do, accommodating the scope of Scottish involvement in the Second World War in displays and collections that had previously been categorised by the traditionally dominant structures of Scottish military service.

Air gunner Sergeant George Melville and his fellow Lancaster crewmen return from a 1942 bombing raid. All were killed on another raid just days later.

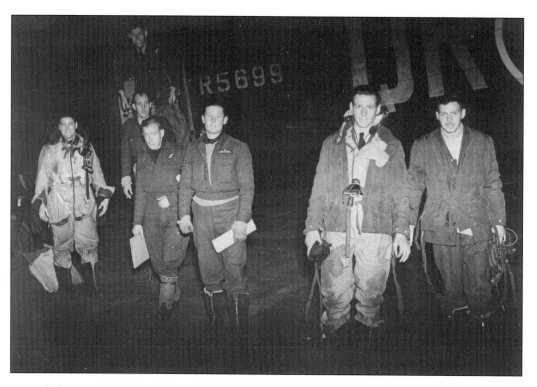

Conscription was not something entirely new in Scottish society. In the late eighteenth and early nineteenth centuries compulsory manpower levies on Scottish parishes had filled militia regiments for home garrisons while the regulars fought French armies overseas; similar levies were one method whereby seventeenth-century armies and navies were raised. But in 1945 the post-war continuation of conscription, of National Service, represented a departure for the British state. British military organisation had not previously relied on universal, compulsory general military service in peacetime in such a way. First World War conscription had ceased in 1919 and demobilisation had gradually seen a return to pre-war regular service practice, where the need for recruits was filled in the traditional manner, and where economic depression kept up the supply. The recruiting posters put out by the Scottish regiments in the 1920s and '30s show some appeal to the emerging mass popular culture (most frequently with pictorial hint of seemingly unlimited opportunities to play organised football), but the traditional fare of the Scottish military image remained their staple, largely unchanged by the war. In 1945, however, with the dismantling of a politically volatile empire to control, and with the crippling cost of victory and national survival all too clear, nationalisation was applied to military service and the question of empire just as it was soon to be applied to the problems of industry and social welfare. Peacetime National Service, which at its height commandeered eighteen months from the lives of the young men of Great Britain, projected the wartime ethos of the services, particularly of the army, forward into the Cold War years of the 1950s and '60s. As well as filling imperial garrisons worldwide, often amidst dangerous political disturbance, young Scottish conscripts took their place along-side their regular service counterparts for active service in counter-insurgency campaigns in such far-flung theatres as Malaya and Kenya and in a full-blown conventional war in Korea.

The National Service experience of military life was nevertheless played out while the emerging strategic realities of post-war British economic and military power, brought home by Anglo-French humili-ation in the disastrous 1956 Suez Crisis, were shaping a rather different role for the armed services. The last National Servicemen returned to civilian life in 1963 at a time when British defence spending was begin-ning to concentrate on the NATO strategy of nuclear deterrence. Gradual retreat from a world-power role meant that, in the broadest terms, Britain was once again to rely on a small professional army, and the reduction that ensued was brought about through disbandments and amalgamations that affected the army in Scotland. This time, signifi-cantly, the Royal Navy was to follow, concentrating on its nuclear submarines and a surface fleet role greatly reduced and relatively close to home. In the post-National Service era prospects in regular service life were drawn in as the end of empire ceased to be a process and became a fact. Recruiting practices were altered to suit the services' requirement for specialist technicians, even in infantry battalions. Shorter periods of service, linked to the opportunity to learn a trade for return to civilian life, displaced the traditional, and diminishing, attractions of foreign travel and adventure.

Meantime, the exponential growth of the welfare state had taken from the services their long-standing, if unofficial, function as an alternative to unemployment and the poor house. To remain attractive to a workforce that had a greater degree of choice, the services had to make themselves more palatable and flexible as an employment option. In this, the traditional aspects of Scottish service were not well placed – the infantry, and so too the appeal of the Scottish regiments, being among the least technical and specialist roles on offer.

The Cold War entailed a Royal Navy and Royal Air Force presence in Scotland alluded to in the previous chapter but, while this was strategically important, it was not strong in manpower terms and was not characterised by a Scottish recruitment profile, however much the various establishments attempted to cultivate a local connection. With ongoing commitment to the NATO presence in Germany, and with the re-ignition of communal strife and terrorism in Northern Ireland,

Men of B Company, 1st Battalion Royal Scots, on patrol in Belfast, 1970.

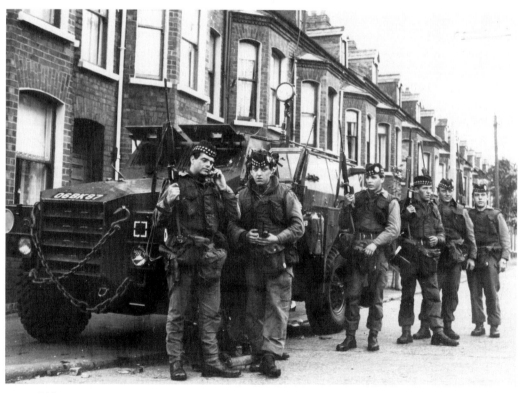

the British army of the 1970s and '80s continued to need soldiers from Scotland. Scottish regiments managed to maintain recruiting levels with the help of judicious allocations within the recruiting and training structure of the Scottish Division. The manpower resource of prime recruiting areas in west central Scotland could be spread to top up regiments where population and economic conditions were not conducive to recruitment, such as in the North Sea oil boom that spread through the north and north-east of the country.

When the collapse of the Soviet Union in the early 1990s removed the strategic threat that had underpinned British military thinking since the end of the Second World War, this was taken by the government as a defence spending windfall and an immediate reduction in the size of the services followed. Revival in the Scottish economy in the late 1980s had already made recruiting more difficult, and the sudden threat of 'peace dividend' amalgamations among the Scottish regiments prompted public protest campaigns that reinforced the climate of uncertainty and the impression of an occupation in decline. Just as it had in the wake of defence cuts in the 1960s, the drive for economy impacted on reserve forces, significantly reordering the structure and reducing the size of the Territorial Army and remaining elements of the naval and air force reserves. The closure of naval reserve establishments more or less reduced the Royal Navy's presence in Scotland to the one base at Faslane. For the army, the loss of numerous local TA units in towns across Scotland, particularly in the north, all but removed the military presence from the local life of large areas of the country, a development with as yet unquantifiable consequences for regular recruiting.

In 1997, in a dramatic, rain-swept ceremony, the Union flag was lowered for the last time over the British colony of Hong Kong. The Black Watch, the first highland regiment to be raised for the British army, was prominent as the world's media covered British withdrawal from one of the last significant possessions of the empire. For the army, this was the last of the overseas postings that offered a flavour of what had once been the norm of peacetime imperial soldiering. In place of long-term garrison service in settled and possibly agreeable destinations worldwide, the small army of the 1990s offered a diet of home service and Northern Ireland duty with increasingly frequent short-term operational postings to trouble spots in the Balkans, Africa and the Middle East. For the 1991 Gulf War they were joined, through necessity, by personnel called up from the Territorial Army. This practice has prevailed since, partly made possible by a shift in the labour market away from secure permanent employment towards short-term contract work and even by virtue of long-term unemployment. It is a recourse which has impacted upon the pressures and attractions of part-time military service.

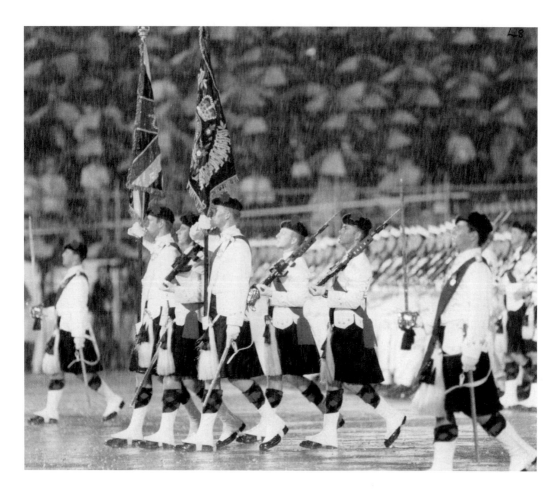

48

The Colours of the 1st Battalion Black Watch are marched on in the Farewell Ceremony, Hong Kong, June 1997.

Fostered by membership of the United Nations and the European Union, and by British governments not shy to deploy military power in support of foreign policy, high levels of operational commitment at the end of the century were not accompanied by significant rises in defence spending or by enlargement of the armed forces. The term 'over-stretch' entered media parlance as a piece of jargon relating to the discrepancy between growing British military commitments and limited British military resources, not least of manpower. The uncertainties of the early 1990s created a crisis in service recruitment which strongly affected the Scottish regiments. Recognising that their survival as institutions was under threat, recruitment and retention became a priority and was pursued in Scotland through advertising and endeavour with some success. One other tactic was to look elsewhere for recruits, much as the Scottish regiments had to do in the middle decades of the nineteenth century. In 1996 the Royal Scots was one of three British infantry battalions to receive a company on attachment from the Royal Gurhka Rifles, and the same battalion had success, through connections made at the Edinburgh

Military Tattoo, in attracting an influx of recruits from Fiji, which has since become a source of manpower tapped into across the army.

Image, recruitment and retention remain a problem nonetheless. The institutional culture of military organisations – characterised by single-sex profile, barrack life, peripatetic overseas service, discipline and the overriding influence of hierarchy and group identity – can be at odds with some of the expectations and mores of contemporary Scottish society. The social pressure on young men to have what is regarded as normal lives, complete with stable relationships, families and the requisite quota of material possessions, has been something the services have made efforts to lean towards but cannot always render compatible with the requirements of military service. Perhaps most difficult to square is the element of physical danger that military service necessarily entails, something which appears an ever more extraordinary contrast to a civil culture in which risk avoidance, health and safety, liability and litigation have become ensconced. The armed services have also felt the effects of broad social changes of recent decades which have seen greater opportunities for, and economic pressure upon, women to follow a career. One consequence has been the compounding of the difficulties in retention of men in their service careers, since their contentment with the round of military postings often relies on the mobility of spouses and families. However, the services have also been able to take advantage of the same change and have turned to women as a significant source of recruitment. Female recruits now represent a substantial and growing element of the Royal Navy and Royal Air Force in particular. Decisions to allow women to serve at sea, as combat aircrew and in combat support roles in the army, indicate that the Ministry of Defence is serious in its desire, and need, to benefit from this previously under-used resource. However, the exclusion of women from close combat roles on the ground precludes their full participation in the most identifiably Scottish of military units.

In 2004 government plans for the army centred on ending the practice of moving single-battalion regiments through a sequence of posting and roles, and replacing this 'Arms Plot' system with larger multi-battalion regiments each with a fixed location and role, with the intention that during their career individual soldiers will move between battalions, locations and roles within the regiment. If realised, this shift may represent the beginning of the end for the remaining Scottish regiments as meaningful separate entities, with all that implies for dearly held traditions and local distinctions. It is, however, an attempt to square operational requirements and economies with the expectations and aspirations of potential recruits. As Scottish society has become more homogenous, the idea of the Scottish soldier has continued to have meaning and appeal, but is not entirely dependent on local and family allegiances to particular regiments and their distinctions.

Like much else in the traditions of Scotland, these have come to appear old-fashioned and have fallen under the eye of a government preoccupied with the idea of modernity, and scrutiny of public expense. Recent recruitment advertising and the display of symbols of Scottish identity among those on active service in recent conflicts, including the 2003- Iraq War, demonstrate that the modern icon of the Scottish soldier continues to be a potent, positive image at least among those who serve and those who might be induced to join up. The creation of a single, multi-battalion Scottish infantry would represent another variation on structures which have sought to employ a sense of Scottish nationhood as an asset to the military requirements of the state. If the planners are proved correct in terms of sustaining military service as a career for Scots, a larger regiment would at least perpetuate the Scottish military life as something distinct. However, in November 2004, government plans to reorganise the infantry clashed with the controversial deployment of a Black Watch battle group in support of US operations in central Iraq. Consequent casualties and intense media speculation re-ignited the public debate about the future of the Scottish regiments. Not for the first time, with a Scottish unit in the spotlight the government had to reckon with the power of national sentiment and its possible implications for votes. 'Modernisation' of the army in Scotland has rarely been a straightforward undertaking.

In the early twenty-first century, the significance of military service as an economic feature of Scottish society is much reduced compared to the situation in 1927, the year of the opening of the Scottish National War Memorial. And yet, the national military reputation has retained a good deal of the potency of that time. It remains to consider how, after the First World War, the standard-bearers of the Scottish military tradition sought to resist and adapt themselves to the pressures of changing circumstances.

---

1 James Ferguson, *Papers Illustrating the History of the Scots Brigade in the Service of the United Netherlands 1572-1782*, volume 1 (Edinburgh: Scottish History Society, 1899), pp.xxiv-vi.

2 R Monro, *Monro, His Expedition with a worthy Scots Regiment (called Mac-Keyes regiment)* (London: 1637), part II, p.75.

3 Andrew Mackillop has stressed how highland landlord recruiters were able to enhance their positions by exploiting out of date and romantic notions of the military potential of the highlands and the clan system held by the British government. A Mackillop, *'More Fruitful than the Soil', Army, Empire and the Scottish Highlands, 1715-1815* (East Linton: Tuckwell Press, 2000).

4 Recruiting bill of the 71st (Fraser's) Highlanders, 1776 (National War Museum of Scotland, M.1982.97). The bill was distributed in the lowland east-coast town of Dundee. Even at

this early stage, highland regiments were recruiting amongst urban populations far from the highlands.

5   D Hamilton, *The Healers. A history of medicine in Scotland* (Edinburgh: Canongate, 1981), pp.129-30.

6   Sir J Pringle, *Observations on the Diseases of the Army* (London: Millar & Wilson, 1752); Sir G Blane, *Observations on the Diseases Incident to Seamen* (London: Cooper, 1785).

7   M Kaufman, *The Regius Chair of Military Surgery in the University of Edinburgh* (Amsterdam: Rodopi, 2003).

8   A Somerville, *History of the British Legion and War in Spain* (London: James Pattie, 1839), p.7.

9   A Alexander, *The Life of Alexander Alexander* (Edinburgh: William Blackwood & Sons, 1830), pp.143-4.

10 A MacKillop, op. cit., p.235.

11 *An Account of the Scottish Regiments with the statistics of each, from 1808 to March 1861. Compiled from the old regimental record books, and monthly returns of each regiment, now rendered to the war department* (Edinburgh: William P Nimmo, 1862).

12 The connection between such occurrences and assumptions about war service is examined in E A Cameron and I J M Robertson, 'Fighting and Bleeding For the Land: the Scottish Highlands in the Great War', in C M M Macdonald and E W McFarland (eds), *Scotland and the Great War* (East Linton: Tuckwell Press, 1999), pp.81-102.

13 L Leneman, *Fit for Heroes? Land Settlement in Scotland after World War I* (Aberdeen: Aberdeen University Press, 1989).

14 L Leneman, *In the Service of Life. The Story of Elsie Inglis and the Scottish Women's Hospitals* (Edinburgh: Mercat Press, 1994), pp.218-9.

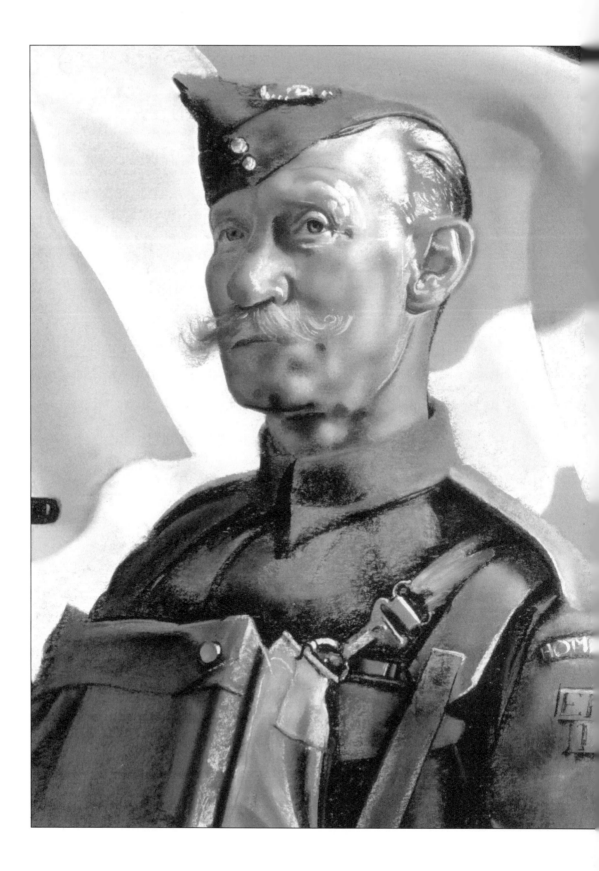

Keep our
Scottish battalions

THE CREATION OF THE SCOTTISH NATIONAL WAR MEMORIAL AND ITS companion Scottish Naval and Military Museum took more than a decade to achieve. In this lapse of years, amid the relief of victory and recognition of the military achievements of 1918, questions had begun to be heard about the cost, conduct and purpose of the Great War, questions that were barely uttered at its close. In the early 1930s, one of the critical voices raised was that of no less a figure than the war-time Prime Minister David Lloyd George, whose published memoirs placed the first question mark against the name of Field Marshal Earl Haig, the victorious wartime Commander-in-Chief of the British army. From such informed, if subjective, criticism of aspects of Haig's direction of the war on the Western Front, Haig's reputation has since passed through the mill of 1930s pacifism and 1960s anti-establishment iconoclasm. Today, despite much written in his defence, Haig's memory still struggles to shake off the virtual ogre status that fell to him in popular perceptions about the history of the First World War. The tendency to demonise Haig as incompetent and heartless perhaps has less to do with specific criticism of his generalship than with the distance that was growing between contemporary British society and the imperial military world that he represented. Haig was a Scottish soldier, a product of the Scottish military tradition in its upper class, anglicised form. Though his immediate family background was not a military one, his calling as a soldier followed the ancestral traditions of the Haigs of Bemersyde and rings familiar here. One of Haig's seventeenth-century ancestors commanded a Scottish cavalry troop in the Swedish army of King Gustavus Aldolphus; his earlier forebears fought back and forth across the Anglo-Scottish border. Haig's rocky posthumous journey through popular memory is an extreme version of the difficult route along which the whole panoply of the Scottish military tradition has found itself travelling through the twentieth century. On his death in 1928, Haig was nothing other than the heroic victor, and a Scottish hero at that. Close on 100,000 people queued to pay their respects as his remains lay in state in St Giles', Edinburgh. How many Scots could be found today to name him as an outstanding Scottish historical figure?

Lance Corporal Robertson, 11th City of Edinburgh Battalion Home Guard by Eric Kennington, 1944.

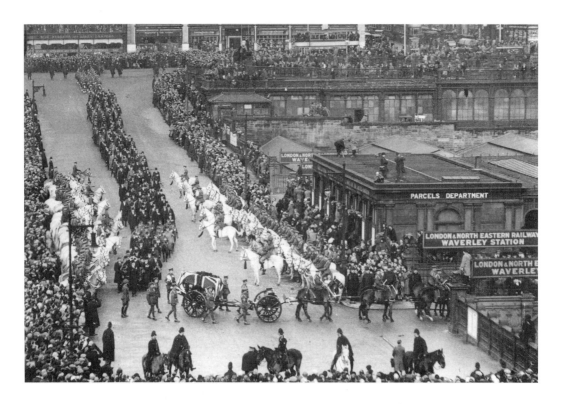

Haig's funeral cortège arrives at Waverley Station en route to his burial at Dryburgh Abbey. His grave was marked by a soldier's simple headstone.

Haig's demotion is more than a matter of the passing of years, and the fading of memory. As a society, Scotland appears to have become less ready to identify with aspects of the military renown that once defined it. Warriors can still be in fashion: the 1990s resurgence of popular interest in William Wallace and King Robert Bruce was evidence enough of that, but these are figures from a different age, far removed from the perceived taint of British imperialism, distant in time and sufficiently free from meaningful class and political associations as to be readily adapted to the myth-making of popular culture. It is true that this change has occurred in a period which ultimately saw the British empire decline, yet that same period also saw British victory in a Second World War greater in scale than the First, and a series of smaller conflicts involving British forces in which Scots have been embroiled as closely as ever. If the association between war and nation has shifted in the popular consciousness it has done so gradually and subtly, and the image has had to accommodate changing popular attitudes to such things as class and imperialism. The immediate inheritors of the tradition, the Scottish regiments and others of the Scottish military community, have worked to preserve it and with it their own position in Scottish life. In this they have often found plentiful support.

The years between the wars brought their share of hardship and dis-illusionment, but it would be wrong to assume that economic depression, the human cost of the war and the progress of socialist politics led the generality of Scots to question their British imperial and martial inheritance. The politics of pacifism were never of the mainstream, while Labour politics were concerned with more immediate economic matters than empire and Scotland's place in it and the nascent Scottish nationalist political parties made little headway with their home rule message. In the area of literature and the arts, the self-regarding 'Scottish Renaissance' of the time was beyond the ken of most Scots, for whom the symbols of the past and the memory of the war were sure things that could be looked to in times of material hardship, uncertainty and political unease. In Eric Linklater's 1934 satire on cultural nationalism *Magnus Merriman*, Magnus, the half-convinced Scottish nationalist, encounters an Edinburgh public house-full of former soldiers, 'slouching dole-men' whose aspect is briefly re-invigorated by talk of the late war:

> High Wood disputed with the Labyrinth, the mud at Louvencourt rivalled as a topic of humour and delight the carnage at Mont St Eloi. In red leather volumes in the Memorial on the Castle Rock were the myriad names of the Scottish dead, and here in the lively squalor of a lousy tavern were their comrades who had survived, and whose names were nowhere written – unless perhaps on the wall of a jakes. But they were alive and, for the moment, rich with their memories. They had marched on foreign soil and killed their country's enemies. Thin-ribbed with hunger, or gross with civilian fat they might be, shambling in their gait and dismal in their dress they were, but once their buttons had been bright, and their shoulders were square, and they were Gordons and Seaforths and Camerons.[1]

It was such men, and the bereaved, and all those who remembered surer times, that filed through the Scottish National War Memorial, that mourned at the obsequies for Haig, that raised memorials in their home parishes, that kept their pride in their war even as they grew unsatisfied and angry with the lot that victory had left to them.

It was of course to their sojourn in the ranks of the Scottish regiments that Linklater ruefully compared his shabby drinkers, 'Gordons and Seaforths and Camerons' signifying all of the Scottish regiments and all that they stood for. For the regiments themselves it was a time for re-establishing in so far as they possibly could the familiar patterns of existence that had been disrupted and broken by the casualties they sustained in the early years of the war, and by their temporary absorption of civilian war volunteers and conscripts. With the latter returned to civilian life, the regiments resumed their pre-war character and role in imperial and home garrisons and tried to pick up where they had left off. Publication of highly detailed, exhaustive regimental histories had begun in the early years of the twentieth century, often funded and written by retired officers, and in the 1920s and '30s new volumes were added to these, each chronicling the respective regiment's part in the war. For this purpose the Royal Scots Fusiliers were able to secure the talents of the literary and political figure John Buchan, who made his work of regimental history a tribute to his brother, killed with the 6th Battalion of the regiment in the battle of Arras, 1917. It was Buchan who officially opened the Scottish Naval and Military Museum in 1933, and his book on the Royal Scots Fusiliers similarly was concerned with more than the war alone: it was a full-blown history beginning with the regiment's formation in 1678. In dealing with the late war as part of this longer story, Buchan recognised how the creation of a mass army had temporarily changed the normal run of things. In a concluding chapter he observed,

> … with the Armistice the great operations closed. Gradually the new battalions disappeared, the survivors were absorbed into civil life, the regiment returned to its old two-battalion basis, and the even tenor of its regimental history was resumed …. In the Great War it had been less a regiment than one of the training schools through which the manhood of the country passed to the field.[2]

In this volume, and in others that did the same work, resumption of the 'even tenor of regimental history' meant the seamless incorporation of this outstandingly different war into the reputations and history of the regular army regiments. The Scottish regiments could go on with things as they had been before, their place in the consciousness and affections of the Scottish people re-enforced by mass participation, but their rather detached existence as part of a small, exclusive professional imperial army quietly restored. And yet storm clouds were gathering. The large-scale withdrawal of the British army from the southern counties of Ireland was the first sign that the old order of the empire was unravelling.

The immediate post-war years were a difficult time of financial stringency for all the services. Despite emerging triumphant and unchallenged as the world's dominant naval power, the Royal Navy fell subject to economy and a new, if short-lived, international effort to moderate the limits of military power. The nascent Royal Air Force struggled for its very existence until the emerging potency of long-range aerial bombing as a strategic dimension of modern warfare gave it an independent future, albeit one essayed on a shoe-string budget. In 1925, the creation of the Auxiliary Air Force, a 'second line' of part-time locally-based units, saw the creation of local air squadrons in Glasgow, Edinburgh and Aberdeenshire, while squadrons were also set up at the Scottish universities. Air warfare had a modern, futuristic aura; the Royal Air Force was the new service and prided itself on its technical, practical

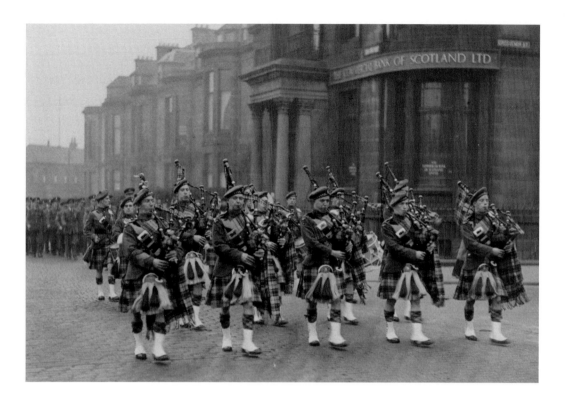

image, and yet it did not take long for the new auxiliary squadrons to identify themselves as Scottish in the traditional manner. Borrowing the long-established symbolism of the Scottish regiments, the Edinburgh and Glasgow auxiliary squadrons had pipe bands organised, with royal permission granted for them to don highland dress in 1933. Officers of the Glasgow Squadron also adopted kilts for mess dress. Kilts and pipers could hardly inspire the airman in battle, and the squadrons were concerned with rather more pressing preparations than the selection of appropriate tartan – 'Grey Douglas' in the event, in honour of squadron connections to the family of the Duke of Hamilton – but they were a way of building *esprit de corps*. In an identifiably Scottish fighting unit of any description at this period, the absence of such cultural emblems was an anomaly requiring correction.

An indication of the public profile still enjoyed by the Scottish regiments was given in an unveiling ceremony held on the esplanade of Edinburgh Castle in 1938. To the Victorian regimental monuments lining the fringes of the esplanade had already been added, in 1923, an equestrian statue of Earl Haig, the tribute of the Bombay merchant Sir Dhunjibhoy Bomanji. But the next monument added to the array, in 1938, was to another Scottish military hero of rather more humble rank, a long-dead hero of Waterloo. In 1936 the grave of Charles Ewart had been discovered in a timber merchant's yard, formerly the graveyard of

Pipers lead 603 (City of Edinburgh) Squadron Auxiliary Air Force through Edinburgh, 1937.

a Swedenborgian church in Salford, Manchester. At Waterloo in 1815, as a sergeant in the 2nd or Royal North British Dragoons (otherwise known as the Scots Greys), Ewart had valiantly, and violently, captured the eagle-topped standard of the French 45th Regiment. There were many individual heroes of that famous British victory, but in Scotland Ewart had been the man of the hour. That his fame, and with it his remains, should have fallen so far from the sight of posterity in the following century was naturally a concern to the officers of the Royal Scots Greys. A grand commemoration for Ewart also represented an opportunity for the Greys, a cavalry regiment without the tartan elements of the Scottish infantry identity, to stress their solidly Scottish roots. Influential support ensured that official reservations over the incongruity of an actual burial on Edinburgh Castle's esplanade were overcome. Ewart's mortal remains were exhumed from obscurity and reinterred in that 'honoured place'.[3] Today, subject to the demands of mass tourism, the esplanade serves as a car and coach park and has rather less of a hallowed atmosphere. Ewart's imposing tomb spends part of the year all but hidden behind the temporary stands erected for spectators at the Edinburgh Military Tattoo. But in 1938, only a year before the outbreak of the Second World War, the Scottish regiments had a special call on what had been the Castle's parade ground and had assumed the quality of a national ceremonial space.

The unveiling of Ensign Ewart's tomb on Edinburgh Castle esplanade, April 1938.

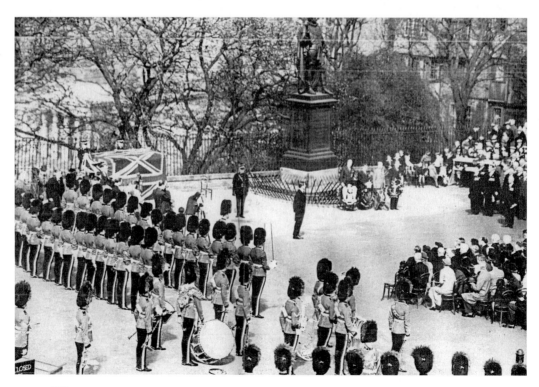

128

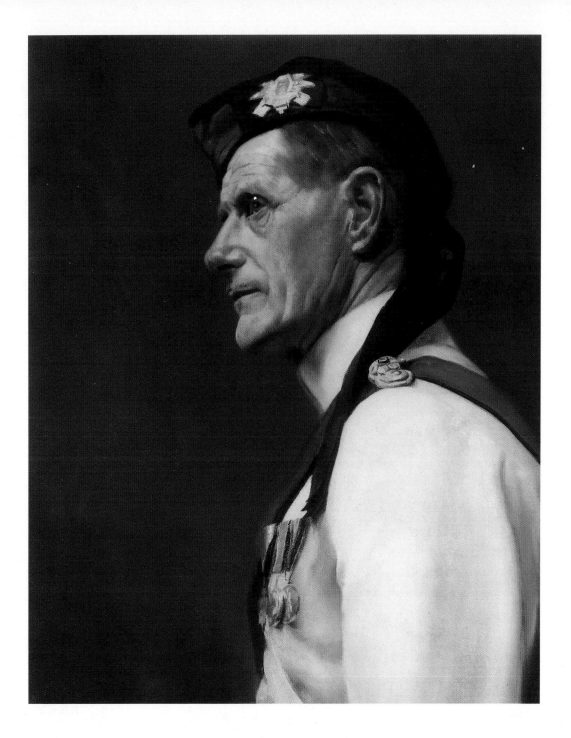

Plate 4.1 This unknown senior Black Watch officer was painted in the 1920s by society artist John Bulloch Souter. Souter's other work of the period warned of the degradation of civilisation following the catastrophe of war. The sense of experience and moral toughness evoked in this archetypal portrait of the Scottish military caste suggest the opposite.

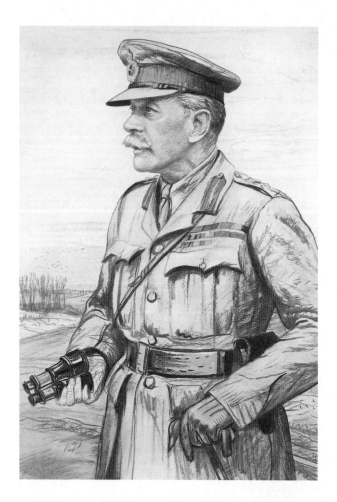

Plate 4.2 This portrait of Field Marshal Sir Douglas Haig was one of a series of British generals and admirals by war artist Francis Dodd, 1917. As a cavalry and staff officer, Haig's career had no overtly Scottish associations, but his Borders origins, Presbyterian faith, his character and demeanour were familiar to the Scottish public.

Plate 4.3 Partisans in Crete kept this Scottish royal standard during four years of German occupation after the fall of the island in 1941. It is believed to have been a headquarters flag of D Company, 23rd Battalion New Zealand Expeditionary Force, recruited from Otago, a New Zealand province with a particular Scottish immigrant character.

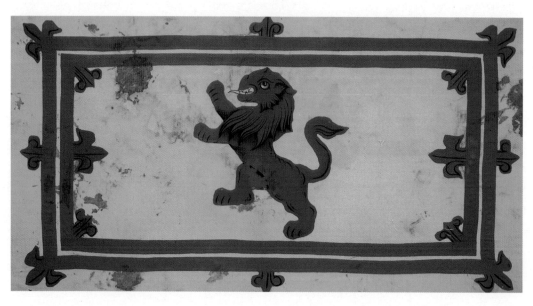

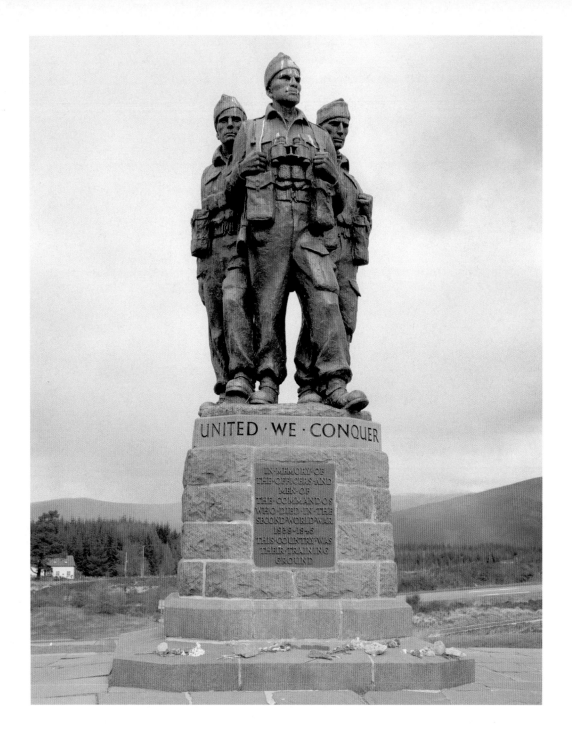

Plate 4.4 The Commando Memorial at Spean Bridge was placed against the dramatic highland landscape in which Commandos underwent their specialist training during the Second World War. The new special forces of several allied nations trained in Scotland and took the methods home. Annual commemorations at the Memorial are international events.

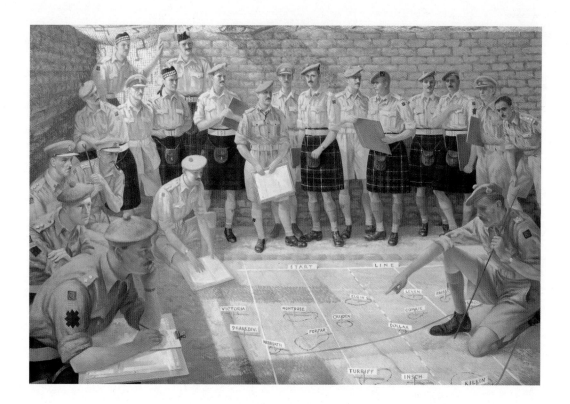

Plate 4.5 *The 51st Highland Division Plans El Alamein* by Ian Eadie records a pre-battle briefing by Major General Douglas Wimberley using a sand-table model of the plan of attack. To aid recognition in the desert landscape, each battalion was allotted objectives whose code-names were named after towns in their home recruiting areas.

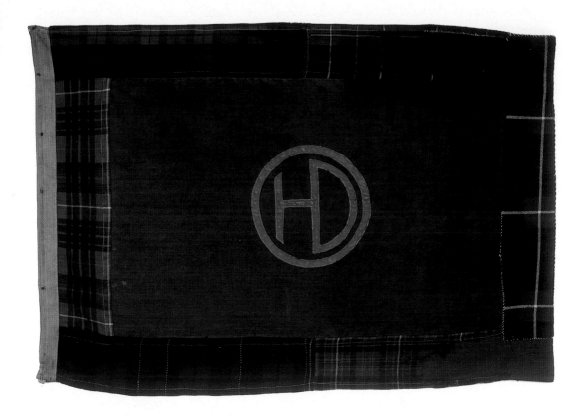

Plates 4.6a and b The headquarters flag of the 51st (Highland) Division flown at the battle of El Alamein, 1942 incorporates the regimental tartans of component units of the Division. The distinctive divisional sign in the centre was part of the 51st's popular image. Appearing on uniforms and vehicles, it was also daubed on buildings and roads to announce the Division's advance, earning the sobriquet 'Highway Decorators'.

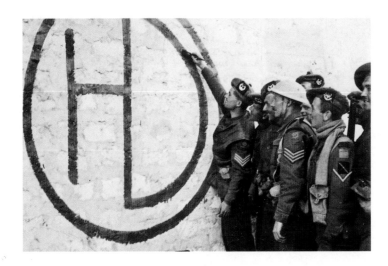

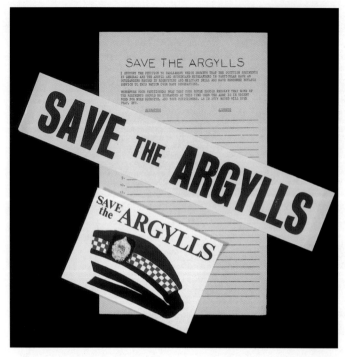

Plate 4.7 In the late 1960s cuts in defence spending, linked to withdrawal from empire, provoked a particular reaction in Scotland. The threat to one highland regiment prompted a public campaign of opposition. A petition which claimed to carry a million signatures was submitted to put pressure on a government facing a general election.

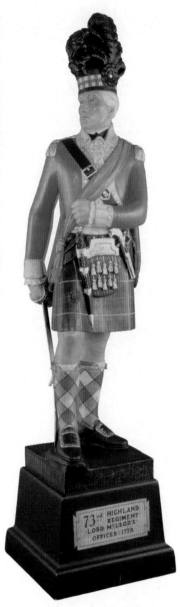

Plate 4.8 This figure of an officer of the 73rd Highland Regiment is one of the 83 oak statuettes created by the sculptor Charles D'Orville Pilkington Jackson for the opening of the Scottish Naval and Military Museum. Commissioned to show the variety and development of the Scottish regiments, their figurative style was intended to suggest strength and continuity.

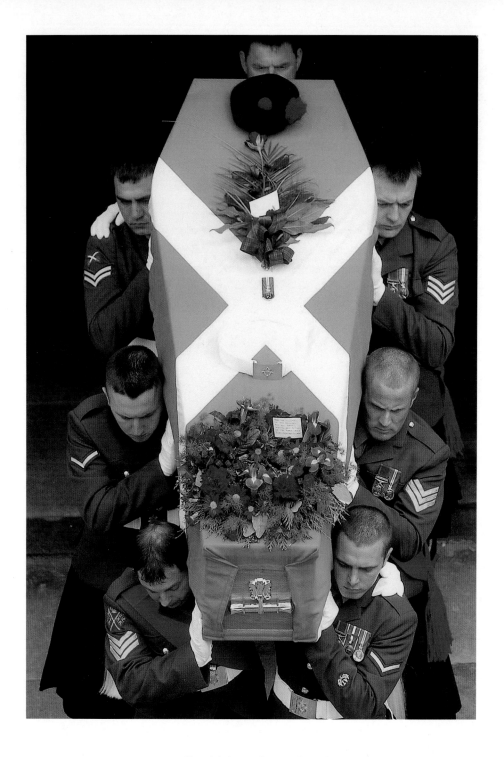

Plate 4.9 Lance Corporal Barry Stephen, 1st Black Watch, was killed in action during the invasion of Iraq in March 2003. His body was brought home for a funeral in Perth. His family's particular choice of the Saltire for his coffin, in place of the customary Union flag, was a poignant expression of the identity of this Scottish soldier of the British army.

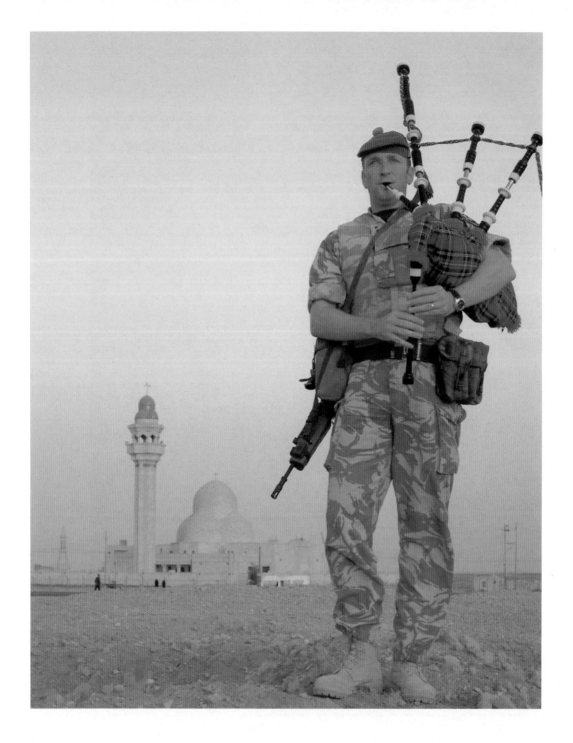

Plate 4.10 The traditional Scottish military image endures, as British forces continue to deploy across the globe. Pipe Major of the 1st Battalion Royal Scots, WO2 A J Cuthbertson, plays in Az Zubayr, southern Iraq, in early 2004.

In the meantime the Royal Scots Greys remained a regiment of cavalry in the truest sense, mounted on the horses that had largely kept them from a frontline role during the First World War. Although without any official status in this respect, their ceremonial presence in such affairs as the lying in state and funeral of Earl Haig hinted at a role as a homegrown Scottish equivalent of the Household Cavalry. In 1938, the year of the Czech crisis, and the flickering of the last hopes that a major European conflict could be avoided, the Royal Scots Greys were still operating on horseback and they were not fully converted into an armoured regiment until 1941. This was not entirely the anachronism it might seem, since the regiment's operational task from 1938-41 was to police the warring factions in Palestine, a role to which the mounted soldier was well suited. Nevertheless, the pace of technological and tactical change in warfare had outstripped the willingness of British governments to commit sufficient military spending for much of the inter-war period, leaving the British services even less well equipped for a major European war than they had been in 1914.

The situation of the Royal Scots Greys was but one example of how Britain had faced difficulty in adapting its imperial military role and existing commitments to new circumstances. The traditional image of the Scottish regiments was an integral part of a military culture, the product of a past of imperial soldiering, that was about to face the critical challenge of the resurgence of German military potential. The power of Nazi Germany was based on an all-powerful state, a rapid rearmament programme of heavy state spending on tanks, aircraft and submarines, and on a mass-conscript army. It also represented a revolution in think-ing, in strategic doctrine, characterised by Hitler's displacement of senior German commanders whose traditional approach, and traditional military ethos, was deemed out of date.

The ultimate Allied victory over Nazi Germany in 1945 was to require an absolute transformation in the British armed services and their methods of waging war, a change even greater than had been achieved in the course of the First World War. This was a slow, painful process but, remarkably, through these new approaches to warfare, to its technology and to its organisation, the traditional Scottish military character survived and flourished. At first this was almost by default. Belated efforts to modernise the British army had not taken full effect by the time the German army was first encountered in combat. The introduction of updated uniform and equipment brought the advent of battledress uniform in 1940, and with it the demise of the kilt on opera-tional service, but this was not before Scottish soldiers, notably those of the 51st (Highland) Division, had already been sent to France. It is clear that some of these at least went into action against the German advance in June 1940 before receiving the new battledress and therefore still wearing the kilt. What they and other British forces then encountered was a devastating defeat, rolled back by an apparently unstoppable, mobile, well-equipped force operating with close air support.

With German success and the fall of France came a particularly heavy blow to Scottish military prestige, the surrender of much of the 51st (Highland) Division at St Valéry-en-caux, with some 10,000 men taken into captivity for the rest of the war. Like the 15th (Scottish) and 52nd (Lowland) Division, the 51st had inherited its title, essence and emblems of identity from a celebrated First World War forebear, and the 51st in particular had emerged from that earlier conflict with a formidable fighting reputation. St Valéry was the darkest day the image of the highland soldier had seen since defeats by the Boers at Majuba and Magersfontein. As in these Victorian traumas, the reputation of the fighting highlander absorbed the surrender at St Valéry with the consolation of gallantry and tenacity in face of the greater calamity that swept the division up. But such a reversal brought forth action to wipe out the stain of defeat, as though the honour of Scotland itself rested on restoring the 51st's position. It was not lightly that, a matter of weeks after the loss of the division, 9th (Highland) Division, recruited from the same area, was renumbered as the 51st, its brigades and battalions re-numbered to match the organisational structure of its illustrious parent, all to keep alive this precious identity. For the men of the original 51st, the privation and frustration of captivity in prisoner-of-war camps was leavened with diversions that included such patriotic demonstrations as highland games and, in at least two camps, the formation of a pipe band. To anyone who has since been presented with the task of mastering it quickly, it will come as no surprise to learn that the steps of the popular highland dance 'The Reel of the 51st Highland Division' were devised by prisoners-of-war, men with time on their hands. Scottish identity might have been propounded in the prisoner-of-war camps, but it was not necessarily an advantage. At least one soldier of the 51st taken prisoner at St Valéry remembers being singled out for treatment by a German guard with a particular dislike for the Scots.[4]

Similar calamities were to follow. British forces held their own and prevailed over the Italians in the Middle East, but retreat and defeat were suffered again when Rommel's German Afrika Korps arrived in North Africa, as German forces bolstered the efforts of the Italians, swept into Greece, then launched a successful airborne assault on the island of Crete. One singular memento of the defence of Crete, a Scottish 'lion rampant' flag, subsequently found its way into the collection of the National War Museum of Scotland. This ancient standard of the Scottish kings has very limited official function in the heraldry of the British armed forces but, like the saltire national flag, it has appeared in the form of headquarters flags and personal banners. The flag from

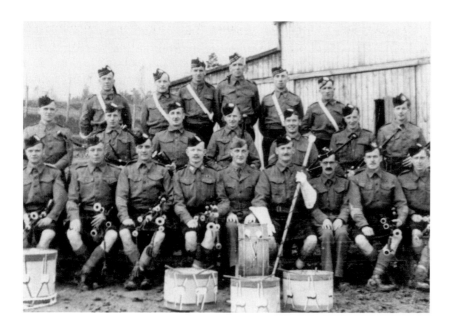

Crete was left behind when British forces withdrew after a fierce action around the village of Galatas. Found and kept safe by local partisans, it was returned ceremoniously to the British military authorities when Crete was liberated in 1945. This Scottish flag belonged not, strictly speaking, to a Scottish battalion, as the partisans had assumed, but to a unit of the New Zealand Expeditionary Force recruited from the strongly Scottish Otago area of New Zealand's South Island. As such it is an interesting representation of the links between war, Scottish identity and the spread of British imperial settlement, all symbolised by a heraldic device used by the kings of Scotland since the 13th century. The same national emblem was held onto in extremity by Scottish soldiers caught up in another, even greater calamity that befell British forces. Scottish infantry battalions in the Far East were among the 130,000 Allied forces captured at the fall of Singapore in February 1942, at the conclusion of a rapid Japanese campaign that struck into Malaya from across the Thailand border and took the strategically, and psychologically, important colony in a little over a month. For those who fell into the hands of the Japanese, the mental preservation of an existence as something other than a prisoner, the maintenance of every possible link with one's own identity, individually and collectively, seems to have been an aid to survival and integrity. For Scots in captivity, Scottish national pride could be one of these aids. Still in the possession of the Argyll and Sutherland Highlanders is a lion rampant Scottish Royal Standard, one soldier's private possession, which was used in funerals of the men of the regiment's 2nd Battalion who died as forced labourers along the Burma-Siam railway.

Pipes and Drums organised by prisoners-of-war from 51st (Highland) Division.

The reversals of the early years of the war had already forced the British military leadership to innovate in order to take the war to the enemy in an offensive spirit, despite the parlous strategic situation and the seriously depleted military resources available. The development of raiding forces to strike at enemy-occupied Europe was one high-profile tactic that was developed, and one that had a strong Scottish dimension. This was not only a matter of the use of Scottish highland terrain for irregular warfare training. Through the influence of place, but also through the background of many officers and men who were involved, drawn from Scottish regiments and from a Scottish background, elements of the traditional Scottish military image appeared as part of the culture of the new irregular forces that evolved. The offensive operations conducted by such units, shock assaults at close quarters, were designed to spread confusion and fear in the enemy, and the heritage of the highland soldier had all the necessary associations for the task. The memory of eighteenth-century irregular warfare in the highlands, recalled in their own training, gave to the new forces a range of ready-made imagery. This ethos was, on occasion, self-consciously carried into action. Colonel Jack Churchill of No.3 Commando carried bagpipes and a highland basket-hilted sword into the raid on the Norwegian island of Vaagso in December 1941. The following March, on the successful raid on the dry dock and submarine pens at St Nazaire, the kilt was worn into action by some men of the Commando demolition parties.

Encountering the traditional symbol of Scottish military prowess in such circumstances, the enemy does seems to have retained a strong, less than appreciative recognition of the Scottish military identity and what it might mean for them. On the disastrous raid on Tobruk in September 1941, Commando officers of 1st Special Service Battalion who had previous service in highland regiments wore the kilt. The Commandos had been driven across the desert by the Long Range Desert Group to penetrate the Tobruk defences and secure a beach-head, all of which was achieved successfully, but, when the complex joint-service plan of co-ordinated beach assaults unravelled, the Commandos were left to try to fight their way out again. As the Italian garrison hemmed them in and capture became inevitable, Lieutenant Hugh Davidson Sillito took the precaution of changing into shorts and hiding his Argyll and Sutherland Highlanders kilt in a cave 'because Scots were especially marked men to an enemy who hated the "ladies from hell"'.[5]

The Scottish touch remained in evidence as irregular forces expanded. Although the Commandos and other forces like the Special Air Service recruited widely from conventional elements of the army, they were happy to adopt Scottish credentials as one effective emblem of what they stood for. The best remembered manifestation of the Scottish touch was the presence of a piper in the Normandy landings. On D-Day 1944, as

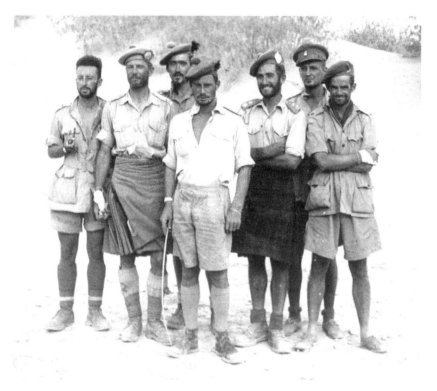

Commando officers in the desert before the Tobruk raid in 1942, from a film taken from a captured Commando and developed in Italy nearly twenty years later.

the Commandos of No.1 Special Service Brigade landed under fire on 'Sword' beach, their commander was the Scottish highland aristocrat Brigadier the Lord Lovat, who had been an influential figure in the early days of raiding. He had with him his 'personal' Commando piper who played the troops ashore.

Back in the mainstream of military operations, the new 51st (Highland) Division had undergone a year of training and moulding at the hands of its charismatic commander, Major-General Sir Douglas Wimberley. Wimberley deliberately set out to foster a Scottish national spirit within the division by maintaining a Scottish recruitment profile and encouraging *esprit de corps* through identification with traditional military virtues in discipline and turn-out. This reaffirmation of conventional British military ethos was coupled with Wimberley's unwillingness to accept some of the new thinking emerging from the War Office. Such was the feeling of complete defeat in 1940, some senior voices advocated that British troops must adopt a doctrine of explicit aggression and hatred towards the enemy. Wimberley was one of those who believed that the traditional virtues of the Scottish military tradition still had practical value in this modern war. The success of the 51st in action in North Africa and Sicily vindicated his convictions. The image of the division was given added visibility by its penchant for painting the divisional formation sign along the roads of its advance. The progress of the 51st was closely followed at home, where news of the division's successes in the British victory at El Alamein and onwards was greeted with relief and enthusiasm. It was also taken up by the Commander of the British 8th Army, General Bernard Montgomery, who came to appreciate the belief within the division's own ranks that it was the best. The result was that Montgomery tended to use and re-use the 51st as one of his favoured attack formations, a commitment to action that kept the 51st fighting at the forefront of the campaigns in North Africa and Sicily before being withdrawn home to prepare for a similar role in the assault on north-west Europe. Success bred expectation, but the earlier months of regular engagement with the enemy, of the stress of battle, and of sustaining casualties, had blunted the division's ability to live up to the reputation it had created. The 51st eventually came to a halt in failed attacks during the struggle to break out from the Normandy beach-heads and it took a change in senior command to revive its capability. The 51st was not the only Scottish formation but, with its combat reputation established and recognised, the principal expectations of traditional Scottish military prowess were vested in it. Its uncharacteristic failure, after so much success, is perhaps an indication that this was too heavy a burden for one formation to carry in a conflict of such magnitude and length.

Through six years of warfare in which unprecedented numbers of Scottish people were directly involved, the influence of Scottish identity on military service overall is harder to discern. The 18,000 men of the 51st were only a tiny proportion, and not all Scots at that. What has particularly coloured much of the popular memory of Great Britain's part in the war is not so much the failures and successes of the overseas campaigns, but rather the impact of the conflict on the civilian population. Scotland's 'Home Front' position and experience have already been described; some of these new experiences and sacrifices were articulated in a way that formulated a Scottish national dimension to the war effort as it was popularly understood. The destruction and devastation of the Clydebank Blitz became, in the very name by which it was known, a badge of honour demonstrating solidarity and the sharing of suffering with populations in the English industrial centres that came under more sustained attack. It has since also become part of a self-consciously 'working class' story of the war, in which the resilience of urban populations to danger and hardship has been presented as part of Scotland's socialist credentials, in company with volunteering for the Spanish Civil War and the championing of war production for the aid of the Soviet Union.

Immediate post-war political developments suggest that many people, although they would not have subscribed to that particular interpretation, nevertheless wanted to see British society take a new direction. The results of the 1945 general election demonstrated that significant sections of Scottish political opinion, like that of British society as a whole, had broadly swung behind the idea of state intervention in all aspects of the economic and social life of the nation – the form of government that had proved successful in wartime. The state had mobilised and directed the industrial and rural workforce towards the war effort with more sweeping and lasting effect than in the previous war, opening, for example, new areas of employment to Scottish women, and even intervening, through the necessity of rationing, in the diet of the people. The interventionist measures introduced in Scotland under Secretary of State Tom Johnston were followed up in the economic boom years of the late 1940s and early 1950s by the expansion of the welfare state, the nationalisation of industry and the construction of public housing. For a time, there was a sense that this all represented a deliberate break from the past, and was an expression of the general desire that sacrifice and victory should carry a social dividend of the sort that failed to be realised after the First World War. This very idea had arisen among those in the wartime armed services, encouraged by promotion of idealism in information and education programmes provided by the Army Bureau of Current Affairs and its equivalents. In the midst of the sense of optimism, the cherishing of peace and desire for a changed society, it might be expected that the old military tradition of Scotland – a tradition associated with past wars and with empire – could have slipped into abeyance. This was not the case: the image was sufficiently robust to be adapted to the times and for Scots across the broad range of society to keep faith with it, as indeed they kept faith with the idea of empire even as the empire's future seemed in doubt. The issues of the late war seemed sound; its conduct and purpose was not questioned in the way of the 1930s. The merger of the armed services with civilian society had been even more comprehensive than before. Victory was credited to the people – of which the military (and civil) establishment represented only one element. The military traditions of Scotland could be appropriated by all those who had played their part.

Despite being accommodated into existing approaches developed in the aftermath of the First World War, Second World War remembrance also reflected the atmosphere in which the best tribute to wartime sacrifice was seen to be a utilitarian commitment to building a better future. War memorials were not widely erected in the manner of 1918-19 and the practice of adding new strings of Second World War names to existing First World War memorials seemed appropriate, not least in having the complimentary merit of being relatively inexpensive. This too applied to the Scottish National War Memorial, where new books of remembrance were added into the existing bays. The desire to create 'useful' functional memorials, a departure from the monumental symbolism more typical of First World War remembrance, was suggested

135

by such schemes as the memorial to Corporal Thomas Hunter, a posthumous winner of the Victoria Cross for his gallantry in action with No.43 Royal Marine Commando at Lake Commachio, Italy, in April 1945. There are other memorials to Hunter, including a cairn erected at Leith in 2002, but the line of houses for disabled veterans built in his memory near to his former home in the council housing estate of Stenhouse, Edinburgh, dedicated in 1954, was in keeping with the utilitarian, future-building ethos of the time.

The functional spirit of commemoration had a Scottish wartime precedent. In 1941 the American-born, Aberdeenshire landowner Lady MacRobert donated £25,000 to the Air Ministry as a memorial to the loss of her three sons, all airmen, two of whom had been killed on active service with the Royal Air Force. The money was to be put to buying a bomber aircraft, a Short Stirling given the title 'MacRobert's Reply', to help carry on the fight. This gesture of defiance corresponded to Britain's then parlous position in the war. The following year, as the German invasion of the Soviet Union faltered, Lady MacRobert made a further donation that put four new Hurricane fighters into RAF service. Three were named after her sons, and the fourth for 'The Lady', as 'MacRobert's Salute to Russia', a singular gesture of goodwill and solidarity between allies of a rather different complexion. The loss of the MacRobert sons, heirs to a fortune made by their father in British India, led Lady MacRobert to place assets into charitable trusts directed towards the interests of servicemen and their families. In wartime this entailed the conversion of one of the family homes into a rest centre for RAF air crew on leave from active service. After the war, MacRobert money continued to provide facilities for serving and retired airmen and helped to support the work of the Erskine Hospital near Glasgow, itself set up in 1916 to care for the returning wounded.

The few Second World War public monuments that did appear in Scotland also convey something of a subtly different spirit of commemoration. The most prominent was the creation of the Dundee sculptor Scott Sutherland: his Commando Memorial outside Spean Bridge, unveiled in 1952, has become a highland landmark. Set against the imposing background of the Nevis mountain range and in the territory across which the Commandos trained, the Memorial's three figures have a heroic quality, but also a naturalism that is distinct from the figures of many First World War monuments. Sutherland used life models, one at least a former Commando, and these successfully evoke the spirit of exceptional endeavour on which the Commando idea was based.

The Second World War might easily have seen the end of one example of First World War commemoration in the Scottish military tradition. The Scottish Naval and Military Museum at Edinburgh Castle closed in 1939, and its collection was put into safe storage for the duration of hostilities. With administrative arrangements uncertain, and with antique military tradition somewhat out of fashion, the museum continued to languish at the war's end and its future existence was far from assured. That it eventually re-opened in 1949 was largely thanks to one man's belief in its importance. David Lowe Macintyre VC CB was a senior civil servant, Under-Secretary to the Ministry of Works, the government department that took on the running of the museum at his behest. Macintyre was also a living embodiment of the Scottish military tradition, a Gaelic-speaking highland officer who volunteered for the army in 1915 and was awarded a Victoria Cross for gallantry while serving on the Western Front in August 1918. This hero of an earlier war saw to it that the connections to Scotland's military past exemplified by the museum's collection would

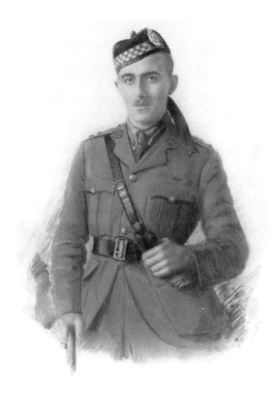

Lieutenant David L Macintyre was awarded the Victoria Cross for leadership under fire and for single-handedly capturing a German machine-gun position, 1918.

remain open for Scots and visitors to Scotland to appreciate. At the official re-opening, the General Officer Commanding in Scotland acknowledged that the museum's purpose was not at that moment a fashionable one: 'I have found in recent years a tendency to decry anything that is old, traditional or historical. Nothing could be more wrong.'[6]

Amongst those who lived and breathed the tradition, the museum's preservation for the future had been kept in mind even while they were on active service during the war. Although the museum was closed, it acquired some significant contemporary objects direct from source. Principal among these was a donation from Major-General Sir Douglas Wimberley. In December 1942 he despatched to the museum the flag flown by 51st Divisional Headquarters at the battle of El Alamein only weeks before. Such was the reputation of the division, and so heightened was public awareness of a Scottish dimension to the El Alamein victory, arrangements were made immediately to put the flag on public display elsewhere in Edinburgh. The General was himself steeped in the Scottish military tradition. He had served in a regiment of the first 51st (Highland) Division during the First World War and had been decorated for gallantry. His grandfather had served in the same regiment, the Cameron Highlanders, during the Indian Mutiny of 1857. In 1942 General Wimberley saw the force under his command in historical terms, as natural successors of the celebrated Highland Brigade of the

1850s, archetypes of Scottish military history as it had been commemorated in the museum at Edinburgh Castle.

The Second World War was nevertheless also a conscript's war, and National Service in its wartime and post-war forms, by immersing a significant section of the Scottish population in the military life and military culture, created a renewed constituency of support for the armed services in Scotland. A handful of cases of conscientious objection on the grounds of Scottish nationalist political conviction were hardly typical.[7] Though doubtless often glad when the experience was over, many of those who served as conscripts naturally retained a sympathy for the military institutions through which they had passed. For the post-war National Servicemen, who had no more choice as to postings than did their wartime counterparts, their allotted time was likely to be served in the army (the Royal Navy and Royal Air Force had quickly contracted from their wartime commitments and strengths) and, inevitably, for many it was seen through in the Scottish infantry regiments. The last National Serviceman returned to civilian life in 1963 and so this constituency is today a dwindling one, but through the second half of the twentieth century men with a background of military experience, albeit temporary, were to be found in all walks of civilian life.

For some, this was sustained through the ex-service social and welfare organisations common to both regular and conscript. Regimental associations catering to the welfare of ex-soldiers and their families had been a feature of most army regiments since before the Second World War, formed from amalgamations of earlier regimental clubs and small associations in different localities. In Edinburgh alone during the 1930s there were no fewer than thirty-six regimental and service association premises in operation, including three for women.[8] The Scottish regimental associations, endorsed and contributed to by the serving regiments, were a social network for former soldiers that connected the serving with the retired, the regulars with the reservists, and the regiments with the local cadet force. Similarly, a feature of many towns and villages across the land was 'the Legion' – the local social clubs of the Royal British Legion Scotland, a union of national ex-service organisations created in the years after the First World War with Earl Haig as its figurehead. With direct links, through the Earl Haig Fund, to annual Remembrance appeals and public commemorations, the Legion was a visible presence in post-war Scotland and by the 1950s had taken on much of the role of the various clubs and associations of the pre-war era. The Legion's involvement in Scottish civil life was not political, but, in addition to its specific concern for the interests of ex-service men and women, it tended to reflect as a matter of course a conservative attitude of public service, stability and civil co-operation which by the 1960s was also imbibed, through associate membership, by those who had never themselves served in the forces. Such organisations represented only one formal manifestation of a broad identification with the military ethos that existed at different levels of society, and it was to this kind of constituency that supporters of the Scottish regiments were able to appeal when, in the post-imperial era, the future of the regiments began seriously to be questioned.

The first signs of the likely fate of the regular regiments in a shrinking British army began to be seen shortly after the Second World War ended. The contraction of most infantry regiments from two battalions into one was effected by 1949.[9] Nevertheless, and indeed consequent upon such cutbacks, there was no shortage of work for Scottish regiments in the post-war years – a result of the activities of communist and nationalist forces in Korea and several parts of the British empire. In these campaigns and crises the separate identities and reputations of the Scottish regiments re-emerged, free from the larger unit identities of the mass wartime army. National Servicemen formed a substantial portion of their manpower, but for those National Servicemen who served with Scottish regiments in the post-war era, the experience was more closely involved with the regiment in its traditional, regular form than had been the case for the wartime conscripts. In garrisons and on active operations they were deployed fully integrated with their regular counterparts as the individual infantry battalion enjoyed something of a renaissance as a unit of military organisation. In counter-insurgency campaigns in such places as the Malayan jungle, units smaller than the large formations of the recent world war fought in a more isolated and self-contained way, becoming the focus of media attention and popular approbation. Even in the more conventional operations of the Korean War of 1950-51, it was individual battalions, rather than larger formations, that came to be associated with specific actions – like the repulse of a Chinese attack at the battle of the Hook by 1st Black Watch, or the 'highland charge' of 1st Argyll and Sutherland Highlanders in the battalion attack on Chinese positions on Hill 282.

Despite such conspicuous service on the part of the traditional regiments, harder cuts, cuts that bit into dearly held traditions and reputations, came in the late 1950s as British defence policy pushed funding towards the maintenance of a nuclear deterrent and away from the operation of large conventional armed forces. With most British infantry consisting of single battalions only, regiments themselves, and not parts thereof, were to go and some famous names faced demise. In Scotland the axe fell first of all on the Royal Scots Fusiliers and the Highland Light Infantry, two Scottish regiments of long-standing with all the cultural weight of the Scottish military tradition, lowland and highland, heavy between them. In the same deliberations of the Army Council, the Seaforth Highlanders and the Queen's Own Cameron

Highlanders, no less renowned, were also marked for amalgamation. With these, and with other, later amalgamations, the hurt wrought by the dilution of venerable, much-loved and successful institutions, the horse-trading over name, uniform and other details that was largely left to the regiments, through their councils and colonels, to sort out, is shrouded in the bald statements of fact regarding regimental amalgamations that appear in subsequent regimental histories and in the laudably forward-looking language of regimental journals at the time of amalgamation. As far as resistance to amalgamations was concerned, serving soldiers, including senior officers, were in no position to make too vocal their opposition to the will of government and consequent decisions of the Army Council. The fight was necessarily left to the retired soldiers, particularly the retired officers; indeed it was, perhaps, the latter who felt the pain most acutely when the regiment in which they served was slated for change. The Seaforths and the Camerons ultimately accepted amalgamation with great regret but without great outward upset. However, the threat to the future of the Highland Light Infantry attracted the backing of an organised public protest campaign and considerable national media attention. Although the HLI had long been centred and recruited in Glasgow, this amalgamation involved the loss of its 'highland regiment' status, a point of particular sensitivity, and with it the loss of the kilt which it had lobbied its way back into as recently as 1949. The corporation of the city of Glasgow took up the cudgel on the regiment's behalf, lobbying the government and, with the energetic activity of one city councillor who had served in the regiment, organised a phenomenal protest march through the city centre in September 1957. None of this was to any great immediate avail: the amalgamation went ahead and the new regiment, the Royal Highland Fusiliers, was to wear not the kilt but the trews of a lowland regiment. Yet the campaign was a demonstration of the extent to which a seam of Scottish society identified with the reputation of the regiments and an example of how the support of these people could be mobilised. A precedent had been set for future public and press campaigns in support of Scottish regiments. In their future designs on the size of the army, governments would have to consider the possible political implications of their actions in Scotland.

Popular opposition to disbandments and amalgamations was spontaneous; the stirring of strong feelings into active popular protest was not. Responses to cuts in the army varied according to the character of the battalions affected and the personalities involved. When, in the late 1960s, another government reassessment of British strategic commitments demanded the sacrifice of further Scottish battalions, the reaction from those two regiments chosen for the cull was rather different. With no appetite for the compromise represented by amalgamation with another regiment, the Cameronians chose disbandment instead, bringing at least the comforts of what today is understood today by the term 'closure'. For the Cameronians closure came at a final conventicle parade in 1968. The regiment's tradition of conventicles – open-air church parades with armed guards posted – recalled the seventeenth-century practice of secret worship, a tradition from the time when the radical presbyterian followers of the Reverend Richard Cameron were hunted as rebels against the Crown. The Cameronians was an old Scottish regiment with a history pre-dating the existence of the unitary British state that, in 1968, ordained its end, and whose last vestiges of empire it had been policing in the Middle East only months before. The senior Church of Scotland minister present made a stirring address to the final parade, marking it 'a grievous day for Scotland, seeing that your roots have been so closely intertwined with the troubled history of church and state in this land'.[10]

If the Cameronians passed sombrely, and relatively quietly, into history in 1968, the same could not have been said of the second Scottish regiment that was slated for reduction. The furore over the future of the Argyll and Sutherland Highlanders raised even more dust than had the fate of Highland Light Infantry ten years previously. On this occasion the man raising much of the dust was the 1st Battalion's flamboyant commanding officer Lieutenant-Colonel Colin Mitchell. With a talent for publicity and a sense of its potential value as the regiment fell under threat, Mitchell attracted the close attention of the press during his battalion's tour of duty in the small British Middle East colony of Aden. Amidst violent nationalist anticipation of the colony's independence, the Crater district of the colony had been illegally taken over by the Aden Armed Police and it fell to the Argyll and Sutherland Highlanders to

Disbandment service of the 1st Battalion Cameronians (Scottish Rifles), May 1968. On the Communion table is the sword of the first commanding officer, killed in action in 1689.

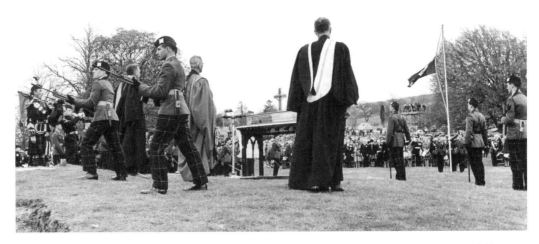

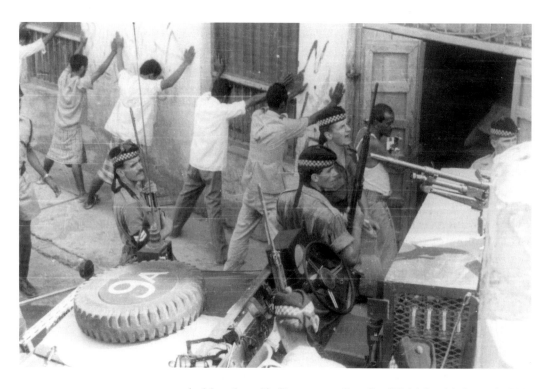

The 1st Battalion Argyll and Sutherland Highlanders search for weapons in the Crater district of Aden, 1967.

re-occupy, hold and pacify Crater pending final British withdrawal. This dangerous and controversial mission was achieved with some dash and with no little controversy over the Argyll's 'no-nonsense' approach to the insurgents and the local population, considered in some quarters to be excessive. It all made for sensational news copy, with a strong focus on Mitchell himself, dubbed 'Mad Mitch' by the headline writers. Amidst doubts over British policy in Aden, concerns were voiced not only about Mitchell's methods but also the appropriateness of his public persona, however there was no doubt that he had made his regiment 'the Argylls' a household name and given to it an image that associated traditional elements of the Scottish military identity with modern military circumstances and capabilities. To sections of the popular press, the toughness, competence and resolution they associated with the Argylls' performance in Crater were held in glowing contrast to what was considered to be equivocation and weakness on the part of the British government over its abandonment of Aden and the loss of empire overall. A matter of months after Mitchell and the Argylls returned from Aden, the disbandment of the regiment was announced, with predictable results. Mitchell had by then left the army and was free to add his name to the campaign mounted to save the regiment.[11] The pitting of an unpopular Labour government against its favourite regiment was manna to the Scottish conservative popular press, and to the regiment's great champion, the *Scottish Daily Express*, in particular.

The 'Save the Argylls' campaign, with its petition claimed to carry a million signatures, demonstrated again the popular feeling that could be mobilised for the Scottish regiments, and the political leverage that it could give them. The regiment's protagonist in Parliament was the Conservative MP George Younger, one of those in public life who carried forward a regimental connection – to the Argyll and Sutherland Highlanders – through past experience as a National Serviceman. The Conservative opposition and the Liberals stood foursquare behind the 'Save the Argylls' campaign, while the Scottish National Party and many in the governing Labour Party would not set themselves against it. For the Conservatives it was a chance to respond to the challenge of the Scottish Nationalists by positioning themselves as the party defending Scottish interests within the Union, and support for a famous Scottish regiment fitted this purpose well. Each of the government's opponents pointed to the planned disbandment as the measure of an administration that could be accused of not understanding Scotland. The issue of what was referred to as 'Argyll Law' in Crater reared up again, polarising political opinion. After denouncing the regiment's Crater record in a House of Commons debate on the proposed defence reductions, the Labour MP Tam Dalyell was vilified in the letter columns of the conservative Scottish press. The hate mail he received personally revealed the murky associations some people made between Scottish identity, religious denomination, race, and notions of manliness.[12]

In face of all this the Argylls were indeed saved, albeit in a much-reduced form, virtually suspended animation, following a change of government. Although Colin Mitchell was himself elected to Parliament, Conservative victory in the 1970 general election was not reflected in any significant gains in Scotland and the implication of Labour in the reduction of the Argylls did not seem to do it any deep electoral damage. The rapid revival of the Argylls to battalion strength was consistent with the support that had earlier been expressed by Scottish Conservative MPs for the 'Save the Argylls' campaign, but owed as much to the emergence of the Northern Ireland conflict as a situation requiring a substantial presence of British military manpower. The Argyll and Sutherland Highlanders were not tampered with thereafter, although, together with the other Scottish infantry regiments, they now face the consequences of the Ministry of Defence's current 'big regiment' plans.

A situation not unlike that faced by the Argylls in Crater was to become the regular diet of Scottish infantry regiments for the next two decades as the British army deployed in Northern Ireland. There seems to be little evidence that Scottish soldiers were regarded or treated on either side – loyalist or republican – in any distinct way from the British military presence as a whole, either of amity or animosity, as a consequence of their national identity and of the historic connections and links of sympathy between the two communities in Ulster and their related constituencies in central Scotland. Indeed, recruiting for the ranks of the Scottish regiments was concentrated in those same areas, and brought into the army both Protestants and Catholics familiar with the equivalent Scottish world of sectarian loyalties. Whatever the sympathies of individual soldiers within the battalions might have been, any sentimental notions of a special Scottish understanding of the situation were rapidly extinguished as attitudes hardened on all sides.[13] The initial, fragile nationalist support for the army's deployment soon melted away and Scottish troops were involved in the first confrontations with rioters in west Belfast in 1970 shortly before a Belfast petrol bomber died under the fire of the King's Own Scottish Borderers. The deaths of three off-duty Royal Highland Fusiliers, shot in cold blood by the Provisional IRA in March 1971, instilled in the army a bitter understanding of the ruthlessness of their enemy. In the most dangerous localities of communal conflict, the army thenceforth acted as soldiers in enemy territory rather than as an aid to policing in part of the United Kingdom. The army's role in direct support of the institutions of law and order in Northern Ireland naturally identified it with the Unionist position, but if the cultural affinities between working-class Protestant Scottish soldiers and loyalist Ulstermen gave the former any proclivity toward loyalist sympathies, this was largely counteracted by the very different social origin of the officers of Scottish infantry regiments for whom any such cultural associations would have had little meaning. Years of repeated short tours of service in Northern Ireland also tended to encourage a 'plague on both your houses' attitude that identified the civilian populations on either side as little other than the source of unreasonableness and intransigence that had created the deadly conflict the soldiers found themselves involved in. On the other hand, it is possible that longer postings of units, or of individuals to staff appointments or to the Ulster Defence Regiment, might have engendered a more partial perspective.

Northern Ireland duties drew in not only the Scottish infantry battalions, but also the Scots Guards and the armoured regiment, the Royal Scots Greys. The latter nevertheless became another victim of the round of army cuts. With the help of a healthy recruiting profile in Scotland, the Royal Scots Greys ensured that its amalgamation with the 3rd Carabiniers (a regiment with English and Welsh roots) was a heavily Scottish affair. The Greys shared with their new partners the traditions of the British cavalry regiments, rather different from the Scottish infantry image, but to these they had added such decidedly Scottish assets as a pipe band, acquired in 1946 by inheritance from the mobile reconnaissance units of 52nd (Lowland) Division. In 1971 the Royal Scots Greys and the 3rd Carabiniers metamorphosed into the Royal Scots Dragoon Guards and embarked on a concerted public image and recruiting exercise in Scotland, presenting themselves as 'Scotland's Cavalry'. This public relations task was aided in singular fashion by the sudden fame of the regiment's Pipes and Drums and Military Band, which together achieved the unexpected feat of an international hit single with a recording of the hymn *Amazing Grace*, originally recorded for a long-playing record of more conventionally modest sales entitled *Farewell to the Greys*.

The attraction of the Scottish image so successfully projected by the Royal Scots Dragoon Guards was not lost on another armoured unit, the Fourth Royal Tank Regiment, which set up its own, initially unofficial, Pipes and Drums in 1973. As creations of the First World War, the tank regiments were the original pioneering armoured units of the British army and the Fourth RTR had a modern technical image rather different from the heritage of the old Scottish regiments or from the British cavalry tradition. However, in 1959 the tank regiments had also felt the run-down in the British army and, following amalgamations, the crucial matter of recruitment was reorganised for the regiments that remained. Scotland was denoted the recruiting ground of the Fourth RTR, which set about stressing its Caledonian connections. Its desire to enter the Scottish regimental club, designating itself 'Scotland's Own Royal Tank Regiment', was entirely logical from the perspective of recruiting, and of survival. A similar connection with Scotland was to be emphasised within the Royal Artillery as territorial designations and recruiting areas were adopted by two field regiments, the 40th and 19th, thereafter known as unofficially 'the Lowland Gunners' and 'the Highland Gunners'. It was an approach shared with numerous non-regular units of the territorial and reserve forces, of yeomanry, artillery, signals, *etc*, who in the post-war years identified and allied themselves in a similar way, emphasising historic connections to wartime Scottish formations, melding their own distinctive local amateur identities and traits with the greater-Scottish military image.

In the event, Fourth Royal Tank Regiment survived as such only until 1993 – when the next significant round of defence cuts bit further into the size of the army. The Fourth RTR's Scottish profile merged into the new 1st Royal Tank Regiment, which absorbed Scotland as part of its recruiting area and retained the pipes and drums. The government's 'Options For Change' defence spending review sought to adjust capability and expenditure to new strategic circumstances generated by the collapse of the Soviet Union and the end of the Cold War. The review cast doubt over the futures of several British regiments and, once again, it was to be in Scotland that trouble broke out with greatest noise. On this occasion four of the Scottish regiments were earmarked for amalgamation – the Royal Scots with the King's Own Scottish Borderers, and the Queen's Own Highlanders with the Gordon

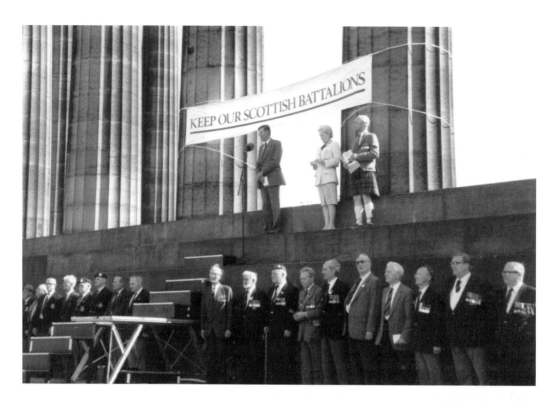

Launch of the
campaign against
cuts in the Scottish
regiments, at the
National Monument
on Edinburgh's
Calton Hill, 1991.

Highlanders. While protest campaigns were organised on behalf of the King's Own Scottish Borderers and the Gordon Highlanders specifically, a Scottish umbrella campaign was set up under the title 'Keep Our Scottish Battalions', whose acronym KOSB echoed that of one of the threatened regiments. Notably, this was a network of opposition concerned only with the Scottish regiments – although plenty of other British units were affected. The campaign organisers had an argument based on broader questions of British strategic requirements, but it was on the sentimental popular attachment to the Scottish regiments that any public campaign could best hope to generate support. They could rightly point to the political situation peculiar to Scotland where the Conservative government making the cuts on this occasion had little representation in Parliament and stood to lose more. It was the Conservatives who had been most forthright in opposition to the previous amalgamations and, with these factors in mind, one campaign tactic was a strong focus on parliamentary constituencies connected to the regiments under threat where the sitting Member of Parliament was a Conservative.

Despite a campaign that successfully revisited the methods and high public profile of the 'Save the Argylls' campaign of twenty-five years before, only one of the proposed amalgamations was stopped, and the other, that of the Queens Own Highlanders and the Gordon

Highlanders, went ahead in 1994. The political fallout from this measure was hard to judge, since the political difficulty of the measure was enough to lead the government to save one pair of regiments, but not the other, and the totality of Conservative defeat in the general election of 1997 clouded any specific effect the issue of the Scottish regiments might have had. Popular backing for the regiments was not universal: the campaign attracted limited attention outside the home areas of the regiments threatened. It was noticeable however that, in the course of the campaigns to save the regiments, representatives of all of the opposition parties in Scotland, including the Scottish National Party, publicly expressed support for a reprieve, while, with elections pending, the Conservatives did what they could to allay fears that the amalgamations would go ahead. There were a few lonely voices welcoming the demise of the Scottish agents of British imperialism, but even candidates of the Scottish Green Party, not given to support for military organisations and then enjoying a brief electoral and media prominence, would not condemn the regiments.[14]

As the Scottish regiments diminished in number, paradoxically one of their principal public relations outlets went from strength to strength. The Edinburgh Military Tattoo began during the late 1940s in small displays of military music, drill and dancing arranged to complement Edinburgh's nascent Festival of Music and Drama. As the latter developed into the Edinburgh International Festival, and, with its Fringe, became one of the world's premier annual cultural events, the Edinburgh Military Tattoo grew in scale and popularity and its month-long run of performances has become a significant international tourist attraction in itself. At the core of the every Tattoo programme is the Massed Pipes and Drums, a sound and a sight that may perhaps be regarded as the quintessential symbol of Scottish identity as it is perceived by the rest of the world. The Tattoo was only the most prominent among many such events staged regularly around the world. Performances and tours by pipe bands and military bands served a public relations exercise for their regiments and indeed for the army as a whole, something of no little importance in such awkward situations as that facing post-war garrisons in Germany and their changing relationship with the civilian population. Nor was the powerful appeal of the pipes and drums the sole preserve of the army: the pipe bands of the Scottish auxiliary air squadrons of the 1930s were only the beginning of the piping tradition in the Royal Air Force. RAF stations in Scotland and RAF units with Scottish links formed their own pipes and drums in the late twentieth century and these too have performed across the world and in the Edinburgh Military Tattoo.

For all its extraordinary success, the Tattoo nevertheless reflects some of the apparent contradictions faced by the armed services in

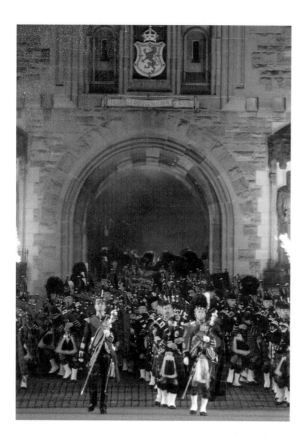

The massed Pipes and Drums of the Scottish regiments open the annual Edinburgh Military Tattoo.

Scotland in the post-imperial era. The early Tattoo programmes drew principally on the home-grown musical resources of the British army, with the Scottish element naturally to the fore. The subsequent shrinkage of the army, of its Scottish elements, and its musical elements, have seen the Tattoo diversify and rely more heavily on civilian contributions and the participation of units from Commonwealth and foreign armies. To fill the Castle esplanade with the massed pipes and drums increasingly requires the contribution of pipers and drummers from Canada, South Africa, Australia and New Zealand, and the pipes and drums of other British units such as the Royal Gurkha Rifles to bolster the numerical presence of the core Scottish contingent. If this change reflects the contraction of the Scottish regiments in recent decades, it also demonstrates how the Tattoo, and the image of Scotland it projects, continues to depend on the legacy of the British empire for its principal appeal. Visitors to Scotland will tend to respond with interest and enthusiasm to the familiar tartan and pipes image that is marketed to them as potential tourists at home and as actual tourists in Scotland, but the Tattoo imagery retains its greatest resonance for visitors to Scotland from the English-speaking world of former parts of the British empire including the United States. For the Scottish-descended inhabitants of former British territories such as Canada, Australia and New Zealand, ready identification with these military symbols of identity rests on a genuine inheritance from the Scotland of the nineteenth and early twentieth century that their forbears left, and that was defined in cultural terms by its British imperial role. Visitors to the Tattoo from countries such as Nepal, India and Pakistan, and numerous countries of the Middle East, are fully familiar with the piping tradition and might be pleased, but not at all surprised, to see it represented in the performance by the military pipe bands of their own armed forces.

Until relatively recently, most Scots would have had little hesitation in identifying with the Scottish military image in much the same way. Many still do. Yet it is certainly the case in post-imperial Great Britain that the idea of British imperialism, even as a fond memory, has become decidedly unfashionable to many, especially the young, and remains, as it has ever been, anathema to some. Political developments – the Scottish home rule question and the creation of the devolved Scottish Parliament – have been accompanied by discernible changes in the way Scotland is perceived among its own people. In the past the sense of difference, that is to say difference from the English, could find expression in such visually and culturally distinct things as the Scottish regiments. Today, the unfashionable taint of imperialism has relegated somewhat these symbols from the high position they once enjoyed in popular expressions of national belonging and the tendency instead is to seek something of Scotland that is untouched by that aspect of the past. There is a political element to this. Among others, the proponents of Scottish devolution and independence have sought to encourage a search for a more modern image of Scotland, one that does not rest on the tenets of empire, that is set against tradition, and incorporates a world view in which patriotism, British patriotism especially, is belittled.

Perhaps stronger is the generation element – the passage of time from the last major European war, the time since British people last faced the serious threat of military subjugation, the ageing of the national service generation, and the shrinking of the armed forces themselves. This effect has probably worked through fully only in the last twenty years. As late as the 1970s the popular culture absorbed by children growing up in Scotland was dominated by stories and images of the Second World War. This was still the stuff of many action films, certainly those shown on television, but has since been supplanted by science fiction and action heroes of a more singular variety. Publishers, most prolifically DC Thomson of Dundee, produced boys' comics such as *Victor* in the 1960s and *Warlord* in the 1970s, and the popular *Commando* comic books whose stories of heroism and derring-do could be outlandish, but followed the thread of real Second World War contexts and events. In reading matter, toys and playground games, recent British military history was second nature to many a Scottish child, in a way that has become much less the case in the last two decades. To younger Scottish visitors to Edinburgh Castle and the National War Museum of Scotland in the early twenty-first century, the Scottish military past that it represents is not necessarily the familiar ground it surely was to preceding generations.

Meanwhile Scots young and old continue to adopt and adapt the traditional imagery of Scottish regimental identity – the kilts and glengarry bonnets sported by Scottish football and rugby supporters for example – as marks of distinction. Whether they would readily connect that image to Scotland's military role in the British empire is another matter. Popular notions of Scotland as a warlike nation remain strong, but the fashion in recent years, encouraged by the fleeting attentions of the film industry, has been to make connections further back in Scottish history, skipping the period in which that reputation was honed and transmitted to the wider world.

The end of the British empire, the amalgamation and disbandment of Scottish regiments, a new constitutional relationship for Scotland within the United Kingdom, a military image that means less to rising generations of Scots than it did to those that are passing: all might be taken to suggest that the Scottish military tradition might be in failing health. There are undoubtedly those who see military Scotland as something firmly of the past; as part of a British imperial inheritance to be dismissed as an unwelcome aberration in Scotland's history. In wishing this inheritance away altogether, they are likely to be disappointed. There is no evidence to suggest the world at large will cease to see Scotland in anything other than the terms that, for those looking from afar, still define it – the traditional imagery that is so closely bound up with Scotland's military reputation. In the interests of tourism, that image is the one which, for the foreseeable future, will be promoted by public funding as well as private enterprise, as witnessed in the annual Tartan Day pageant now being marketed in the USA. Visitors will not be drawn to Scotland by its aspirations to modernity. Although they are beginning to notice the ambivalence with which the Scots relate to their past, foreign visitors will continue to seek out the cultural distinction that has a ever-present military tinge, an inheritance that, however much it is distorted and exploited for commercial purposes, is not bogus, but is the product of centuries of real Scottish history in which the British imperial experience was an essential factor.

As far as its future place in the mindset of home-grown Scots is concerned, the Scottish military image is nothing if not adaptable. It retains an appeal that at least sees it remain instantly recognisable across broad sections of Scottish society, sufficiently so still to be employed as an aid to army recruitment. Nor is it an image that is about to disappear from public life, whatever reorganisation and stringency are required of the British armed forces in the near future. At the opening of the new Scottish Parliament in Edinburgh on the first of July in 1999, the accompanying ceremonial and festivities attempted a symbolic marriage of the traditional and the 'new' Scotland. The Queen was accompanied by the full paraphernalia of state, including the Life Guards of the Household Cavalry, a military institution not immediately connected with Scotland in the public mind, but the Scottish Crown was brought out of Edinburgh Castle and escorted to the Parliament by soldiers of the 1st Battalion Argyll and Sutherland Highlanders. And it was not only these ancient ceremonial symbols of Scottish sovereignty that had a military escort. The procession of civic leaders, schoolchildren and newly elected Members of the Scottish Parliament that walked from the old pre-Union

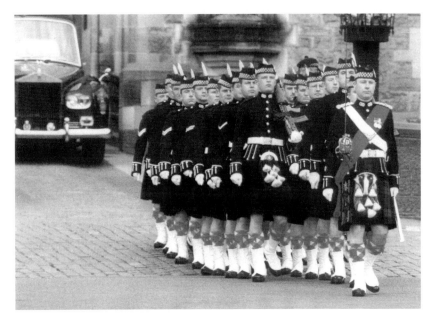

Men of the 1st Battalion Argyll and Sutherland Highlanders escort the Scottish royal crown and regalia to the ceremonial opening of the new Scottish Parliament, July 1999.

Parliament Hall to the new Parliament's temporary accommodation on the Mound – the 'new' aspect of the proceedings – was led by the 1st Battalion Black Watch with its Pipes and Drums. With them were the Highland and Lowland Bands of the Scottish Division.

In the twenty-first century the Scottish media continue to find the bearers of the Scottish military image highly newsworthy, both in the context of politics and of war, as clear an indication as any of popular interest in the performance and fate of the regiments and a willingness to consider them in national terms. In the initial stages of the 2003 Iraq War, the involvement of the Black Watch and Royal Scots Dragoon Guards was the front page news of the Scottish popular press.

Even as Scottish public opinion divided over the political arguments for war, there was a positive interest in what the Scottish units deployed were experiencing and achieving. As so often in the past, this was reported in a manner suggesting the presence of Scottish units in combat represented a Scottish national involvement in the fighting. In a further post-devolution twist, the media turned for comment to the First Minister of the devolved Scottish Executive who, despite having no constitutional role in the area of defence and foreign policy, was expected to speak for the nation in acknowledging its particular concern and support for the Scots on active service. Ongoing controversy over the British involvement in Iraq has seen the media continue to report the presence of Scottish units, and the loss of Scottish lives, as a national story. Again, the connection that is implied between the presence of Scottish troops and the will and concerns of Scottish people is not one that reflects the constitutional realities of how British military power is used.

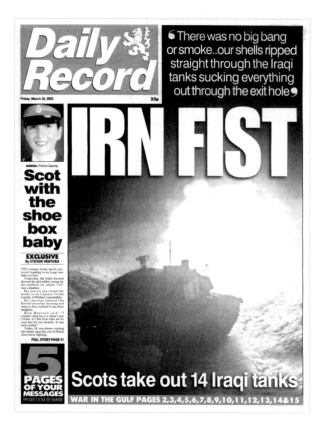

This is one uncharted area in which sentiments of greater Scottish autonomy might possibly impact on the future constitutional workings of the British state. Those who oppose the presence of the British nuclear deterrent in Scotland might hope to mobilise such sentiments with similar impact. Meanwhile, the political heat generated by questions over the future number and identity of the Scottish regiments appears greater than that proceeding from the concentration of British nuclear warfare capability in the Gare Loch, a further indication of how tradition and reputation continue to dominate perceptions of Scotland's military situation.

During the 2003 Iraq War, the Scottish media again reported the involvement of the Scottish regiments as a natural focus of national interest.

To mark the founding of the Scottish Naval and Military Museum in 1930, the leading Scottish sculptor Charles d'Orville Pilkington Jackson was commissioned to create a series of carved and painted oak statuettes representing the Scottish regiments from 1633 to 1918. Still on display in the National War Museum of Scotland, the statuettes suggest an idea of the resolute qualities of the Scottish soldier that Pilkington Jackson deliberately conveyed as something timeless. Placed together, the eighty-three figures also hint at the scale and longevity of the Scottish propensity for military service. One of the generation of Scots who served in the First World War, Pilkington Jackson had already worked on the Scottish National War Memorial. Stylistically, the museum statuettes bear close relation to Pilkington Jackson's later, best-known work: the equestrian statue of King Robert the Bruce at Bannockburn, site of the celebrated Scottish victory over an English army in 1314. Pilkington Jackson was also one of the artistic contributors to a monument raised in 1952 in Edinburgh's Princes Street Gardens, a tribute to the service of the oldest Scottish regiment, the Royal Scots. Its stone monoliths bear images and emblems of this oldest of British infantry regiments and display the battle honours it won across the British empire. Between them is a connecting grille which carries the text of the Declaration of Arbroath, the 1320 letter of the Scottish barons to the Pope proclaiming the Scottish independence won by King Robert Bruce in his wars against the English, the essential historic expression of sovereign Scottish nationhood. Like all the Scottish regiments, the Royal Scots saw themselves as representative of a national tradition and history that connected back to just that. Forming part of the British armed services, among the most centralised of British state organisations, the armed forces in Scotland carry a shared British history of imperial military power, and (with particular reference to the two world wars of the twentieth century) a shared memory of crisis and of sacrifice. But the Scottish regiments were, and are, vehicles through which, especially at times of military and economic success, the Scottish sense of nationhood has been celebrated and reinforced. For a nation without a nation state, national institutions were emblems of Scotland's status within the Union. The oldest Scottish regiments predate the creation of the British state and along with the Scottish institutions of church, law, and education, the existence of them all has been cherished as a demonstration that Scotland did not cease to exist in 1707.

By no means all Scots have shared, or share, the view that connects war, military service and Scottish nationhood in this way. Some might regard this story as the manifestation of a shameful militarism put to the service of an imperial past in which they take no pride. A greater number might feel uneasiness over the finding of national redemption in the conduct of warfare, with all its consequences of destruction, suffering and loss. It is not the purpose of this historical study to pronounce on the rights and wrongs of what occurred, but rather to consider one strand of our history that helps to explain why Scotland is as it is. An aptitude for war is one of the stories Scots in the past have been happy to tell about themselves. Like any historical phenomenon, that aptitude was the product of a unique set of circumstances – proceeding from Scotland's global position and from the need for its people to make a living – that built, one upon another, to create one of the supports on which Scottish nationhood rests.

1   E Linklater, *Magnus Merriman* (Edinburgh: Canongate Classic Edition, 2001), p.40.
2   J Buchan, *The History of the Royal Scots Fusiliers (1678-1918)* (London: Thomas Nelson & Sons Ltd), 1925, p.451.
3   Ministry of Works files (National Archives of Scotland, MW1/965, MW1/1335).
4   Author's conversation with the late Mr G McLennan, formerly 5/7th Gordon Highlanders.
5   G Landsborough, *Tobruk Commando* (London: Greenhill, 1989), p.163. After much resistance the depleted Commando force surrendered. Many Italians had been killed by the

Commandos in the operation to secure the beach-head, and the Commandos were saved from the vengeance of the Italian garrison only by the arrival of German troops who surrounded the prisoners for their own protection.

6   Speech of General Sir Gordon H A MacMillan, GOC Scottish Command, opening the Scottish United Services Museum, quoted in the *Edinburgh Evening Dispatch*, 14th April 1949.

7   In 1942 the chairman of the Scottish National Party was imprisoned for refusing conscription. In 1952 Michael Grieve, son of the poet Hugh MacDiarmid, pursued a similar case against peacetime National Service with the same result. See T Royle, *The Best Years of their Lives. The National Service Experience 1945-63* (London: Michael Joseph, 1986), pp.32-6.

8   These were all represented at the official opening of the Scottish Naval and Military Museum in 1933.

9   This stringency generated an optimistic practice, surviving into the twenty-first century, whereby the infantry regiment's single regular battalion is designated the First Battalion (*ie* '1 Royal Scots', *etc*), as though the advent of war or crisis might reactivate its 'suspended' second battalion and prompt the raising of further battalions as had been done during the First and Second World Wars.

10 Dr Donald McDonald quoted in J Baynes, *The History of the Cameronians (Scottish Rifles), Volume IV, The Close of Empire 1948-1968* (London: Cassell, 1971), p.226.

11 Mitchell responded in print to his critics over Aden. His autobiography, *Having Been A Soldier*, (London: Hamish Hamilton Ltd), was published in 1969.

12 A selection is quoted in I Wood, 'Protestantism and Scottish military tradition', in G Walker and T Gallacher, *Sermons and Battle Hymns. Protestant Popular Culture in Modern Scotland* (Edinburgh: Edinburgh University Press, 1990), pp.112-36.

13 I Wood, 'Thin Red Line? – Scottish Soldiers in the Troubles', in I Wood (ed), *Scotland & Ulster* (Edinburgh: Mercat Press, 1994), pp.150-71.

14 The stated position of the candidates in the Kincardine and Deeside by-election of 1991, in which the future amalgamation of the Gordon Highlanders was a significant issue, is given in D Fairgrieve, *A Regiment Saved. The inside story of Operation Borderer: the fight to save the King's Own Scottish Borderers* (Edinburgh: B & W Publishing, 1993). For an analysis of post-war defence cuts and the response of the regiments of the British army, see H Strachan, *The Politics of the British Army* (Oxford: Clarendon Press, 1997), pp.214-33.

SELECT BIBLIOGRAPHY

Bird, A, *A Separate Little War. The Banff Coastal Command Strike Wing versus the Kriegsmarine and the Luftwaffe 1944-45* (London: Grub Street, 2003).

Broun, D, Finlay, R and M Lynch (eds), *Image and Identity. The Making and Re-Making of Scotland Through the Ages* (Edinburgh: John Donald, 1998).

Carswell, A, *For Your Freedom and Ours. Poland, Scotland and the Second World War* (Edinburgh: National Museums of Scotland, 1993).

Chalmers, M and W Walker, *Uncharted Waters. The UK, Nuclear Weapons and the Scottish Question* (East Linton: Tuckwell Press, 2001).

Colley, L, *Britons. Forging the Nation 1707-1837* (New Haven: Yale University Press, 1992).

Cookson, J, *The British Armed Nation, 1793-1815* (Oxford: Clarendon Press, 1997).

Devine, T, *Scotland's Empire 1600-1815* (London: Allen Lane, 2003).

Devine, T and J Young (eds), *Eighteenth Century Scotland: New Perspectives* (East Linton: Tuckwell, 1999).

Finlay, R, *A Partnership For Good? Scottish Politics and the Union since 1880* (Edinburgh: John Donald, 1997).

Fry, M, *The Dundas Despotism* (Edinburgh: Edinburgh University Press, 1992).

Fry, M, *The Scottish Empire* (East Linton: Tuckwell Press, and Edinburgh: Birlinn, 2001).

Graham, E, *A Maritime History of Scotland 1650-1790* (East Linton: Tuckwell Press, 2002).

Hay, I, *Their Name Liveth, The Book of the Scottish National War Memorial* (Edinburgh: Trustees of the Scottish National War Memorial, 1985).

Henderson, D, *Highland Soldier 1820-1920* (Edinburgh: John Donald, 1989).

Henderson, D, *The Lion and the Eagle. Polish Second World War Veterans in Scotland* (Dunfermline: Cualann Press, 2001).

Hunter, J, *A Dance Called America. The Scottish Highlands, the United States and Canada* (Edinburgh: Mainstream, 1994).

Hutchison, I, *A Political History of Scotland 1832-1924. Parties, Elections and Issues* (Edinburgh: John Donald, 1986).

Jamison, B (ed), *Scotland and the Cold War* (Dunfermline: Cualann Press, 2003).

Lavery, B, *The Royal Navy and Scotland* (East Linton: Tuckwell Press, 2001).

Leneman, L, *In the Service of Life. The Story of Elsie Inglis and the Scottish Women's Hospitals* (Edinburgh: Mercat Press, 1994).

McCorry, H (ed), *The Thistle at War. An anthology of the Scottish experience of war, in the services and at home* (Edinburgh: National Museums of Scotland, 1997.

Macdonald, C M M and E W McFarland (eds), *Scotland and the Great War* (East Linton: Tuckwell Press, 1999).

MacDougall, I, *Voices from war and some labour struggles: personal recollections of war in our century by Scottish men and women* (Edinburgh: Mercat Press, 1995).

Macdougall, N (ed), *Scotland and War AD79-1918* (Edinburgh: John Donald, 1991).

Mackillop, A, *'More Fruitful than the Soil', Army, Empire and the Scottish Highlands, 1715-1815* (East Linton: Tuckwell Press, 2000).

Mackillop, A and S Murdoch (eds), *Military Governors and Imperial Frontiers, c.1600-1800. A Study of Scotland and Empires* (Leiden: Brill, 2003).

McRoberts, D, *Lions Rampant. The Story of 602 Squadron* (London: William Kimber, 1985).

Merriman, M, *The Rough Wooings. Mary Queen of Scots, 1542-1551* (East Linton: Tuckwell Press, 2000).

Murdoch, S and A Mackillop (eds), *Fighting For Identity. Scottish Military Experience, 1550-1900* (Leiden: Brill, 2002).

Murdoch, S (ed), *Scotland and the Thirty Years' War, 1618-1648* (Leiden: Brill, 2001).

Paterson, L, *The Autonomy of Modern Scotland* (Edinburgh: Edinburgh University Press, 1994).

Peebles, H, *Warshipbuilding on the Clyde. Naval Orders and the Prosperity of the Clyde Shipbuilding Industry, 1889-1939* (Edinburgh: John Donald, 1987).

Prebble, J, *Mutiny. Highland Regiments in revolt, 1743-1804* (London: Secker & Warburg, 1975).

Robertson, J, *The Scottish Enlightenment and the Militia Issue* (Edinburgh: John Donald, 1985).

Robertson, J (ed), *A Union for Empire. Political Thought and the British Union of 1707* (Cambridge: University Press, 1995).

Robertson, J Irvine, *The First Highlander. Major-General David Stewart of Garth CB, 1768-1829* (East Linton: Tuckwell Press, 1998).

Ross, D, Blanche, B and W Simpson, *'The Greatest Squadron of Them All'. The Definitive History of 603 (City of Edinburgh) RAUXAF*, 2 volumes (London: Grub Street, 2003).

Royle, T, *Death Before Dishonour. The True Story of Fighting Mac* (Edinburgh: Mainstream, 1982).

Royle, T, *The Best Years of their Lives. The National Service Experience 1945-63* (London: Michael Joseph, 1986).

Simpson, G (ed), *The Scottish Soldier Abroad, 1247-1967* (Edinburgh: John Donald, 1992).

Strachan, H, *The Politics of the British Army* (Oxford: Clarendon Press, 1997).

Tabraham, C and D Grove, *Fortress Scotland and the Jacobites* (London: B T Batsford/Historic Scotland, 1995).

Walker, G and T Gallacher, *Sermons and Battle Hymns. Protestant Popular Culture in Modern Scotland* (Edinburgh: Edinburgh University Press, 1990).

Wood, I (ed), *Scotland & Ulster* (Edinburgh: Mercat Press, 1994).

Wood, S, *The Scottish Soldier* (Manchester: Archive Publications, 1987).

Wood, S, *The Auld Alliance. Scotland and France: The Military Connection* (Edinburgh: Mainstream, 1989).

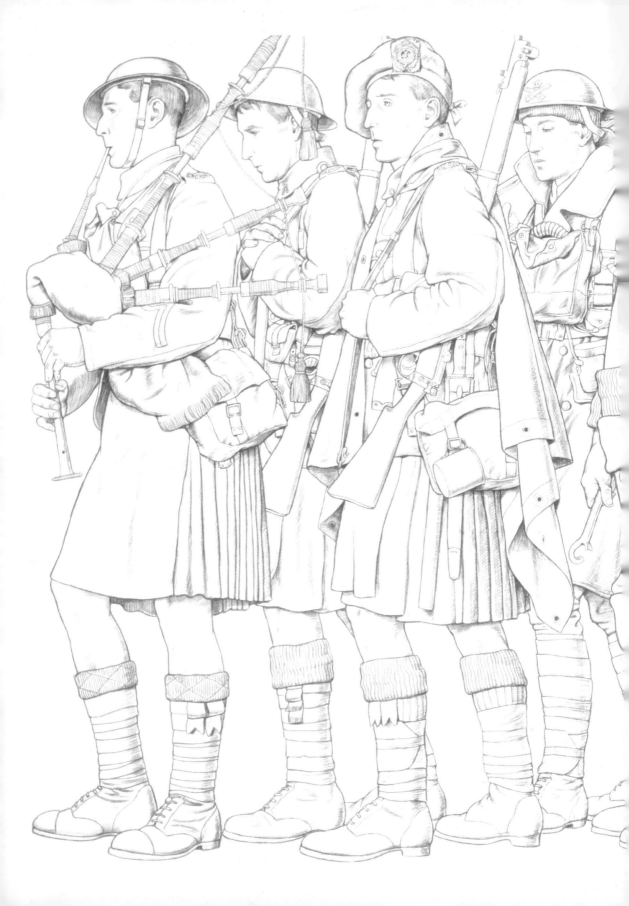